STUDIES OF THE MODERN CORPORATION
COLUMBIA UNIVERSITY GRADUATE SCHOOL OF BUSINESS

Francis Joseph Aguilar, *Scanning the Business Environment*

Herman W. Bevis, *Corporate Financial Reporting in a Competitive Economy*

Richard Eells, *The Corporation and the Arts*

Jay W. Lorsch, *Product Innovation and Organization*

Irving Pfeffer, *The Financing of Small Business*

George A. Steiner and Warren M. Cannon, *Multinational Corporate Planning*

George A. Steiner and William G. Ryan, *Industrial Project Management*

Gus Tyler, *The Political Imperative*

Clarence Walton and Richard Eells, *The Business System* (3 volumes)

The
Political
Imperative

The
Political

THE CORPORATE

GUS TYLER

Imperative

CHARACTER OF UNIONS

Introduction by F. S. C. Northrop

AN ARKVILLE PRESS BOOK

THE MACMILLAN COMPANY, NEW YORK

COLLIER-MACMILLAN LIMITED, LONDON

First Printing

STUDIES OF THE MODERN CORPORATION
Columbia University Graduate School of Business

The Program for Studies of the Modern Corporation is devoted to the advancement and dissemination of knowledge about the corporation. Its publications are designed to stimulate inquiry, research, criticism, and reflection. They fall into four categories: works by outstanding businessmen, scholars, and professional men from a variety of backgrounds and academic disciplines; prizewinning doctoral dissertations relating to the corporation; annotated and edited selections of business literature; and business classics that merit republication. The studies are supported by outside grants from private business, professional, and philanthropic institutions interested in the program's objectives.

Richard Eells
EDITOR

INTRODUCTION

By F. S. C. Northrop

Sterling Professor Emeritus of Philosophy and Law
Yale University Law School

▶ Two of the most vital entities in today's world are the business corporation and the labor union. Both have to be reckoned with. Countless piecemeal factual studies have been made of each. Because the present book is much more than this, it merits special attention.

When we turn to the question of what all the previous factual studies add up to by way of a theory, or philosophy, within the present historical and cultural context, the situation of the businessman and his corporation is quite different from that of the laborer and his equally "incorporated" unions. There is a plethora of theoretical and philosophical books on the business corporation. Many have considerable factual warrant and persisting current influence. For comparable books on labor unions, one looks, as Mr. Tyler notes, well-nigh in vain. At least this is true in the English-speaking, and especially the American, world. It is by way of initiating a remedy to this situation that this book achieves both its novelty and its seminal importance.

Mr. Tyler's book has come at a time when both businessmen and labor union leaders are re-examining their traditional conceptions of what their present respective associations are or should be. Goal values as well as instrumental pragmatic considerations are in question.

The leaders of the most dynamic business and labor corporations, as well as students in the graduate schools of business and departments of economics in our universities, have discovered that there is a considerable gap—if not a contradiction that frequently hinders the corporation's growth—between the traditional Adam Smithian philosophy that many present businessmen may continue to profess and what, purely from a successful businessman's point of view, they not merely must but ought to do. In short, most of the present business leaders and their corporations have moved out from underneath their traditional conception of themselves. A new philosophy of the business corporation is in the making.

It will help us to appreciate the need for Mr. Tyler's book and why he, in his modesty, emphasizes that it is but a beginning, if we list a few of the modern books on the theory and philosophy of the business corporation. This list will indicate the degree to which such theory and philosophy is being reconceived and remade, as compared with what lies ahead for studies of the labor union. We restrict ourselves to the English-speaking world and only to some of the more theoretical, philosophically significant, and practically influential books.

Still in the influential category is Adam Smith's *Wealth of Nations*. The businessmen who profess this philosophy today usually dismiss professional philosophy as useless, referring to themselves as being concerned only with hard facts or with what some social scientists have called brass tacks. It is not irrelevant to note in this regard that Adam Smith was not a businessman who had to meet a payroll at the weekend. Rather, he was during the earlier portion of his life a professional philosopher at the University of Glasgow. Even worse, in 1752 he was its Professor of Moral Philosophy. At that time, he formulated the business philosophy he later published. He refers, moreover, to the duration of this professorship as the most useful period of his life.

These historical considerations remind us that anyone who says he has no philosophy or that he is concerned only with hard facts is likely to be caught at the back of the neck by an antiquated professional philosophy (factually reasonable in part in its day) that he has never critically examined. Unconsciously acquired, such a philosophy makes him incapable of seeing any facts, hard or soft, brassy or more modest, that do not fit it. As the cultural anthropologist Clyde Kluckhohn has noted concerning associations of peoples in the world's diverse cultures, there is no such thing as a culture without its philosophy; the only question is whether its specific philosophy is overt or covert. Similarly, for the individual person, the only difference between one who says he has a philosophy and one who says he does not, is that the former is more likely to know what his philosophy is and to have critically examined its validity in the light of present as well as past facts and alternative theories of the facts.

The degree to which this has occurred with respect to business corporations since Adam Smith's *Wealth of Nations* is illustrated by the following additional theories and theoretically oriented publications: the Marshallian or Austrian neoclassical economic theory; the latter with Keynes' postulate of full employment added; A. A. Berle Jr.'s institutional theory and its critique of any purely economic theory of business corporations; Thurman Arnold's *The Folklore of Capitalism; The Corporate Take-Over* (edited by Andrew Hacker); John Kenneth Galbraith's *The New Industrial State;* D. T. Bazelon's *The Paper Economy; The Corporation in Modern Society* (edited by Edward Mason); John R. Bunting's *The Hidden Face of Free Enterprise;* Peter F. Drucker's *The Concept of the Corporation;* and Andrew Shonfield's *Modern Capitalism: The Changing Balance of Public and Private Power.*

Like the present book by Mr. Tyler on the *raison d'être* and theory of trade unions, Mr. Shonfield's treatise presents a comparative descriptive theory of contemporary business corporations. An analytic theory comparable to the first three listed above, but more adequate to what is described, must come later. In his descriptive theory, Mr. Shonfield specifies the essential characteristics that today's British, American, French, West German, Italian, Japanese, and other business corporations have in common. These characteristics have important differences from those of previous corporations in any one of these countries and hence suggest the need for a richer analytic theory than now exists. Mr. Shonfield also gives the specific characteristics that distinguish the contemporary business corporations in any one of these nations from those in any other. Correlating these differences with the respective annual percentage increases in the gross national product of these nations and also with their differing traditional philosophies of the corporation, he suggests the degree to which in each particular nation the traditional theory of the corporation functions as a generator of or as a roadblock to an increase of the gross national product.

One can hardly imagine more suggestive evidence than Mr. Shonfield's philosophically important conclusions. First, the need, if they are not to put mental blind spots in the way of their own best interests, for both labor leaders and businessmen to bring their theories of themselves and their incorporated associations abreast of their present novel character and problematic situation. Second, the realization that neither the members nor the leaders of an incorporated entity such as a business corporation or a labor union respond merely to facts; also involved is their way of conceiving the facts. If the latter is partial or antiquated in the face of present facts and problems, the behavior is likely to be also. Hence, Mr. Shonfield's discovery of "ideological roadblocks."

The cure for them is not, as so many suppose, to rid oneself of all ideology. This is impossible. Instead, it is to bring the ideology one inevitably has, be it covert or overt, up to date.

Interestingly, the comparative descriptive judgment of the British Mr. Shonfield is that these traditional ideological roadblocks are greater in the most modern of British industrial organizations than they are in the American, and are greater in the American than in their French counterparts. This is one reason why, were we to consider French as well as Anglo-American books on the theory and philosophy of the business corporation, François Bloch-Lainé's *Pour une Réforme de l'Enterprise* would have to be given high priority.

Even though labor unions are as corporate in the broad sense as are business corporations, there are few theoretical studies of the trade unions comparable to those of business corporations in the English-speaking world. The Webbs and Shaw might be cited as exceptions in England, but they can hardly be described as great labor union theoreticians. Laski clearly was an exception, but with roots in the theories of Saint-Simon, Proudhon, and Marx, his philosophy typifies that of the Continental labor leaders with their Ph.D.'s rather than British trade union shop leaders.

Bentham's philosophy had a prodigious influence. But his was the British Liberal Party's theory, which laborers soon found wanting. Moreover, it was not a theory concerned primarily with labor unions in the sense of restricting itself, as most of the theoretical books listed above restrict themselves, to a more adequate theory of business corporations or the business cycle.

"The Philosophy of the British Labour Party" by Lord Lindsay (the post-World War II Labor Government's first labor lord) in *Ideological Differences and World Order* (edited by F. S. C. Northrop) does, however, express a trade union political policy with considerable British popular as well as labor support. It is a combination of the liberal Humean component of Adam Smith's philosophy with intuitive middle-class nonconformist Protestant egalitarianism, reinforced in Lord Lindsay's own personal and professional case (he, too, was by profession a philosopher) by Kant's rationalist moral imperative of a universal lawfulness before which all men are in their rights and correlative obligations equal. The impact of even this philosophical import from the pre-Hegelian German culture of Kant was by no means negligible in its British vote-catching appeal, since it dominated the thinking of Oxford and the Scottish universities into World War II. Besides being a practicing nonconformist Protestant, the Master of

Oxford's Balliol College, and a Kantian as well as a liberal Humean in his ethics, economics, and politics, Lord Lindsay of Birker was a Scot.

In the American historical scene, such conceptualizations of the trade union movement have been fewer and far between. Probably more important than anything else in making American labor unions different from those anywhere else in the world, is Samuel Gompers' decision against a labor political party.

Nevertheless, John R. Commons did develop a theory of trade unionism many years ago. Mr. Tyler tells me that extensions of that theory have been ably carried forward by Selig Perlman and Philip Taft but that these developments have been limited to the historico-economic schools. Frank Tannenbaum, to whom Mr. Tyler expresses his indebtedness, offered a theory of the trade union movement in *A Philosophy of Labor*, which is based less on economic than on sociologic premises. The Marxist influence —whether Socialist or Communist—has also had its spokesmen. In addition, there have been variants on these themes. But Mr. Tyler informs me also all these theories assumed two unstated premises: first, the union is analyzed as a special institution rather than as a variant in a more inclusive category; second, the disciplines applied are the traditional economics, history, sociology, or political science without the benefit of other or more recent insights of psychology, philosophy, theology, ecology, and ethology. Mr. Tyler seeks to correlate the labor union with other human associations and to do so through the multiple contributions of current disciplines.

The Marxist influence in present day labor theory makes Locke's seventeenth-century labor theory of economic value of considerable present relevance. It persisted in England until Ricardo, and in the mid-nineteenth century was taken over by Marx as the economic (as distinct from the Hegelian historical, dialectically deterministic) warrant for his communism. Its influence on the thinking of Continental European trade-union and labor-party leaders, non-Marxist as well as Marxist, is still considerable. This Lockean labor theory of economics affirms that the economic value of any manufacturer's product or laborer's services in exchange is determined by the number of material foot pounds of work that goes into the making of it.

Initially, the impact on British workers was great. Laborers in the pubs of London discussed it as a serious basis for their own policy. But Locke had hardly published it before his own more thorough and analytic *Essay Concerning Human Understanding* was to entail implicitly what Jevons made explicit later; namely, that the labor theory of the value of anything in economic exchange is, on Locke's own theory of human knowledge, theoretically meaningless and without warrant. Independent empirical considerations confirm this conclusion. The final result in the entire English-speaking world was the introspective, psychological theory of the value-in-exchange of the manufacturer's goods and the laborer's services, referred to above, of the nineteenth-century British Liberal Party and of the economists, Jevons, Marshall, Lord (Lionel) Robbins, Keynes, and their many present American followers.

This economic philosophy, apart from Keynes' *ad hoc* political postulate of full employment, derives straight from Locke's *Essay* by way of Bentham, Jevons, and Marshall. Today, even for businessmen, it serves more as a theory of what they would like to be the case for laborers than as a theory of what they themselves (with their many mergers, similar competitive prices, large governmental orders, and separation of management from ownership) do *in fact*. The point, moreover, increasingly seems to be, not that what businessmen are now doing or what both labor unions and government find it necessary to do to them is wrong, but instead that our traditional theories or philosophies of these matters, moral ("wrong" is a moral word) and political as well as economic, are at the very least only trustworthy in part.

With respect to laborers and their unions, the situation is

similar but more distressing. Such is the case whether Keynes' *ad hoc* postulate of full employment be added politically to his introspective psychological theory of economics or not. The plight of many laborers, in the slums of Birmingham in the nineteenth century and in American cities today, makes this evident to everybody.

But if neither (i) the Adam Smithian philosophy of the conservatives, or (ii) the introspective psychological theory of economic values-in-exchange of the British and American economic liberals, nor (iii) the labor theory of the early Locke, Ricardo, and the Marxists will do, what then is to be the *raison d'être* of labor unions? Or, for that matter, of business corporations? Or the rôle of government?

This is where all of us are today. It is also where, for the labor unions' portion of this predicament, Mr. Tyler begins his timely, incisively written, and descriptively seminal book.

PREFACE

▶ Labor unions belong to the genus corporation in the great tradition of monasteries, guilds, universities, municipalities, charitable societies, and business enterprises. Hence insights on unions offer insights on corporations.

In the nature and dynamics of all these institutions may also be found clues to the mystery of man, one of whose eternal expressions is the corporation.

It is the contention of this volume that the union, like its corporate counterparts, is a political entity, with the word *political* used in four senses. First, it is political in the Aristotelian sense that "man is, by nature, a political animal," who congregates around a *polis* including the *polis* of occupation. Second, it is political in the Lasswellian sense of "who gets what" in the world of the economy. Third, it is political in the vulgate sense of participating in governmental processes. Finally, it is political in the Machiavellian sense of the *homo politicus* manipulating men and their minds.

Hence, while this is a study of unions (and corporations) it is simultaneously a study of man, the political animal. It is an effort to look into the phenomenon of life through the piercing eye of an institution—the labor organization.

The author leans on two sources: on himself as one with more than three decades of experience in the labor movement; and on students of anthropology, ethology, theology, biology, economics, politics, history, psychology, sociology and cooperative life who have explored facets of man's existence.

This book is intended to be nonjudgmental. It does not argue that unions are good or bad; it tries to state what they are—in themselves and as a complex expression of man's dilemmas.

The author realizes that in the writing of this book he has violated an ancient trade union principle; namely, the jurisdiction of the craft. He has invaded the territories of disciplines in which he has no formal standing and has, therefore, undoubtedly invited the ire of those upon whose intellectual property he has trespassed. The author expects to be chastised, but begs that he be beat with mercy. If he has crossed strange boundaries, it was out of admiration for the strange great trees of knowledge whose apples he could not resist.

GUS TYLER

CONTENTS

I

The Labor Interrogatives

By 1976 American trade unionism will be about two centuries old, yet there are open questions about its role in the total culture which have persisted throughout labor history. The major queries apply to the nature of the unions themselves and to their impact on the economy, the government, and the free society. Each generation asks the questions anew as if they had never been asked before. And each generation seeks answers by reference to immediate conditions as if there were nothing to be learned from the past.

What are these eternal interrogatives?

First, will there continue to be a labor movement—or will it lose influence and ultimately disappear? Second, what is the role of the union in collective bargaining—the ends and the means of trade unionism in the economy? Third, what is the role of organized labor in government—its program and its practices? Finally, what are the aspirations and ambitions of trade union leaders—democrats or bureaucrats?

In the second half of the twentieth century, these questions are reopened, as they will be again and again in the coming decades. They are perennial queries that will only yield their secrets to eternal truths. Yet, because the questions seem to arise out of immediate circumstances, answers are usually sought in fleeting situations. This inquiry is an attempt to unearth the roots of unionism, entailing an investigation into the past to reveal the dynamics of the present as they shape the future. The term *past* will not be limited to the recent past, traditionally dating back to the industrial revolution. It is a thesis of this work that the relevant past goes back to the guilds and the ecclesiastical corporations, and before that to man's innate associative habit, and even before that to man's prehistory and the instincts that he inherited from his less sapient vertebrate ancestors.

Lest this undertaking appear to be as pretentious as it is ambitious, it may be well to consider the need for this sort of comprehensive venture into understanding the labor movement. At present, the study of unionism is a narrow science. It has become a subheading in economics and gamesmanship, the measuring of money and the manipulation of men. There are endless studies on labor and the labor market, on wages and costs, on production and efficiency, on contracts and clauses, on automation and employment. The unions are viewed as an item in econometrics. The dynamics of the movement—that is, collective bargaining, organization drives, strikes, arbitration, settlements—are handled as a by-product in the new science of gamesmanship, studies in how-it-was-done or advice on how-to-do-it.

Although econometrics and gamesmanship are valuable and vital sciences, especially for the daily practitioner, they have only limited worth. A man can be taught to drive a car skillfully while knowing little about what makes the car run, even less about the origins of the combustion engine, and absolutely nothing about the nature of physical movement. Likewise, a man can be taught to organize a plant, or break a strike, or settle a controversy without his knowing about the basic nature of the labor movement.

For a period, there was considerable interest among labor scholars in unions as institutions rather than as mere instruments. The classic history of American labor by John R. Commons is one such investigation into the institutional roots and social dynamics of the movement.[1] A handful of scholars continue the work. But it is a striking evidence of the decline of such institutionalists that in the decades since Commons' great landmark work, there has been nothing comparable with this monumental undertaking. The study of the total institution has made way for bits and fragments of history about different unions, different

1. John R. Commons and Associates, *History of Labor in the United States* (New York: Macmillan Company, 1926).

periods, different interpretations of specific events. And, while many of these studies are as useful as they are scholarly, they provide little insight into the role of organized labor as a continuing force in American civilization.

The institutional study of unions has, since Commons, become a subheading of history, often limited to economic history. Occasionally, some concession is made to politics as it affected the economy and hence the unions—and there it ends.

Statements on the long-range origins and purposes of the labor movement have become the special preserve of absolutists, generally the ideologic children of Marx. They see the movement arise as an antithesis to capitalism. They see it growing in might and militancy until such day as the proletariat takes power to transform the bourgeois thesis into a socialist synthesis. Where the movement fails to go along its prescribed course, the absolutist attributes this to the bad judgment or motives of the leaders, to the backwardness of the mass, or to some momentary happenstance that will, at most, merely delay the inevitable day of deliverance.

Some of the absolutists, having become disillusioned with their illusions, have abandoned their messianic view of the labor movement. It was all a bad dream. The movement never was a movement; the unions are merely pillars of the Establishment; soon they will be a forgotten footnote in the development of corporate capitalism.

Yet in the years since Marx and Commons, the intellectual world has developed new disciplines to understand man and his man-made institutions: state, church, corporation, juvenile gang, ethnic enclave. Anthropology, sociology, ethology, psychology (especially psychoanalysis) provide new instruments to probe human behavior. These more recent disciplines turn their attention to all sorts of social institutions, from the family to the organization man, from the cocktail party to the political party, from tribalism to nationalism. No one and nothing is sacred as the new sciences invade the older humanities of economics, history, law, government, business.

Yet somehow unionism has been immune—with a few rare and startling exceptions. As a study, unions have been left to the economists, now sharing their monopoly with the gamesmen, with an occasional crumb to the historian.

This inquiry assumes that the new knowledge that man has of himself is relevant to unionism—as relevant, let us say, as it is to the corporation. The study of unionism should not be confined to its relations to itself or just to the production process or even to the economy. Unions are a product of a total culture that derives its most stubborn habits from a primeval past.

Because the wish for omniscience does not automatically confer omniscience, this undertaking will be limited by man's still inadequate knowledge of man, and even more limited by the author's measured share of that informational store. Yet, lest a massive movement in American life remain an intellectual *terra incognita*, this work will venture into the precarious realm of labor's long-neglected institutional origins and imperatives, equipped with untested weapons and uproven thoughts, with the hope that the dead bones of our failures will leave a trail for others to follow.

The compulsion to undertake this perilous journey derives from something more than curiosity. There are immediate questions before us—ancient interrogatives restated in fresh terms. They beg for an answer—or, at least, for an intelligent dialogue. Here is the way these perennials appear this season: Will there be a labor movement? Will there continue to be a labor movement? This latter question became fashionable during the mid-1950s after the merger of the American Federation of Labor and the Congress of Industrial Organizations. Out of the marriage much was awaited but little occurred. The unorganized were not organized; some unions lost membership; the percentage of unionists fell. Viewed in the short run, a forecast of doom appeared valid: all the indices were negative. What the forecast lacked was philosophy: the nature of unions as rooted in the phenomenon of man. The nay-sayers saw labor organizations as the products of a current industrial circumstance and not as eternal expressions of man's being. The *now* blinded them to the *hereafter*. There were associations of workmen, tightly knit unions, in the Greek and Roman Empires. There were unions of craft journeymen in medieval Europe. There were unions in Colonial America. It is hardly likely that, with roots so deep and ubiquitous, unions should choose to vanish in our times when they are more powerful and more widely accepted than at any time in their centuries-old history.

The question about labor's future is, of course, not new in this country. In the opening decade of the nineteenth century, court decisions in the cases of the cordwainers placed all unionism in jeopardy: A union was a conspiracy and, if it was not so per se, it was so because of its inevitable antisocial misbehavior. Following that decision, unions sagged. With the depression in the late 1820s unionism seemed on the way out. But by the mid-1830s, unions were once more flourishing, grouped around a central labor federation of considerable influence. With the depression of the late '30s, however, the unions collapsed again. In their stead came a steady stream of social reformers. There seemed little need or hope for labor organizations per se.

Yet immediately following the Civil War, great organizations of working people again appeared, the most notable being the Noble and Holy Order of the Knights of Labor. Their lofty sentiments resounded throughout the land; their rough, tough rank and file took on the giants of industry in bloody combat and won victories. For two decades, the Knights dominated the labor-management arena, inspiring workers, frightening employers, yet before the century was out, the movement had declined.

In the first decade of the new century, a new labor federation picked up where the Knights had left off. The American Federation of Labor, born in the 1880s, came into its own in the years from 1900 to 1904, establishing an almost undisputed hegemony over American trade unionism. Rising and falling with the business cycle (more or less), it continued as a solid and stolid force until the early 1930s and the great collapse of the economy. Once more the old question: would there be a labor movement?

In the mid-1930s, a new sector of the labor force was organized into the Committee for Industrial Organizations. The unskilled and semiskilled in mass production were unionized. From 1935 to 1955, AFL and CIO engaged in continuous war and they both grew bigger and stronger in the process. And then they merged into AFL-CIO. Whereas they both grew while fighting each other, they now began to decline while uniting with each other. Once more, the old question recurred. The immediate fear was that the union could not organize the "new labor force." These were the employees in the service trades and in white-collar jobs who were now the majority over the old blue-collar workers in production. Prominent in this new labor force, as an ever-growing sector, were the professionals and those working for nonprofit institutions, especially government.

Will the trade unions be able to take hold in this new labor force? Answers can be sought in many ways. The simplest is to find out whether unions are having any success among the workers in these new and now dominant sectors of the economy. This is the usual econometric approach: a kind of bookkeeper's judgment about the phenomenon of man. Another way is to conduct polls, surveys, questionnaires in depth to discover the mental makeup of the new breed. This is a form of sociometrics: predicting the future outcome by measuring the present mood, like taking a poll to forecast an election. Still another approach is a consultation with history: to find analogues to the present dilemma.

While all these approaches are useful, and the author has indulged in their use regularly, it is here suggested that a more basic approach is timely: to find out whether there is not something in the very nature of man, including the working man, that does not mandate the inevitable appearance of unions among the new members of the labor force. For want of a better name, this might be called an anthropologic investigation of unions: the missing link between man's relationship to the apes and to his employer.

As eternal as the question of labor's continued being is the matter of the union's role in collective bargaining. Some insight here may be derived from looking into the behavior of the modern union's forbears—the guild—not simply to note similarities but also to underline the continuing nature of unions from era to era.

It is folklore that the organization of workers to put unionized (united) pressure on employers is a child of the industrial revolution. This widespread belief has inhibited many historians of the movement from digging into the medieval past to the era of guildism to uncover the roots of unionism. Traditionally, guilds and unions are viewed as unconnected phenomena.

In truth, however, there were organizations, strikes, and rules for the settlement of conflicts that run back many centuries before the modern era linking guilds to unions. And the questions raised then are questions that persist to the present.

Consider this ordinance of the shearman of London, for instance, dated 1350:[2]

Whereas heretofore, if there was any dispute between a master in the said trade and his man, such man has been wont to go to all the men within the city of the same trade; and then, by covin and conspiracy between them made, they would order that no one among them should work, or serve his own master until the said master and his servant, or man, had come to an agreement; by reason whereof the masters in the said trade have been in great trouble, and the people left unserved;—it is ordained that from henceforth, if there be any dispute moved between any master and his man in the said

2. *Memorials of London*, pp. 247–248, quoted by John P. Davis, *Corporations* (New York: Capricorn Books, 1961; original edition, 1897), pp. 184–185.

trade, such dispute shall be settled by the wardens of the trade. And if the man who shall have offended, or shall have badly behaved himself towards his master, will not submit to be tried before the said wardens, then such man shall be arrested by a sergeant of the Chamber, at the suit of the said wardens, and brought before the Mayor and the Aldermen; and before them let him be punished, at their discretion.

In these two sentences, drawn from an ordinance written more than half a millennium ago, are contained all the crucial elements of collective bargaining. Here are described the origin of a union, a strike, the injured parties, a private instrument for settling the strike, and the use of governmental power to enforce the rule. Thus was it in 1350 and thus was it in 1950. Consider, one by one, the almost imperishable elements of the drama:

The action begins with a man going "to all the men . . . of the same trade." It is significant that he does not go to all workingmen, but to his craft kin, an early foreshadowing of what later came to be called business or job-conscious unionism. In the "union" of the skill, the man feels his strength.

Although the ordinance describes the man as "wont to go to all the men within the city of the same trade," it is truly unrealistic to believe that every time a man felt aggrieved he had to undertake a personal organizing drive to attain his ends. It is more likely that the men "of the same trade" were in fairly regular contact with one another. There also is a mountain of evidence, as we shall note later, that such guilds of craftsmen existed on a going basis. If they did not, the master would have had little to concern him, for it would have been an endless exercise in futility for the complainant to create an organization on an ad hoc basis for each grievance.

The second action is the strike, in which it was ordered that "no man among them should work." Indeed, this definition of a strike is as exact for the present as it was for the fourteenth century. And the way in which the strike ended is likewise exactly the same, right down to the use of the same term. They had to "come to an agreement."

The attitude of the masters, in their reaction toward this cessation of work, was classic in its content. First, they complained that, as a result of the strike, the masters of the trade have been in great trouble. Then, they added, the inevitable appeal to the public interest; namely, "the people left unserved." Finally, they invoked the pejorative stigma for the combination of their workingmen, naming it an act of "covin and conspiracy."

From then to the present almost identical appeals and protests have come from "masters" confronting organizations of their "men." Because strikes have brought "great trouble" to management, the latter have sued unions for damages—and, on many occasions, have collected handsomely. Because strikes inconvenience the consumer, employers have appealed to public opinion to turn against unions. And, finally, since unions are a combination of men endangering both wealth and commonwealth, employers have beseeched courts to hold that unions, or certain acts of unions, are a "conspiracy" and should be treated accordingly. In the fourteenth-century ordinance, machinery is established to deal with the conspiracy. The wardens of the trade have the final word. And if any man refuses to recognize the authority of the wardens—the big rulers of their little private governments—then the man can be forcibly hailed before the Mayor and Alderman for appropriate punishment.

In the centuries since 1350, the methods for channeling or checking the "strike" have been defined and refined over and over. But eternally there stands the question of how far the right to strike may be extended.

In the second half of the twentieth century, this is still a wide open question. Shall a nationwide strike in any industry be permitted or shall all strikes be limited to local areas? Shall a union have the right to strike an industry affecting the national health and welfare, especially in a moment of national crisis? Shall public employees have the right to strike, and if so, which public employees?

As open as the question of the right to strike is the question of how to hasten or compel an agreement. Shall it be by purely voluntary actions on the part of the disputants? Or shall some government agency act as conciliation or mediation service? Or shall there be compulsory arbitration? Or shall the President of the United States or the mayor of a city be provided with an arsenal of weapons to be used at his discretion? Every one of these questions is presently before local councils and federal legislature in a variety of forms. They are merely restatements of an ancient problem of how to deal with the strike.

The medieval ordinance does not touch on the reason why the men go on strike. As a rule, ordinances and industrial relations legislation do not go into the causes of the strife, except in some general terms in the preamble to certain bits of law. But it would not take much research or imagination to know the causes of conflict. Undoubtedly, they involve pay for work done, work conditions, and work rules. The basic reasons why men strike have not changed in essence though they have changed in form.

Through the ages, conflict between master and servant breaks out over three central points: power, prices, and production. Power involves the relative rights and prerogatives of the contending parties. Prices involve the cost of labor as well as the selling price of the service or commodity, thereby also affecting profits. Production involves the work methodology as defined by management and modified or adjusted according to the pressures of labor.

The ordinance of 1350 deals solely with the first eternal interrogative: power. It does not go into prices or production. It decides who has the last word in the dispute. It tries to answer the simple query: Who's in charge here? In the centuries that have followed, this matter has recurred incessantly. It is still unsettled.

In the latter half of the twentieth century the question arises in the form of management prerogatives. There is little quarrel in present day America that a union has the right to be recognized and to engage in a dialogue with the employer over matters of wages and hours, although even in this elementary area there are grey zones. But there certainly is no agreement about whether a union has the right to demand a share in profits, to examine employers' books, to control contract work, to block new production techniques, to control hiring and firing, to pass on plant removal. These are but samplings of some of the hottest questions in labor relations in the twentieth century. And they all come down to the question of who has the final say over what—the question of power.

Over the years, the relative power of master and servant has gone through many changes. In 1303, notes the *Liber Custumarum*, "the Cordwainers had found it advisable to forbid by ordinance that their journeymen should meet to make provisions to the prejudice of the craft or the damage of the common people, on pain of imprisonment."[3] In effect, this was a sweeping decree against the journeyman's freedom of assemblage to push his special interest. The master cordwainer was unquestioned master. In the following centuries, the power of the "servant" has risen to challenge the unilateral power of the master to rule the workplace. But the exact boundaries remain unfixed because in the very nature of the struggle between boss and bossed—as in the struggle of nations, churches, street gangs, staphylococci, or male kobs—boundaries are defined by strength, whether physical, aesthetic, mental, or supernatural.

It is part of our thesis that the workplace is a small planet. It is a microcosm, like a jungle in Uganda with its inter- and intraspecific wars or like a cubic inch of soil with its microscopic belligerents. In the microcosm of the company or industry, a union seeks to exert power. In the larger world of the government

3. Quoted by Davis, *op. cit.*, p. 185.

and society, a union likewise seeks to exert power. In both cases, the union—the organization of the worker—is the means whereby the laboring man makes his presence known in the community.

It is a popular myth that organizations representing working people did not have any voice in government until the late eighteenth or early nineteenth century. The dates coincide with the great democratic revolutions in America and France and with the subsequent extension of the franchise to the propertyless classes. The workingmen's parties of the late 1820s in the United States—a product of the revolution and the extended franchise—are generally believed to be the first sally of labor organizations into politics.

Yet, if one does not limit the concept of organized labor to the modern type of union but enlarges the idea to include the craft guilds, there is evidence that these early prototypes of unions were deeply involved in the politics of their times and, indeed, represented the main, if not the sole, channel whereby the toiler could make his presence known in governing councils. The evolution of the craftsman from a societal nonentity to a political voice in the English towns is the narrative of the rise of the guilds in the middle ages.

In eleventh- and twelfth-century England, the craftsman was something of a pariah, an official second class citizen. He was denied the right of burgess-ship (citizenship) and found himself in a servile state. He could not bring an accusation against a townsman, nor could the latter be convicted on the testimony of the former. If a craftsman wished to become a burgess, he had to forsake his craft, bidding farewell to both his guild and his tools. In brief, the mark of the guild was a mark of shame, a lowly status without the normal rights of free men.

After about two and a half centuries of such shame, the craftsman and his guild began to emerge into respectability. By the end of the thirteenth century the craftsman could become a citizen. In explaining the reason for the upward transition, it is suggested "(a) that the craftsmen were increasing in number, (b) that many who had been serfs of the feudal lords became free, and (c) that they increased in prosperity and consequently in wealth."[4] In any event, guild no longer meant exclusion from citizenship.

As the guilds further increased membership and gained their rights and riches, they began to turn exclusive. They would no longer accept just plain people into their old societies of new status; a man had to be a burgess before he could get membership in the craft. The early mold had been turned inside out: once a guildsman was denied citizenship and now a craftsman had to be a citizen to get into a guild. The badge of dishonor had become a symbol of status—not an uncommon twist when the once disowned become owners.

In this period, membership in the guild and membership in the town—standing as craftsman and as burgess—became so intertwined that one became almost indistinguishable from the other. The guilds became the entrance to the political realm and vice versa. The cordwainers and sawyers prescribed (1375) "that no one of said trade shall keep house within the franchise, if he be not free of the said city, and one knowing his trade; and that no one shall be admitted to the freedom without the presence of the wardens of the said trade, bearing witness to his standing." In short, the wardens of the trade stood vigilance at the doors of the town and the trade: to get into either, one had to pass muster before these potentates. What was true of the cordwainers was true of the scriveners of London who were not permitted to practice their skill if they were not "free of the city, made free in the same craft, and that, by men of the craft." As late as the seventeenth century it was custom in Chester "that no man can use or exercise any trade unless—besides his freedom of the Cittie— he be alsoe admitted, sworne, and made free of the same Company whereof he desires to trade."

4. Davis, *op. cit.*, p. 199.

Many of these practices had grown up through custom or the private law of a guild. Inevitably, these social habits were formalized into ordinances that could be enforced by public agencies. From there it was only one short step to endowing the guilds with official standing in the governing councils of the town. Thus, for instance, the Council of Durham, by its charter of 1602, was composed of a mayor, twelve lifetime aldermen, and twenty-four guild representatives—two selected from each of twelve crafts. "In some towns," notes Davis, "the domination of the guilds was carried so far that the town government was constitutionally nothing more than a federation of guilds."[5]

Although these developments took place many centuries ago, they present a striking analogy to many subsequent social orders and utopias. A government composed of federated guilds inevitably invites comparison with the soviets of the communists, the corporate state of the fascists, the guild socialism of some British Fabians or the industrial republic of Daniel de Leon. In all these cases, the occupational institution (guild, union, corporation, soviet) becomes the base of the government, indeed, forms the state itself. If one equates the guilds with soviets (and why not?), then many towns of Elizabethan England were the prototypes of the U.S.S.R.

Actually, the notion that the guilds (or the soviets) were (or are) the true government is an illusion. By the time the guilds were admitted to the governing circles, they were bureaucratized by the political leaders within the guilds, who had now risen to positions of personal wealth and power and were running the treasuries and real estate of the guilds as if they were all the private preserve of the guild hierarchy. Admitted to the governing clique, this "new class" of institutional bureaucrats now used their public posts further to enlarge their riches and their influence. The guilds themselves changed character, becoming less

5. Davis, *op. cit.*, p. 200.

14

trade and job conscious and more political and government conscious. "Instead of being organizations of tradesmen and craftsmen in the town, they tended to become merely sections of the town population, the pivot around which their social life revolved being participation in town life and not engagement in trade or craft. Accordingly the combination of guilds became frequent, when the centripetal force of burgess-ship became stronger and the centrifugal force of economic interests became weaker."[6] In short, as the guilds entered government, they (or at least their leaders) became statesmen, more concerned with the problems of the community than with their one-time special interest, using the guilds as a power base, and allowing their original form and role to atrophy.

Surely, the same may be said of the evolution of the Russian soviets. As envisioned by Lenin in his *State and Revolution,* the soviets were to replace both Czar and Duma, both the monarch and the parliament. Worker, farmer, and soldier—through his separate little soviet—would be the government, thereby giving every lowly soul a big direct voice in high places. To Lenin, the soviet was the ultimate in democracy: a pluralist government in which every one would be most effectively involved through representatives speaking for the special interests of his occupational grouping. In the great parliament of occupations—the supreme soviet—would blossom the perfect democracy. This dream of Lenin's was soon a nightmare, as Communist Party commissars took control of the soviets and as an inner clique took control of the Communist Party; the "democracy" became a dictatorship and pluralism became totalitarianism.

The role of the guild in the political structure of the middle ages is mentioned here to indicate how old is the question of labor organizations in politics. At a later point, we will deal with this question at some length. In this introduction, however, it

6. *Ibid.*, p. 201.

should be noted that this has been one of the great subjects of inner controversy within the American labor movement: should unions be economic or political institutions?

In the early years of the American Federation of Labor, this question separated socialists from pure-and-simple trade unionists. The former group was primarily political; the latter, primarily occupational. The former thought of the union as a base of governmental power; the latter thought of the union as the base of industrial pressure. The wars between the socialists and the followers of the Gompers school were long, repetitive, and indecisive.

After the AFL-CIO merger in the mid-1950s it appeared that the labor movement had come to a consensus: to do both industrial and political work. But the consensus covered up all the nuances of emphasis on how much industrial and how much political. And over such matters the debate within the labor movement continues, as it will for many decades, and it is expressed less in well-ordered arguments than in specific actions or inactions.

The role of unions in politics, however, is not simply a subject of internal union debate. The question comes regularly before Congress as legislation is introduced to limit unions to collective bargaining and to curb their political influence and instrumentalities. Those who oppose union political power do so for a spectrum of good reasons extending from fear that labor's influence will create an inimical climate for business to fear that the unions will be the base of an American Soviet.

While this debate rages within and without the labor movement, the unions continue to evolve attitudes toward political action that are less the product of sheer argument, logic, and deliberative decision-making than they are the inevitable expression of laws at work within man and the human community. These laws of group behavior were as meaningful in Elizabethan England and Jacksonian America as in the conduct of the AFL-

CIO Committee on Political Education in the mid-twentieth century. In the deepest sense, the basic drive behind labor politics is to be found in the compulsions of living creatures to work out a modus vivendi within the environment. And since man is the supreme virtuoso in this calling, rising above all other creatures precisely because he is relentlessly dedicated to affecting his environment, it may be expected that the workingman, one of the subspecies of man, will pursue the common purpose of the species, through the great ritual of politics.

The social institutions that develop within the United States are regularly appraised in terms of their impact on the official dream: the democratic way of life. Unions have not, and probably should not, escape such repetitive assessment. Even when a culture does not formally put its constituent parts to the test, the civilization has sly, hidden ways of making its institutions behave. Political party, church, economic system, corporation, and union are constantly disciplined by the common ethos. For example, in speaking of the ethical basis of the economic order, Manning Nash holds that "the economy is not so different from the rest of society so that one set of values holds there, and other values hold in other contexts. The economic system does not exhibit an ethic counterposed to the regnant value system."[7]

While this bit of insight on the relationship between economy and culture—a statement broad enough to underpin a total science of economic anthropology—may well go unchallenged, it is much more difficult to apply the same concept to trade unions: namely, that the labor movement "is not so different" and that it does not "exhibit an ethic counterposed to the regnant value system." After all, unions do come into being as a counterforce, as a challenge to the economic and political establishment. At times the challenge even rises to revolutionary assault on the immorality

7. Manning Nash, "The Organization of Economic Life," in *Horizons of Anthropology,* ed. Sol Tax (Chicago: Aldine Publishing Co., 1964), p. 177.

of the ancient regime. Surely, the identity of values between labor and the culture has been questioned.

What is the impact of unions on the democratic way of life? In part, this question has been posed in the discussions of unions in relation to the economy and politics. In recent years, however, unions have been assessed for their impact in terms of their internal structure and operation. The bureaucratization of American unions is a subject of fairly recent vintage. In their earliest days, unions had minimal bureaucratic problems because there was minimal bureaucracy. As in every primitive grouping, the prevailing poverty in the first unions made it impossible to maintain a cadre of full-time leaders. But, just as in all other civilizations, when there was enough income to provide for a permanent corps of aristocrats—priests or kings—a bureaucracy appeared; so, too, in the trade unions.

In the democratic lexicon, the word *bureaucrat* is pejorative, although the most democratic nation of the second half of the twentieth century could not make its libertarian method nor its humanitarian aspirations effective without a steady proliferation of bureaus and bureaucrats. So, too, in unions, especially in those with loftier traditions, the concept of the bureaucrat is repulsive. Hence, unions will, out of hand, deny the existence of bureaucrats, although if they are without them, they are the only stable institutions that have ever existed in this unstructured state. To embarrass unions, their critics try to pin an even more obnoxious label on union leaders by calling them "labor bosses."

Responding to these taunting words, unions trot out their lares and penates, the household gods of democracy. They point to their past deeds in winning for the worker a voice in economy and government—the birth and development of industrial and political democracy—and to their egalitarian constitutions and the election of officers, from president to sergeant-at-arms. They point to the rejection (or approval) of contracts by rank and file; to the origins of the top men, risen from the workbench to the high seats of union office; and to the daily involvement of workers in union life at the plant level. The case is solidly based in history and current events.

Yet none of this evidence really settles the question of bureaucracy and democracy in the labor movement. There have been union presidents, albeit few, who have been elected for life. Many union conventions are rituals to confirm an existing hierarchy and a preordained policy. Oppositionists to existing leadership have, in some notable cases, been treated as outlaws and liquidated through summary justice or straight murder. Occasionally, a union is taken over by gangsters who run the union as if it were a gangster state. These individual transgressions against the democratic ideal—whether they be few or many—are sufficiently dramatic to call into question the impact of unionism, as a system of internal government, on a free society. Under the auspices of a Senate committee, there has been a continuing investigation of internal union operations for many years. Out of these investigations came a modification of the labor-management act, entitled the Taft-Hartley Act, that placed unions under legislative controls so far as their internal conduct was concerned. For many decades to come, the relations of union leaders to members will continue to be a matter of concern to both the labor movement and the nation.

In trying to understand by what inner mechanisms unions are controlled, we will find that little understanding can be derived from the necessarily limiting investigations of unions per se. The answers partially lie in history: in the development of the guilds, in the evolution of corporations, in the bureaucratization of nations. And beyond that the answers will have to be found in the kind of conclusion Robert Michels reached about all political organizations or Machiavelli assumed in his advice to the Prince. And even then we will not have reached the end, as the investigation leads on to the role of leadership in the tribe and the problems of ethics and power.

2

The Aristotelian Imperative

▶   "Man is, by nature, a political animal," said Aristotle. What did he mean? He surely did not mean that every man runs for political office or even casts a vote. This has never been true and certainly was not true of ancient Greece. According to one popularized version, in Athens there were "about 250,000 people but only 35,000 had the vote. Only full-fledged, high-octane, hereditary, pure-blooded male Athenian citizens were allowed any part in public affairs. The other 86 per cent of the population, some 215,000 people had no voice at all."[1] Despite this, Aristotle held to his sweeping generalization about the nature of man.

What Aristotle meant was that somewhere in man's bones is a congregational compulsion. Man is a gregarious animal. In ancient Greece, the group in which he gathered, his organized community, was called the *polis* (city). Hence, man is a *political* animal. Man gathers in his *polis* not by accident nor by design but by nature. He is re-enacting in a civilized state the primeval habit he inherited with his animal origins: the herd instinct.

The natural groupings of man are generally conceived in territorial terms: the city-state or the nation. Yet, such groupings certainly do not exhaust the forms in which men congregate. The nomadic tribe, as one obvious example, does not cling to one piece of politically bounded real estate; it wanders. The ancient history of the Hebrews is probably the most famous record of a movable *polis*. And in the Diaspora, the wandering Jew again finds his *polis*—his culture identity—in unexpected corners of the earth.

The congregational compulsion is an open instinct that ex-

1. Advertisement of the Amalgamated Lithographers in *The New York Times*, December 6, 1956.

presses itself in multiple groupings within the great cultural groupings of mankind. Among these subcultures is the polity of the occupation, springing from the *polis* of the workplace. The trade union is one such polity, an expression of man's political nature based on a man's skill, trade, or profession. Although such organizations find rational explanations for being, the underlying drive is the instinct of occupational birds to flock together.

Although the many forms in which men group are diverse, they hold certain traits in common—whether they be a nation, gang, guild, corporation, or religion. They have recorded these traits in the etymology of several words derived from the Greek *polis*, such as polity, policy, politics, and police. Put together they define the nature of groups. *Polity* is defined by Webster as the "form or constitution of government of a state, or of any institution or organization similarly administered"; it is the more or less formal, written or unwritten composition of the group, expressed through constitution, mores, customs, rituals. *Policy* is the program of the polity; it may be stated in some literary form, such as the preamble to a constitution or in the Decalogue, or in codified legislation, or in a tribal leader's call to hunt the elephant, a general's command to charge the enemy, or a union leader's pleas to strike the boss. *Politics* is the process of making policy; it is the complex game of who does what, of leader and led, of authority and freedom, of rule and revolt. *Police* enforce policy; they are the disciplinary element in the polity—the instrument of the politico-in-charge to carry through his will (policy) within the rules of the polity.

This cluster of relationships, deriving etymologically from *polis*, are valid for man, the political animal, in the great territorial groupings of mankind and in the subgroupings called unions. They spring from the herd instinct, the congregational compulsion. The concept of the congregational compulsion is repugnant to the American mood. The notion of any compulsion, whether imposed from without or within, is repulsive to a free people. In addition, as children of the Enlightenment, we prefer to believe that our acts are the results of conscious reason and not unconscious instincts. The Aristotelian concept of the herd man smacks too much of the closed society. As a people, our folklore opts for social compact over social compulsion.

Much of the American experience tends to reinforce the notion that social systems are the product of a social compact, a broad-based agreement reached by free men. The nation began with a written document—a compact penned on the Mayflower —that was drafted and ratified by free men. In all respects this was an example of Rousseau's romantic notion about the origins of society: free individuals voluntarily joining together into a social contract. When a Roger Williams or an Ann Hutchinson became displeased with the contract, they removed themselves and their followers to another spot where they once more seemed to be re-enacting the Mayflower Compact as free individuals freely associated. When the separate colonies joined forces against the British, they pledged their honor, mutual fortunes, and lives in the common cause—again as freely associated entities. When the Revolution ended, they wrote a new compact called the Articles of Confederation, and later, still another compact in the form of the Constitution. In all cases, these written agreements started with a preamble that declared the purpose and then proceeded to spell out the social forms agreed upon to pursue the purpose. Against such a background it is only natural that Americans should viscerally feel that social organization is the purposeful act of individuals drawn together in an act of reason.

This piece of autochthonous mythology was inevitably reinforced by the experience of the frontier. Here again the drama of the Mayflower was re-enacted. Men and their families arrived in new lands, not as ocean voyagers, but by flat boats down the Ohio River, by covered wagons, by narrow trails. Each man carved his way in the wilderness or erected his log castle on the lone prairies. He established his sovereignty as an individual with his ax and his gun. When towns and territory were composed, they were based on still another written document: the Northwest Ordinance, a highly egalitarian statement of purpose.

The social fluidity of America further reinforced the myth that social organization is the result of individual will rather than societal instinct. The American workman was not bound by the Tudor Industrial Code that froze him into an occupational category almost from birth, that bound him to his job and his earnings by law, that restricted his movement from place to place by necessity and his movement from craft to craft by governmental decree. The American workman could move both horizontally (from place to place) and vertically (from poor to rich or, occasionally, vice versa). His movement was facilitated by the shortage of skilled workers in the colonies that effectively nullified any attempts to apply the Tudor caste system in the new world. For these reasons, the guild system never sank real roots in the colonies, and organizations of artisans came into being as voluntary associations, a further re-enactment of the social compact in the *polis* of the workplace.

The dramatic experience of the American Revolution—a free people rebelling against formal authority—added a militant ethos to the myth of the social compact. Aristocracy was an abomination, the usurpation of power by force, ritual, and pretense. The revolutionary struggle was distilled down to freedom versus autocracy, the individual versus the government. That government was best that governed least. The utopian dream that people could do without government altogether sought historic justification in the fantasy that social organization was the handiwork of man's individual desire.

In such a people there were open ears for a Jean Jacques Rousseau or a Henry David Thoreau. Rousseau preached the gospel of the social contract and the innate goodness of man before corruption by the ways of government. Thoreau proved, by his example, that the resourceful man could live happily as a hermit,

For three centuries, American life was dominated by the ideologies of an agricultural people. Up to 1900, the nation was statistically rural. From 1900 on, much of the nation was mythologically rural, clinging with desperation and longing to the notion of the "rugged individual," able to resist forced involvement with his fellow men under the compulsion of either law or circumstance. This rural self-image—the happy, lone, independent man of the soil—found political props in an American legislative structure that perpetuated rural dominance long after rural America had become a rapidly shrinking minority of the nation. This cultural lag—the dominance of rural mythology over metropolitan reality—kept alive the notion of man as a free agent, joining in association with others only when and how he decided, consciously and with good reason, to do so.

The advance of industrialism and metropolitanism tended, perversely, to strengthen the myth of "rugged individualism." As the new order began to make its demands on the ancient regime, the mind of the past hardened in its resistance to the change. Small-town America began to put its habits into words, to pile up an arsenal of clichés with which to fight off encroaching urbanism. Because of inflated rural strength in the American legislative structure, these clichés found formal expression in written law, thereby putting legal flesh on the bones of a bucolic skeleton.

Right into the latter half of the twentieth century, the folk heroes are the men of the "Marlborough country," the lone ranger roaming the open prairie. Our most enduring heroes come out of the west, out of the last frontiers. They are individuals against the crowd, man against destiny, errant and noble and unafraid. They are the rebirth of Columbus on the wide seas, Daniel Boone in the wilderness, Lewis and Clarke in the far northwest. They are the reincarnation of the great American myth—man as the lonely hunter.

To such a people, steeped in such a past, it is repugnant to view any human association as an expression of compulsions out-

2 4

side the conscious decision of the individual. To assume that man is a tribal animal appears to smack of those ideologies we have come to link with the closed society. Thus Karl Raimund Popper speaks of tribalism as "the emphasis on the supreme importance of the tribe without which the individual is nothing at all."[2] To Americans, even the most minute hint that the nation is all and the individual is nothing is anathema. Hence Americans—who are members of many, many tribes at the geographic, social, economic, and ethnic levels—reject almost out of hand any explanation of their associativeness, their great proclivity to join up, based on the tribal character of man.

Despite the natural disinclination of a free people to think of *man* as a collective noun, the evidence of history and the testimony of the present compel the basic assumption that organizations such as unions, cities, churches, families, nations, and gangs are variations on one central theme: the political nature of man, using "political" in the Aristotelian sense. The overwhelming proof lies in the findings of post-Aristotelian disciplines.

"The literature of many disciplines agrees, as it does in little else, on the central importance of groups to an understanding of men in their relations with one another," according to Earl Latham.[3]

The whole structure of modern society is associational, adds William Yandell Elliott.[4]

Modern man is literally conducted from the cradle to the grave by groups, for he is born in a family, goes to school in organized classes, goes to church, perhaps, plays with boyhood gangs, joins fraternities, works for a corporation, belongs to various associations,

2. Karl Raimund Popper, *The Open Society and Its Enemies* (Princeton: Princeton University Press, 1963), p. 9.
3. Earl Latham, *The Group Basis of Politics* (Ithaca, N.Y.: Cornell University Press, 1952), p. 1.
4. William Yandell Elliott, *The Pragmatic Revolt in Politics* (New York: Macmillan Co., 1928), p. 434, quoted by Latham, *op. cit.*, p. 1.

cultural, civic, professional and social, and is carried off to his im-
mortal reward by a business enterpriser with the solemnity appropriate to such ceremonies.

In running through the disciplines, Latham states:[5]

Sociology devoted itself to the study of groups. . . . The instru-
mentalist philosophy of John Dewey rejects the abstract individual
as a fictional character. . . . The psychologists, by different routes,
come to the same conclusion. . . . The concept of the group is basic
to certain approaches to jurisprudence, and it has been helpful in
bringing to economics a knowledge of the human institutions through
which men dig coal, make soap and battleships, create credit, and
allocate new resources of production.

The historian John Bowle makes the following commentary:[6]

During the last century and a half, the perspective of thought has
been radically altered by a new apprehension of the antiquity of
man. Modern research, as well as political experience, sees human
society heavily controlled by forces atavistic, instinctive, to logical
analysis often blind, yet for that reason perhaps the more in harmony
with the mysterious tide of life. . . . In view of this evidence, the
ancient assumption that civilization derives from a social compact,
reflecting the deliberate choice of rational individuals, has long disappeared, and history is seen as a branch of a relatively new science
of biology, concerned with a creature which owes much of its success to an intense sociability. . . . When in the Upper Palaeolithic,
homo sapiens became the dominant human type, his societies were
socially solid and mentally co-conscious; they had to be to survive.
The basis of the earliest communities is primarily the pack.

The fact that man is under a constant compulsion to "join up"
does not mean that he does not have a freedom of choice. The
final decision as to what organization to join is a free act, in the
same way that a hungry man's decision on what to order from

5. Latham, *op. cit.*, pp. 3–5.
6. John Bowle, *Western Political Thought* (New York: Oxford University
Press, 1949), p. 15–16.

the menu is a free choice. But the drive to associate—like the need to eat—is nonrational, even if biologically explicable and philosophically justifiable.

In man's freedom to join a group, he is not equally free in all areas at all times. When a man is born into a nation, he is not free to decide whether he will be a citizen, pay taxes, serve in the armed forces when drafted. These are all musts. If a child is born into a primitive tribe, his options are far more limited than if he is born into a home in Brooklyn, U.S.A. Among jungle people, he will be told how to paint his body, whom to follow, when to make an incantation or to dance, what pain to suffer in the rites of passage. For many centuries, a man was told what religion he must recognize as his own and, even today, if some persons marry outside the faith they are as good as dead. In nations where a caste system prevails, a man is born into a trade with which he is cursed or blessed for the rest of his life.

In certain areas of life in free countries, there are many human associations that are utterly free. One may or may not join a hunting and fishing club; one may or may not buy stocks in AT and T or GE; one may or may not join a fraternity or sorority; one may or may not become a Republican or Democrat or Trotskyite. In these cases, association involves minimal compulsion.

Somewhere between the groups that one *must* join and the groups that one *may* join are the many, many groups that one "must" join while appearing to choose freely from among those organizations that one "may" join. Within the individual and within the community, there are subtle influences at work that tend to blur and dim the line between "must" and "may."

The most common of the subtle forces is language. In a cultural grouping, there is a common language—more or less. Some speak it well—like the King's English; some speak it poorly—all slang. And even these dialects and argots reveal themselves as unifying forces, reflecting the subcultures of language within the larger language culture. A common language is more than a way to communicate; it is a common matrix for thought. The words that are symbols of ideas limit, enlarge, or define our thinking. To talk alike is to think alike, even when we are in bitter disagreement. Indeed, it is not even possible to disagree unless the disputants first agree at least on language.

Languages differ not only from country to country but also among regions, classes, races, and trades. Occupational jargon is a cultural divider and unifier. Consider the clergyman and the industrialist; the learned society and the technician; the photoengraver and the garment cutter; the underworld and the lawyer. If any of these so chose, they could conduct a conversation in their special languages that would leave the outsider totally without comprehension.

Among the other subtle forces at work "compelling" the individual to join some given group are education, dress, tradition, and location. One of the most difficult to resist is the pressure of an existing formal group within a culture, especially if that group has the power to apply violence, to ostracize, or to proselytize.

Any individual, of course, is always free to say *No!* to all these musts. He may be able to leave his country and go into exile, but when he does, he will invariably end up in some new nation or in some exotic colony of exiles with its laws and bylaws. A man may leave his trade, or change his neighborhood, or climb the social ladder. But in each case, he must adjust to some new trade, new neighborhood, or new rung on the way up. And typically, the convert to the new way of life—whether it be job, place, or scale—tends to be a more passionate member of the new *polis* than most of its more settled citizens, who live out the old group ways through ancient habit.

Although man's congregational compulsion appears to be antilibertarian in that it appears to deny man's individuality—his desire and ability to go it alone—the truth of the matter is that man has repeatedly defended his freedoms and won new rights precisely through organization. In the eternal conflict between freedom and organization, man has repeatedly surrendered certain freedoms in order to organize and has organized to win certain freedoms.

A later chapter concerning unions will dwell at greater length and depth on the role of the organization as an instrument of freedom. It is noted here, lest our emphasis on the instinctive need of man to move collectively—the concept of man as a political animal—create the impression that man has no instinct to "be himself," whether this means to enjoy freedom, privacy, or property. But in pursuit of this happiness, man does not escape the instincts of the species: he asserts himself through organized groups called nations, and through groups within the larger groups, such as unions, corporations, political clubs, or committees of correspondence.

Consider the paradox of America. We are a nation of free people. We are also a nation of joiners. We like to think of ourselves as individuals who walk alone and, ironically, we compulsively band together into societies, sensible and nonsensical. Yet in that paradox may be buried a truth: we are free because we organize. The many special and distinctive attitudes and actions that differentiate one individual from another can each be protected because we freely associate with others to form groups to protect our freedom to do what we want to do. Hence, the freer we are, the more organizations. And vice versa—the more organizations, the more defenses for freedom. We are free not only because we are "one out of many" (*E pluribus unum*) but also because out of the one we are many.

In discussing the town of Amherst, William L. Doran reported that there were "well more than one hundred Clubs, Lodges, Leagues, Guilds, Tribes, Granges, Circles, Unions, Chapters, Councils, Societies, Associations, Auxiliaries, Brotherhoods and Fellowships. Their specialities or special interests, to name a few, include cards, cameras, stamps, gardens, churches, teachers, speakers, voters, horses, business, service, golf, nature, fishing, eating, gunning, parents, grandparents, ancestors, needlework, temperance, travel and kindergarten."[7]

The American habit of association and the relationship of this popular occurrence to a free society were clearly discerned by De Tocqueville. "Americans of all ages, all conditions, and all dispositions constantly form associations. . . . Wherever at the head of some undertaking, you see the government in France, or a man of rank in England, in the United States you will be sure to find an association. . . . Amongst the laws which rule human societies, there is one which seems to be more precise and clear than all others. If men are to remain civilized, or to become so, the art of associating together must grow and improve in the same ratio in which the equality of conditions is increased."

The urge to join is not just an American habit. The congregational compulsion is universal. In other countries, the channels through which the instinct flows are more limited by social immobility: in some, birth into a caste means a predetermination of friends, marriage, education, residence, dress, diet, language; in others, political choice is limited—often to one party; elsewhere, religious choice is limited to one religion. In all these different lands, man is joined with his like, under internal and external compulsions. In the United States, where there is greater freedom to join, there is more joining, a more varied proliferation of the herd instinct. But no matter the form, the instinct is always there —an open instinct acculturating its expression to place and time.

What is the origin of this herd instinct? Anthropologists are not altogether agreed on the origins of social life. Some say that man took over the habit from other primates; some say that man —quite unlike other primates—is distinctive in his way of life as a community creature. Some hold that the family is the first form of social organization; others insist that, from the beginning, the

7. William L. Doran, *University of Massachusetts Alumni Bulletin 4* (December 1948), quoted by Earl Latham, *op. cit.*, p. 3.

family has been just a subhead of a larger social group, such as a tribe. They are all agreed on one thing: there never was a lonely couple called Adam and Eve walking happily through the Garden of Eden. From the beginning, man is a congregation.

Robert Briffault, writing in the late 1920s, argues passionately that man, unlike the higher vertebrates, was quite distinctive in forming communities. "The association of individuals is not a common feature in the animal world. . . . There is in the animal world very little that is even analogous to social relations. Gregariousness, the local aggregation of life, is not necessarily association. Herding animals are of all the higher animals the most devoid of social instincts."[8] What makes man different from the other primates, according to Briffault, is the central fact of man's social life. This living in a group is the starting point of a new kind of evolution, cultural rather than physical. Because man, unlike the lower orders, is able to conceptualize, he is able to and *must* organize. This capacity to "work by means of mental images" has transplanted "mental life from the sensory and subconscious psychism of animals to a medium of symbols, ideas, values, to a world which is not the creation of an individual, or inherited by him through psychological processes, but it is the transmitted legacy of a social tradition. That mentality is dependent upon the permanent and undying social group, not upon the transitory individual. . . . Evolutionary development has, in the human species, been transferred from organic elements physiologically inherited to social tradition."[9]

It is clear that, writing in the days before Hitler and World War II and at a time when behaviorism hoped to remake men and social revolution remake man, Briffault sharply severed man from the animal. *Homo sapiens* is, above all else, sapient. He is not, like the animals, the prisoner of his senses or his subconscious

8. Robert Briffault, "Evolution of the Human Species," in *The Making of Man*, ed. Y. F. Calverton (New York: The Modern Library, 1931), p. 765.
9. *Ibid.*, p. 763.

psyche. Man's mental life is radically different. And precisely this difference is expressed in man as the political animal, as the organizer of cultures. To Briffault, man makes societies because he can think and without the society his thinking power would atrophy.

Man's view of man has changed during the past several decades. The beast in man came out on parade, goosestepping his way across other men. Science was impelled to take a deeper look into man by taking a deeper look into animals. The new idea was not to study the animal in the cage, where he was subject to the civilizing influences of man, but to study the beast in his natural habitat. Up to mid-twentieth century, animal behavior was generally studied in captivity, which was unfair to both the primate and the professor. The animal did not live a natural life and the scholar reached unnatural conclusions. But, since about 1958, the savants have left their smelly laboratories and wandered into the jungles to live with, and sometimes live like, the animals to learn about primate, and other, life in the raw. By the mid-1960s, the game of on-the-spot primate probing became so popular that "more than fifty persons from eleven countries, including zoologists, psychologists, and anthropologists were engaged in such studies."[10]

What have we found out from this new science of life with forefather? The first is that "primate life is group life." As Yerkes puts it: "One chimpanzee is no chimpanzee." The primate —at least, the ones most like man—is a herd creature.

When we speak of group life among the primates, we are really not including all of them. There appear to be two general categories: the tree dwellers and the ground dwellers. The former act more like birds, nesting in small family formations of relatively short duration; the latter act like people, gathering in long-lasting communities composed of many families. The

10. Irven DeVore, "The Evolution of Social Life," in *Horizons of Anthropology*, p. 26.

32

primates who are man's closest relatives are not the prosimians who live like birds on the wing but the monkeys and apes who are down-to-earth creatures like us. Their social groups are large, stable, and differentiated. The group always includes more than the family. The social order is stable in that it does not fall apart shortly after the business of mating is over and done with. Within this social order, the individual primates play real and differentiated roles, with a kind of division of labor.[11]

According to DeVore, the human family always occurs as part of a larger social unit, never in isolation. This view of the human group as a community embracing several families is not universally accepted among anthropologists. Carleton S. Coon, for instance, points out that investigation of human beings "in a state of social organization no more complicated than those of the subhuman primates" reveals that "among such peoples the largest stable or social unit, the only true institution, was the simple biological family with or without a few dependent individuals. Members of a group of this kind would spend most of their time moving about in search of food. Their relations with other family groups would be infrequent and so lacking in regularity that no larger institutional structure would be possible."[12]

Coon is quick to grant, however, that if the first primitive group is the family, it is far less typical than the larger unit, what he calls a "cultural complexity." It appears that where the family lives in virtual isolation, it does so because it is surviving at the brink of existence: a primitive people trying to exist in the frozen tundra, the dry desert, the fierce jungle, or the chilly, inhospitable coastal lands. But once life becomes more livable and man's terrestrial existence becomes less precarious than the bird's or prosimian's existence on a tree branch, *homo sapiens* moves to a life bigger than family size.

11. *Ibid.*
12. Carleton S. Coon, *A Reader in General Anthropology* (New York: Holt, Rinehart & Winston, 1948), p. 2.

Approaching this matter in terms of what is relevant for understanding man, Coon adds: "The units of human society which can be studied with greatest profit are the groups of individuals who participate in whole cultures, whether these cultures constitute the way of life of a few hundred chilly hunters or that of millions of comfortable Roman citizens. In any one of these simpler societies a band may consist of let us say ten families of, on an average, five persons each, thus making a total of fifty persons."[13]

In this society, there are no strangers. Everybody knows everybody. The group is close, tight, and so monolithic by nature that the individual thinks in terms of collective consciousness, guilt, and penance. Such groups are called "face-to-face, or *natural*, groups." Whatever they are called by social science, they are the original building blocks with which we erect our vast and complicated social institutions—nations and unions—and they confirm Aristotle's dictum that man is a political animal.

Adding the dimensions of philosophy and theology to that of science, Pierre Teilhard de Chardin in *The Future of Man* stresses the universal meaning of "association or, better still, social organization," starting with the vegetable:[14]

No sooner is it constituted by the grouping together of elementary particles, than the living element, whatever its degree of complexity, begins to reproduce itself. But the process does not end there. When it exists in sufficient numbers the separate element tends to link up with others of its kind so as to form with them a more or less differentiated organic whole. In this fashion, the higher plants and the metazoa evolved out of isolated cells, the corals out of fixed or drifting polyps, the termitary out of free neuroptera and the ant-hill or bee-colony out of independent hymenoptera. A similar impulse of group formation seems to have become operative along each zoological branch, but at very different ages of the earth.

13. *Ibid.*
14. Pierre Teilhard de Chardin, *The Future of Man* (New York: Harper & Row, 1964), pp. 37–38.

34

Carrying the argument and the analogy up to man, Teilhard notes that "prehistory teaches us that in the beginning Man must have lived in small autonomous groups, after which links were established, first between families and then between tribes. These associations became more elaborate as time went on." Ultimately, believes Teilhard, these groups will associate in larger and more complex orders to compose a sort of social organization of mankind. Whether Teilhard's vision of the future is valid, his understanding of the past squares with the findings of anthropology and history: man is a political animal.

The nature of man as political animal is immediately relevant to an understanding of trade unionism. The clue, again, is to be found in the origin of the words that often tell us so much about the origin of the species. *Union* means oneness. It is a shorthand way of saying: we are many persons gathered together as if we were one. A union starts with its *organization*, a word that means two things at once: *organic*, which conveys the meaning of life as opposed to death, and *organ* which represents a collection of cells functioning as a unit to perform a defined purpose. The union is an *association*, another word whose origin is telltale. Association is a coming together of individuals—people not necessarily born into the same family or trade but grouped together by a common concern. (At a later point, we will explore the nuances that separate *unions* from other *associations*, a revealing commentary on the class connotations of words.)

The political nature of man is relevant to a study of unionism, however, in still another way: in explaining why men see in unions of their occupation both their ends and means, their Utopia and their ladder to heaven.

Man and many of his close cousins among the primates are distinguished from other animals by a long infancy. This protracted immaturity leaves an indelible and decisive mark on man. The child is father of the man; the experience of the youth shapes the behavior of the adult.

The infancy of primates is not only long by comparison to other animals, but also, from the very outset, child rearing is a *group* activity. This is in striking contrast to the situation found in many animals, where the mother is separated from others of her species during the birth period and lives alone with her offspring until they are able to support themselves. . . . In the primates, the mother is neither separate from the group while her offspring are young, nor does she live in a female harem. On the contrary, she and her infant are surrounded by curious juveniles and adults of all ages, and she depends upon the adult males to protect the young infant from danger.[15]

In human beings the period of gestation and infancy is more protracted than among other primates. Indeed, the relationship of child to parent is so protracted among humans that, in effect, it becomes permanent.

The association of mother and offspring is among all animals, including the apes, a temporary one, coming to an end when the young reach sexual maturity. In the human group by the time that one generation has become sexually mature, new generations have been added to the group. The association between the generations, pronounced in all primates, is greatly increased as regards solidarity in the human group. From being a transitory association, it tends to become a permanent one.[16]

Prolonged infancy is believed by some to make man a dreamer. From the warmth of the womb, the infant moves into the warmth of the group. Both his early unconscious and later conscious life are formed in a relatively secure environment, a miniature heaven. When infancy ends and what to him must seem like infanticide begins, the youth suffers the pains of paradise lost. He is angry, feels betrayed, dreams of suicide or some near future when he will recapture the Utopia-that-was in a Utopia-to-be.

Life in the social group is the incubator of the social dreamer. Because man can dream (perhaps because of that protracted in-

15. DeVore, *op. cit.,* p. 27.
16. Briffault, *op. cit.,* p. 766.

fancy) he seeks the last security of youth in his hopes. Denied or betrayed by the parent culture, he organizes new groups among whom he rediscovers some of the glow of infant association and in which he finds a propitious climate for his aspirations. The group may be the gang, the college fraternity, the protest organization, or a union.

Prolonged infancy imparts to man still another distinctive quality. It gives him greater plasticity, more time, and more opportunity to assimilate the accumulated habits of the culture. If ontogeny recapitulates phylogeny, then maturation recapitulates cultural evolution. The infant has nine months for the first task and about 13 years for the latter. If man matured more rapidly— in a year or so—he would hardly have time to learn what he must know to be the beneficiary of his cultural heritage. But luckily man develops slowly. And since developmental retardation means prolonged plasticity, the process of learning can be lengthened. Thereby "the range of cultural as against mere biological evolution" widens enormously and man can leap ahead without waiting for physical mutation.[17]

This is the paradox of man: an infant with weak teeth and soft brain rises by virtue of his disabilities to lord of all creation. "The helplessness of human young," writes McNeill, "must at first have been an extraordinary hazard to survival. But this handicap had compensations, which in the long run redounded in truly extraordinary fashion to the advantage of mankind. For it opened wide the gates to the possibility of cultural as against merely biological evolution. In due course, cultural evolution became the means whereby the human animal, despite his unimpressive teeth and muscles, rose to undisputed pre-eminence among the beasts of prey."[18] Thus it was that the physically weak and mentally meek have inherited the earth.

17. William H. McNeill, *The Rise of the West* (Chicago: University of Chicago Press, 1962), p. 5.
18. *Ibid.*

As it was in the beginning so has it been since then. Whenever *homo sapiens* feels weak in the presence of his environment, he tends to group in a culture within which he finds the collective strength to survive and the collective knowledge to raise self and the young. In the beginning, such groups battled with the natural environment as they found it. In subsequent centuries, similar groups had to do battle with the social environment as man had made it.

One such group giving battle to the social environment is the union, an instrument whereby those with weaker economic "teeth and muscles" seek to find collective strength and wisdom. The union recapitulates for the adult in the workplace the memorable history of the young in infancy. In both cases, the enfeebled find that "in union there is strength."

The great engine of mankind—cultural evolution—can carry man a long way. And because each man understands this instinctively, he reaches out to his group for strength, for wisdom, and for eternal life—for the group as such will live after the man himself has died. All this a man learns in his prolonged infancy. But also because of that long drawn-out youth—the comfort of the womb extended beyond the womb—man's aspirations vis-à-vis his environment go far, far beyond mere survival. He can dream of an environment in the future that would recapture the lost paradise of an earlier life. As a social being, man survives today, dreams about tomorrow, and develops the intellectual and physical tools to move from now to then.

As a political animal, man does more than get along with his neighbors. He learns to aspire and to educate self and young to attain these aspirations. He envisions ends such as no living creature ever attained and fashions unprecedented means for these dreamed-of ends. He does this as a citizen of the larger state and as a citizen of many lesser "states," such as trade unions.

3

The Universality of Unions

Unions are universal, although they often make their public appearances under an alias. They are the natural grouping of people who share an occupation and are organized into guilds, associations, societies. The labor union, as we know it in the twentieth century, is really only one such union. The modern labor organization is the associative expression of employees, formally organized to negotiate and enforce relations with employers. But employees are not and never have been the only occupational group to organize. Indeed, employees—like slaves— are among the last to organize. And among workers, the very poorest and the most illiterate are usually the least likely to organize.

Organization of social groups begins historically from the top down. The first to set up occupational groups are the people of power, those who come to society with "a book, a bang, or a buck"; that is, the man of the word, the man of war, and the man of wealth—the priests, the warriors, and the owners of property. Organized into tightly knit "unions," they use their power not simply to defend their special interests but also to control the total culture or at least as much of it as they can.

The trade union is a relative newcomer on the scene, dating roughly from the development of manufacture. It does have close kin in the guild, a form of preindustrial unionism, more congenial to an immobile society than the present labor organization. Viewed in the long light of history, however, the union is a close relative of priesthood, royalty, corporation, and guild. This does not mean that unions are the same as these other groups. Unions are distinctive. They have also, at many points in history, fought and opposed church, state, and corporation. Yet just as cats and dogs have much in common, so do modern unions and other class organizations. These common traits make them all *unions* in a very broad and generic sense; namely, the gathering together of practitioners in a given occupation.

In any society, there is often a sub-subgroup that is geographically, politically, and sometimes even economically part of the culture but is in reality outside it. These are the low men on the societal totem pole: the forgotten, the neglected, the withdrawn, the self-isolated. They live in the subcellars of the civilization. They are the perennially poor passing on their poverty as a legacy to their children and their children's children. Such groups also organize. They, too, develop a polity: unwritten and generally unpretty. In recent years, with the official and intellectual discovery of poverty, there have been close-up accounts and studies of this culture of the poor: its special mores, customs, liberties, and sanctions. In these studies are revealed the city within the city. Here, too, man is a political animal—in the *polis* of poverty. Throughout history this bottom group has had minimal impact on the affairs of men. Normally, it is not geared for action to influence the large society but is fundamentally constructed for self-survival, to give physical wherewithal and moral approval to its denizens. Now and then, when society grows riotous and heavy storms stir the lower depths, the bottom comes to the top. But when the calm returns, it sinks to the bottom again, only to be rediscovered now and then by sensitive students who dig into its quaint customs as if it were some primitive tribe in darkest Guinea.

From the wealthy to the poor, then, every sector of the culture organizes. Some do it well, usually at the top; some do it poorly, usually at the bottom. Some organize just to survive; some to influence the total culture; others to dominate the society. But each in its own way is a *union*, the collective expression of the will of an occupational group.

The organization of economic groups within the larger cultural group takes place only when a society has reached a certain level of complexity. Where everybody does the same thing, there is no lasting basis for separate groups. The society tends to be monolithic, unicellular, homogeneous. But when a society becomes complex, it becomes heterogeneous, multicelled, polylithic. In a complex society, there is role differentiation, with different groups practising their expertise. The more complex the society, the greater is the role differentiation. The players of diverse roles organize their societies within the society; whatever these groups call themselves, they are all *unions*.

What are the common traits of all these unions? Let us see what history has to tell us in answer to this question.

The first great revolution in human society occurs when man, instead of living off his environment, tries to change his environment. Instead of hunting animals, he domesticates them; instead of foraging for food, he grows it. In sum, wild beast and wild food are tamed, made subordinate to man's will and decision.

Once man seeks to control his food supply, he must extend his control to other mysterious powers in his environment, such as the weather. Controlling the weather is not easy. As Mark Twain wrily remarked: "Everybody talks about the weather, but nobody does anything about it." But in the year 3500 B.C., there were men who developed a special skill in this area: they proposed that they could do something about the weather.

In ancient Sumer—a community that was temple-oriented—the keepers of the faith claimed a special skill in high demand: the ability to converse with the mysterious powers in the beyond to grant propitious weather. These early mathematicians—sometimes called magicians—had learned the secret of the seasons: the moons, the solstice, the frightening eclipse of the moon or sun. They were guardians of these mysteries and could release their wisdom to the faithful, advising them on when to plant and when to reap. They were the wise men who used their local wisdom to rule a people. With a tutored sense of time, they predicted what was inevitable, thereby winning repute as makers of miracles, like later musicians who, by strumming their guitars to the east made it appear that they caused the sun to rise.

The authority of the priestly colleges was thus very great but their services to the community were correspondingly vital. The priests alone possessed the skills of calculating the seasons, laying out canals, and keeping accounts, without which effective coordination of community effort would have been impossible. Still more important as a basis of sacerdotal power was the supernatural aura enveloping those through whom the great gods deigned to communicate with men. Armed with such authority, the priests were free to develop their organizing capacities in both the practical and religious spheres until they succeeded in raising Sumerian society to the level of primitive civilization.[1]

Although the early priests of Sumer are often depicted as nothing more than makers of mumbo-jumbo, it should be recognized that they served at least three lasting services for all civilization: first, they were the societal engineers and managers; second, they served man's everlasting need for security through rationalized ritual; finally, and most importantly, they preached the scientific doctrine of cause and effect, of an ordered universe, wherein man could, by proper effort, affect his environment.

As opposed to earlier civilizations, whose distinguishable head man was usually the tribe's best hunter, Sumer represented a revolution: a civilization that had undergone a "managerial revolution," with the best-informed men running the city—by magic, by ritual, by pretense, and by superior ability to observe the phenomena of nature. The "union" of managers was the "priestly college"—a body with distinct economic interests, with almost unlimited political ambitions, and with tight hierarchic inner controls.

As the first scientists of recorded civilization—able to calculate seasons, engineer canals, and keep books—these Sumerian

1. McNeill, *op. cit.,* p. 34.

priests organized themselves into a society at the top of the society, a ruling elite, and raised their people to a civilized state. The
people, in return, gave economic support to this leisure class
whose face, instead of turning downward to the stubborn soil,
turned upwards to the gods.

Sumerian theology held that men had been created expressly to
free the gods from the necessity of working for a living. Man was
thus considered to be a slave of the gods, obliged to serve ceaselessly
and assiduously under pain of direct punishment—flood or drought
and consequent starvation. Such ideas . . . probably justified the
earliest beginnings of the practice of concentrating grain and other
goods in temple storehouses, where they were used by priests to
minister to the gods' needs.[2]

The conversion of a little bit of mathematical matter into a
great deal of political energy was not a purely Sumerian phenomenon. On the Salisbury Plains of the British Isles, the same
drama was re-enacted around the awesome rockpile of Stonehenge. Sometime between 1900 and 1600 B.C., these incredibly
massive stones were laid out in an even more incredible design.
Almost two millenniums before Christ, some wise men had calculated a way to place holes, mounds, pillars and lintels so they
could measure the coming and going of the moon, the sun, the
seasons, and eclipses. The planning, engineering, and hauling of
stones were not all done at once. First, there was just one key
stone and several holes; then there was another circle of stones;
and then a third project. The building materials came from afar.
The full job, according to a calculation by astronomer Gerald S.
Hawkins, took a total of 1,497,680 man-days of work.[3] The labor
took over three centuries.

To harness such a labor force, to direct its efforts, and to
maintain the undertaking over three hundred years must have

2. *Ibid.*
3. Gerald S. Hawkins, *Stonehenge Decoded* (New York: Dell Publishing Co.,
1966), p. 73.

required an organization, a continuing "directorate" with high intellectual skill, great authority, and self-renewing life. No doubt, when the work was finished, the members of the "directorate" found their authority greatly enhanced by their handiwork: a magical calendar erected in stone to serve as a center of wisdom and worship.

In explaining why Stonehenge was built, Hawkins suggests that, in addition to the project serving as a form of mental gymnastics for intellectually curious men, it was "a calendar, particularly useful to tell the time for planting crops" and was a way to "create and maintain priestly power, by enabling the priest to call out the multitude to see the spectacular risings and settings of the sun and moon, most especially the midsummer sunrise over the heel stone and the midwinter sunset through the great trilithon."[4]

The priestly college is our first recorded union: an occupational congregation in possession of certain mysteries, organized to promote its ideology, its status, and its influence in the larger society. The fact that this union was also the ruling class does not make it less a union. This was an early white-collar union, an organization of skillful eggheads, who discovered that a little bit of knowledge is a useful thing in an unknowledgeable civilization, an instrument to manage, to direct, and to govern a society.

The Sumerian temple city was a model for many a theocracy in the centuries to follow. So deeply imbedded is the rule of the theocrat in human society that all attempts to break that ancient influence by separation of church and state have been difficult and only partially successful. In a sense, the union of wise men, such as the priestly college of Sumer, has been a continuing force from 3500 B.C. to 1967 A. D.—changing faces, places, and prayers.

What are some of the traits of the priestly college that it holds in common with other unions?

First, all members have a common occupation.

4. *Ibid.,* p. 117.

Second, members are organized into a polity, a structured group. The hierarchy of the priesthood is not only the most ancient but also among the most clearly defined of any occupational grouping.

Third, the college controls admission to its own ranks, imposing long apprenticeships, vows of loyalty, careful screening. While there is no written record concerning the selection of priests of Sumer, there is endless information on how subsequent religions chose their ministers. Selection is severe, and where a given religion is an established and recognized power endowed with worldly as well as spiritual authority, the apprenticeship is long and rigorous, calculated to create a limited elite.

Fourth, the college seeks monopoly control over its calling. Indeed, anyone practicing the trade without authorization is viewed as a heretic and is fit for burning.

Fifth, the college develops an economic point of view and means to assure a stable source of income.

Sixth, the internal relations of the college are determined in a complex political game. The history of any religious order anywhere, anytime, is replete with evidence.

Seventh, the college reaches out for political power in the larger society outside the precinct of faithful tithe-paying parishioners. In Sumer, the college was king, a theocracy as firm as the Massachusetts Bay Colony. Throughout all recorded history, the church-state relationship has been a central political issue.

These traits are common to other unions, such as the nobility. The class of nobles—that is, the entitled gentry—has risen most prominently from chaos. They come to establish order and to do so by physical force. Whereas the priest is a man of words, the noble is first of all a man of war. The latter, like the former, serves the great human hunger for security, for a safer today and tomorrow. The priesthood protects man against angry gods; the war lord protects man against angry neighbors.

In Sumer, by 3000 B.C., the temple cities were warring against one another and were threatened by barbarian invasions. To protect their border and also to establish some administrative order over areas larger than the community of the temple city, there arose a class of military leaders: kings and their retinue.

The institution of kingship stabilized itself in Sumer by superimposing military relationships upon an older religiopolitical system. The authority of field commander over his army served as a prototype for the king's authority over the city; and the rise of kingship may be conceived as a process whereby extraordinary powers delegated in time of war became normal in peacetime. Kings arrogated to themselves supreme military and judicial authority and organized royal households analogous to the divine households of the temple communities.[5]

The special skill of the original nobility was their talent as warriors. The first lords appear to have been men of muscle, carrying social security to their dependents in a mailed fist. "In early times when violence was rife," said Salter in 1894, "the custom was to place one's self under the protection of some brigand rather more honest than the rest and make a bargain with him. The great men of Greek antiquity, and of almost every other antiquity, were professed brigands punctual in their performance and faithful to their word. So, as is well known, in the middle ages, when government was weak or non-existent, small proprietors of freeholds placed themselves under the patronage of powerful lords and became by choice their vassals, or even their serfs."[6]

Whether these men of war are called brigands or robber barons or—in the words that Hammurabi used to describe himself—"The Good Shepherd, the Completer of plenty," they are a class that quickly moves from soldier to statesman, from warrior

5. McNeill, *op. cit.*, p. 43.
6. William Mackintire Salter, *Anarchy or Government* (New York: Thomas Y. Crowell and Co., 1895), p. 17. (Salter leans on Leroy-Beaulieu, *The Modern State*.)

to ruler, from war-maker to law-maker. They come well equipped for the function: they are their own police power since they control arms. The mind of the people is prepared to accept them; the notion of a strong leader precedes settled civilizations, running back to the leader of the hunt. And before that, the lower creatures from whom man arises instinctively accept the concept of the leader of the pack. Where the military man follows the priesthood, the forms of hierarchy are premolded and legitimatized.

Whether the nobility operates under a monarchy deriving its power from the king or as an oligarchy assigning powers to a chosen king is secondary to the fact that in due time a class develops a special claim, talent, and apparatus to govern. This class organizes a polity that is, in effect, a union of military governors.

Because of its unlimited power, especially in times and climes where other unions have not yet arisen to challenge its hegemony, this noble class claims unbounded jurisdiction. Indeed, it plays God. Consider, for instance, Hammurabi's description of his many interests and talents:[7]

As a God, King of the City, knowing and far seeing, I looked to the plantations of Dilbat and constructed its granaries for Ib the God. . . . as Overlord I gave fresh life to Erech, furnishing abundance of water to its people; I completed the tower of Eanna. . . . As a leader and king of the City I made the settlements on the Euphrates to be populous. . . . As the Shepherd of my People, in the midst of Agade of the wide squares, I settled the rules and set straight the Tigris. High of purpose, great King, a very sun of Babylon, I caused light to arise upon Sumer and Akkad.

The great check on the house of lords was, of course, the house of God—and vice versa. Hence the jurisdictional conflict between the two "unions" over property and power, over the economy and the government. "No doubt the relation between

7. Quoted by Bowle, *op. cit.*, p. 31.

king and priest," comments McNeill, "was often an uneasy one. Perhaps accommodation usually occurred without prolonged dispute or open violence, but we are informed that Urukagina, king of Lagash (*ca.* 2400 B.C.), openly set himself against the priests, proposing to restore the good old days by protecting the poor and the weak from priestly oppression. In time, however, royal usurpation became sanctified by myth and ritual, of which the central act was an annual ceremonial marriage between king and goddess of the city."[8]

In subsequent centuries, the priesthood gave legitimacy to the royalty through the divine right of kings. And, in return, the warrior class protected the monopoly of the established church. And periodically, church and nobility have joined hands in holy wars that serve to extend the boundaries of both the nation and the faith. If we view the priestly college and royalty as two of our first unions, then the political coalition of these associations is really the first federation of unions, albeit unions of a ruling elite.

The nobility, like the priesthood, shares the common traits of all unions. The members of the nobility have a common occupation as governors; they are structured in a polity; they control admissions into their ranks, usually limiting entry to birth or marriage, except in those rare cases where titles have been "democratized" on a rationed basis, as in modern England. The lords establish a monopoly in their calling, outlawing all efforts to challenge this power as subversive and yielding only so much of the monopoly as repetitive revolution or revolt may compel. The lords accumulate property, both individually and through the collectivity known as the Crown. They find a way to insure a steady income: a tithe for the church and a tax for the nobility. Internal relations are handled politically. And, of course, this group reaches out for political controls over the total society, a

8. McNeill, *op. cit.,* p. 43.

specialty responsible for the historic success of the nobility over the "mobility"—snob over mob.

The community of scholars and the professions based on higher learning—such as medicine, law, and teaching—share traits in common with the unions of the ruling elite as well as of the modern labor organization.

Out of the Middle Ages arose a class of masters, or teachers, attached to the church. At first, they were neither a group nor a free entity. The teacher was a monk, the *scholasticus*, attached to an abbot. When the body of students grew, the *scholasticus* became a sort of headmaster, known as the *magister scholarum*. As the job of the headmaster became more administrative and less educative, the duties were transferred to the chancellor, the personal representative of the bishop. He, in turn, issued the license to teach (*licentia docendi*) to masters—the lecturers—who now began to form into a new class, gradually grouping into a polity.

The first power of the new group was control over admissions to the trade. Since the chancellor really was not in a position to judge a man's qualifications to teach, he turned to the masters, whose recommendation (or blacklisting) became binding. The masters then began to impose their own code of behavior on colleagues, to write laws for their universities, the new *imperium in imperio*. "The masters made rules (a) prescribing a uniform dress for the members of the body, (b) demanding a designated order in lectures and disputations and (c) requiring the attendance of masters at the funeral services of their dead colleagues."[9]

To enforce these work rules, the masters compacted that they would refuse to work with the nonconformist. "To secure the observance of rules the masters had taken an oath to withdraw their *consortium* from those who should fail or refuse to observe them." This refusal of the masters to work with a "scab" had, in the time of Pope Innocent III in the early thirteenth century, the power of law—as did closed shop contracts in the United States

9. Davis, *op. cit.*, p. 261.

until the passage of the Taft-Hartley Act. When a group of masters sought to readmit one of their expelled colleagues, permission had to be obtained from the Pope.

Their political relations to the outer community pivoted on two points: Crown and town. From the former, the masters, who were now organized into a university, sought privileges; from the latter, the masters demanded subservience. So effective were the universities in winning these objectives that the students as well as the masters won immunities from the crown and dominance over the town.

John P. Davis in his monumental work on corporations, including the educational corporation, tells of a revealing incident in Paris in 1200 A.D. A town-versus-gown conflict had turned into a tavern brawl, and the townfolk had retaliated by stoning the student hostel.

Upon the demand by the students of redress from the king, coupled with an implied threat to migrate from Paris, the king imposed severe punishments on the provost and his fellow citizens that had participated with him in the riot. Furthermore, he conceded to the scholars that such of them as should in future be arrested by either royal or municipal officers should be surrendered at once to the bishop or his representatives for trial. It was further provided that the townsmen should take an oath to respect and protect the privileges of scholars and even assume to inform on their own initiative against citizens who should fail to likewise respect them. The provost, as the representative of the body of townsmen, was to take a similar oath before the assembled masters that he would not violate the privileges of the scholars. Goods of scholars should not be levied on by secular officers and those accused of assault on scholars should not be accorded the choice of trial by battle or ordeal.[10]

The universities proved their power where other privileged groups failed.

10. *Ibid.*, p. 264.

Any privileged class within the town walls, whether protected by King, noble, bishop or abbot, had usually to defend their privileges with vigor if they were not to fall before the strong corporate spirit of the town. As a general rule, the towns succeeded in bringing the privileged classes within them into substantial conformity with their own population. In the case of the universities, however, the town was destined to defeat in its struggle with the privileged class of masters and scholars. In the case of Oxford, the university had so established its early independence and later dominance that "by the middle of the fifteenth century the Town had been crushed, and was almost universally subjugated to the authority of the University. The burghers lived henceforth in their own town as the helots or subjects of a conquering people."[11]

In the world of the Church, the university tried to repeat what it had accomplished in the secular world: privileges from the top and if not dominance over, at least independence from, the local potentate. In its struggle with the Bishop of Lincoln in the latter part of the thirteenth century, Oxford University won the battle, with the bishop yielding as "an act of pure and voluntary grace." But that was only the beginning: a papal bull of 1395 exempted the University from the jurisdictions of all "archbishops, even *legati nati*, bishops and ordinances."

The union of masters knew the power of the strike. In 1209, another one of the recurrent town–gown riots broke out at Oxford when townspeople sought to arrest several students for having killed a woman. The masters, who had on numerous occasions threatened to leave the town and had actually declared a cessation of lectures, now organized a *suspendium clericorum*, a mass walkout estimated to have involved about three thousand. Many of these "strikers" organized the University of Cambridge as their ultimate protest against the townfolk of their former location. The Pope stepped in as arbitrator in this dispute and wrote a contract *ex cathedra* that laid down rules favoring the masters and

11. Hastings Rashdall, *Universities in Europe in the Middle Ages,* Vol. II, p. 411. Cited by Davis, p. 288.

scholars and levied reparations on the town for its misbehavior. As for the "masters who had continued to lecture after the secession of the other masters and of the scholars," they were punished by "suspension for three years from the exercise of the privilege of lecturing."[12] The union of masters would tolerate no scabbing.

In twentieth-century America, the great professions that are derived from university life—law, medicine, education—are organized in well-known and well-established associations: the American Bar Association, the American Medical Association, the National Education Association. Although the very word *union* has been anathema to all three of these associations ever since their foundation, they are unions nevertheless.

In recording the likeness of unions, trade associations, and professional societies, Corinne Lathrop Gilb concludes that they are all three driven by the same compulsion:

"In each case there is need for group cohesion; for control over group boundaries; for establishing, reinforcing, and advancing the position of the group in relation to others. In each case the techniques for accomplishing this are to a remarkable degree the same. Trade associations have their codes of ethics, which attempt to minimize intra-group competition. All kinds of vocational organizations utilize conferences, journals, workshops, group insurance, and so forth, for comparable functional purposes. . . . The professions' efforts to exert some control over income floors and ceilings and to curtail competitive bidding have been matched by trade union efforts to eliminate wage differentials for related categories of workers to discourage the setting of wage levels on the basis of individual merit. Business has made similar efforts, too. Since the Second World War, fair-trade regulation has become so prevalent that to be unethical in the lexicon of some businessmen is to charge below the just price— now a floor rather than a ceiling—or to compete unduly."[13]

12. Davis, *op. cit.*, p. 285.
13. Corinne Lathrop Gilb, *Hidden Hierarchies* (New York: Harper & Row, 1966), p. 228.

The first professional associations in America came into being as social rather than economic entities. They were little self-selected societies for the elite. In a day and age when the number of professionals was relatively small, when they were drawn from about the same social stratum, and when their individual names carried prestige and authority, the club could set the tone for the profession. In its occupational class, this natural aristocracy was the self-legitimatized spokesman.

When the population increased to make once-famous names anonymous, when the growing number of professions drew recruits from new social layers, the informal leadership of the club became inadequate: a polity had to be established for the *polis* of the profession. They organized to set codes and standards for the professions, to control admissions, to establish internal disciplines, to protect their collective and individual property (income, mysteries, hospitals, or schools), to maintain their freedom vis-à-vis other organized groups in the society. They sought to obtain these objectives through their own little governments—the *imperia in imperio*—or, where unable to do so, through law, including laws that conferred on the profession the powers of the state. "In the quarter century between 1890 and 1915, led by only a few people, the professions shook off their inertia, remarshaled their forces, took a strong defensive position in favor of professionalism, and aggressively created or sought from government the tools that would enable them to entrench their new position and eventually to expand it."[14]

As in the case of labor unions, the professional associations found themselves embroiled at an early time in a "class struggle" against the corporations. For doctors and lawyers especially, this was a fight to maintain their standing as self-employed professionals against the threat of proletarianization. Corporations were invading the practice of medicine and law, hiring doctors and

14. *Ibid.,* p. 39.

lawyers as salaried hands. "By the 1890s some corporations began to install medical care plans for their employees, and mutual benefit societies sought to provide medical care for their members at a fixed price." In the field of law, "rapidly growing business institutions—trust companies, banks, land title companies, casualty insurance companies, and so forth—were invading the traditional provinces of the bar, using salaried lawyers to perform legal services for the public."[15] Teachers found themselves in a struggle against political "corporations"; namely, the municipal machines that dispersed jobs to teachers and school administrators as patronage plums to the politically deserving. Against the insecurity and the humiliation of the spoils system in the schools, the teachers organized their professional societies.

In the opening decades of the twentieth century, the professions moved from a class run by men of status to a mass run by elected leaders. Whereas the professional societies once limited membership to preserve their exclusive character, they now used every method of persuasion to force all licensed practitioners into the organization to make certain that it would be all-inclusive. Instead of seeking intimate seclusion for their meetings, they sought great conventions with the public invited to attend through the press. The ivory tower became a battle station.

The desire of the doctor to maintain his occupational independence and not to become a mere employee of the corporation recurred in the profession's resistance to virtually all third-party medicine, especially to such practice under government auspices. Organized medicine has offered many a rationale for its opposition to third-party practice (breaks down doctor-patient relationship, depresses medical services, limits free choice, and so on), but it must also be recognized that the doctor is here re-enacting the role of all other occupational groups in any civilization: the innate compulsion to congregate in defense of its status, its professional terrain, its lebensraum, its income, its prerogatives, its

15. *Ibid.*, p. 36.

freedom. In the case of teachers, who were employees to begin with, they, too, organized to defend their freedom against the "boys in the backroom."

As the professions organized, their societies began to take on many of the police powers of a government, dispensing summary justice to delinquent practitioners. Doctors and lawyers who violated the formal canons or, sometimes, even the informal mores of their associations soon felt the sting of the professional society. They were taught to conform. In the organization of the professions—as in the organization of the priestly college, the nobility, or the latter-day union—freedom has been sought by the individual through conformity with his group, because "the professional association and its impersonal code stand as buffer between the individual and those who might otherwise dictate to him."[16]

Although the underworld of organized crime is in most ways far removed from associations of divines, royalty, and the learned professions, the "honored society" (to use a common phrase applied to the Italian *Mafia*) has more in common with other honored societies than either would care to admit. They are related by the nexus of the human habit to congregate by occupation. Because criminality is an aberration, it is usually not considered as an occupation. Yet crime, especially organized crime, has been a career throughout the history of mankind. It is a way to earn a livelihood. In pursuit of its business interests, organized crime turns to mayhem and murder, less for passion than for profit.

Because organized crime is an identifiable occupational grouping, it displays all the traits of other organized groups. In the *polis* of the underworld, the gang is the union of the outlaw, the corporation of the criminal, a state within the state. The criminal gang is a distinct class within the society. It makes its living from illegal activities, from the investment of its funds and manpower in legal activities, and from a blend of both. To maintain itself, this class must master a variety of skills, from cracking safes to

16. *Ibid.*, p. 54.

"fixing" the police, from smuggling goods to murdering people.

Within this class, there is a polity, an unwritten constitution enforced more thoroughly than most written constitutions and sets of statutes. Within this polity there is provision for a legitimatized hierarchy: leadership, chain of command, decision-making, administration, division of the income. There are processes for choosing new leaders. There is tight control over admissions. There is endless push to maximize demand for underworld services and an equally determined squeeze to limit the number of practitioners in the field.

Organized crime has policies, that apply both to external and internal affairs. Decisions are made on the most profitable fields to infiltrate and invade: prostitution, dope, real estate, unions, business, banking, import, insurance, transportation. Decisions are made on how and when to legitimatize money, to move illicit income into licit operations, to wash the dirty money of crime in the cleansing streams of the accepted economy. Internally, decisions are made on jurisdictions, on division of the income, on chain of command, on enforcement of policy.

Organized crime has its police. Murder Inc. was the police force of the American underworld, playing a decisive role when the many underworld fiefdoms of the pre-1930s were being federated into a national syndicate.

Organized crime has its politics. Ordinarily the politics of the underworld, like the politics of any civilized society, is played out through a harmless ritual of bluster, bluff, pretense, logic, coalitions, and ultimate acceptance. It is war fought out with the bloodless weapons of amicable hostility. Occasionally, the political struggle within the underworld cannot be resolved at a conference table in Appalachia, N.Y., or in Miami, Fla., and the struggle turns bloody: intergang and intragang warfare.

Finally, organized crime is structured. Its mores involve respect for authority, a readiness to suffer for one another, a maintenance of total secrecy. It has a special language, as distinct as

Cockney or Brooklynese: a collection of common symbols to signal the fraternity of unspoken understandings.

As in the case of other societies, the underworld must relate to other groupings. Its most immediate antagonist is the government, the maker and enforcer of the law. Organized crime first tries to escape the law; then it tries to neutralize the law; then it tries to become the law. In this process, the underworld develops a political dimension that starts with bribery and ends with financing political campaigns. The outlaw strives to become the law. In its relationship to corporations and labor unions, the underworld repeats its relationships with government. First, gangs try to steal from unions and corporations, a continuing relationship of antagonism. Then gangs start to infiltrate unions and corporations, to make them arms of the gang.

The resemblance between union and guild is sufficiently striking to warrant the conclusion that the two are congenitally related. Indeed, in Chapter 1 the guilds are described as very early examples of occupational groupings engaged in both economic and political activity and behaving very much like unions of today.

Despite strong resemblance, however, the modern union and the medieval guild are not directly and organically related. The guilds were a thing of the past when the first unions in America came into being. By the sixteenth century the English guilds were either dead or a waning shadow of themselves. The guilds were already a matter of history before Jamestown had been founded.

The remarkable likeness between union and guild is dramatic testimony to the thesis that unions are universal. (Here again the word *union* is used in its generic sense as an occupational grouping with certain definable characteristics held in common with like groupings.) The American union was not a transplant. It was and is indigenous, exactly as were the English guilds.

While guild and union have much in common, they are markedly different. The guild was not a class organization in the sense that Karl Marx or Samuel Gompers might have used the term *class;* namely, as an organization of worker versus boss, or proletarian versus bourgeois. The guild was an occupational grouping that included all strata within a craft or trade, whether master, journeyman or apprentice.

As the guilds matured and hardened over the centuries—the process ran for about five centuries from the years following the Norman Conquest to the sixteenth century—class differentiation began to disrupt and reshape the original guilds. The masters had the decisive voice within the guild. The journeymen organized secretly to combat their masters. The formal guild ultimately became a *company* run by a few members of the board or, in some cases, by an individual holding the company charter from the Crown. The journeymen became just plain workers with no voice in the guild, now turned company. "The craft gild, company or mistery developed, before the end of the sixteenth century, from a self-governing organization of men of a craft into a closed corporation imposing from above a code of regulations to which the men of the craft should conform."[17]

Whereas in medieval England guild lines were drawn vertically to differentiate craft from craft, in the later bourgeois England union lines were drawn horizontally to mark off class from class. The modern union is a product of this latter era, a period during which "the social conditions under which the men of a craft had a common interest in the craft itself were . . . giving way to new conditions under which separate classes in the craft itself would have greater affinity to corresponding classes in other crafts than to other classes in their own craft."[18] In sum, the *craft* struggle was giving place to the *class* struggle.

Union and guild, then, were born centuries apart, under differing circumstances, for different, almost contrary, purposes. Yet they lived the lives of almost identical twins, a fact that should

17. Davis, *op. cit.,* p. 187.
18. *Ibid,* p. 187.

no longer come as a total surprise after one has admitted the universality of unions among a wide variety of occupational groupings.

Both guild and labor unions were, in their earliest years, social organizations. "A gild was an association of persons for the preservation of peace, the promotion of social fellowship, the performance of religious worship or some other phase of *social* activity of common interest to its members."[19] They were also mutual aid societies that assisted their members "in sickness, helpless old age, poverty, commercial failure, loss by shipwreck and fire and other distress, and after their death defrayed, if necessary, the expense of their burial and of masses and prayers for the response of their souls. They aimed, finally, to maintain a standard of morality and fraternal courtesy."[20]

These early guilds—basically social-religious bodies—were very often composed of craftsmen of a given occupation and, so far as their written documents reveal, did not necessarily serve any economic function per se. Contrariwise, later craft guilds, with clearly defined economic purposes in their written charters, did not spell out social-religious functions, although they indulged in them. Because of their differing emphasis on the social and the economic, some historians insist that these two types of guilds—socioreligious and economic—were not sprung one out of the other. (The same point can be made about earliest workingmen's associations and later unions in America.) For the purposes of establishing the universality of unions, it is not necessary to prove that craft guilds were an organic descendant of the socioreligious guilds. Indeed, the argument for the congregational compulsion finding expression in many forms among people of a given polis is *strengthened* if socioreligious and craft guild both started spontaneously.

This point—the congregational compulsion—is further re-

19. *Ibid*, p. 148.
20. *Ibid.*, p. 164.

inforced by the fact that the word *guild* is derived from an organizational form that preceded both the socioreligious and the craft guild. This was the frith-guild of seventh- and eighth-century England. Its members—the Gegilden—composed a kind of blood-fraternity, larger than and different from the family with rules and regulations for group responsibility to pay for crime and to receive retribution for acts committed against any member. The legal responsibilities of the frith-guild for its individual members is known because, as in most legal proceedings, there are written records available to historians. But it may reasonably be inferred that where such "group" liability was law, there must have been an intensely close social grouping conducting many other activities in addition to lawsuits. What the base of the frith-guild was we do not know. Its known contribution is etymologic: a word meaning a group with a sense of mutual responsibility—very much like the latter day guilds and unions.

The craft guilds, like unions—especially skilled craft unions—were very much concerned with control of their market: admissions, quality of the commodity, work rules, internal discipline. They guarded their mysteries, like priests, magicians, doctors, and market analysts. Before the laws of patent and copyright, they set up severe penalties for anyone who revealed their secrets. The word *mystery* originally meant knowing rather than not-knowing. The Greek word *mystes* referred to one who was *close-mouthed* after initiation in the mysteries. He made certain that he knew more by making certain that he did not share what he knew.

To keep the mysteries within controllable confines, the guilds elaborated complex rules on apprenticeship and on who might practice the craft. In the thirteenth century, when the craft guilds were still weak, admission was wide open, depending almost solely on ability to use the craft. In the subsequent centuries, as the guilds began to feel their strength and to define their purpose, they set up a formal system of apprenticeship. The term of training had to run for at least seven years. Bondmen and villains were ineligible. Admission to apprenticeship was disallowed unless the father could pay twenty shillings a year. So vital was this control of admissions and so influential did the guilds become that even a major catastrophe such as the Black Death could not change the practice: to prevent the drift from agriculture into the crafts after the plague, Parliament enacted a law that all who had tilled the soil up until twelve years before must continue to do so. Additional restrictions on admission were the large, even exorbitant, initiation fees and limitation on the number of apprentices per master.

The guilds that were involved in merchant operations made it the cardinal, generally the sole, point in their charter to see to it that "no one who is not of the gild may trade in the said town, except with the consent of the burgesses."[21] Where a trade guild did not have this specific power written into its charter, the guild exercised the power nevertheless. A written grant was omitted because it was taken for granted. Armed with the power to say who had permission to trade, the guilds set forth comprehensive regulations and restrictions to protect their dues-paying members against all comers. Davis describes the following restrictions:

Tolls were levied on nonguildsmen from which guildsmen were exempt. No one who bought for reselling, except a guildsman, might sell many articles at retail, nor might others buy of him except guildsmen or townsmen. Stranger merchants might not remain in town for more than forty days and during their stay had to conduct their business in the presence of guildsmen. A foreigner might not enter into partnership with a guildsman. Guildsmen had the right to pre-empt goods on sale as against a foreigner or even a townsman. Guildsmen had the right to make first offer on goods brought to the port. If a guildsman exercised his right of pre-emption, he had to divide up his purchase with fellow guildsmen if they so wished it. No fish-dealer might cut

21. *Ibid.*, p. 154.

up his fish for sale without a license from the guild; and he would not get a license so long as townsmen had fish to sell. A herring dealer could spend only one day in town. At Reading a foreigner would forfeit his corn if he brought it to market before 3:00 P.M.[22]

From the power to license came the power to police the products of the guildsmen. The regulations were minute and many. Wool threads could not be used for warp. Wool caps were to be made black, white, lana, or grisa. Old caps could not be dyed black because they could too easily be resold as new. When caps of flocks instead of wool were brought into the country from abroad, the offenders were ordered to remove same, to leave security that they would do so, and take an oath never to repeat the offense. Bridles and saddle-bows were under strict examination. Cast iron might not be used; defective materials were outlawed; no painter was to paint a saddle-bow made outside the city until it had been examined and approved by the inspectors of the lorimers. Shoemakers might not sell shoes of bazen as being cordwained, nor shoes of calf-leather for ox-leather. Beef was not to be baked in pies and sold as venison, and rabbits were not to be baked in pies at all. A man who made girdles of silk, wool, leather, or linen had to garnish them with worthy metals such as latten, copper, iron, or steel and not with lead, pewter, tin, or other base metals.

These early guildsmen did not lack a proper sense of public relations. While their many regulations served to protect guildsmen against unregulated competition, in almost exactly the same way that a craft union today seeks regulations to accomplish the same purpose, the guilds went out of their way to convince the people that it was in the public interest to impose these restrictions. Here, for a fascinating example, is an item from the Articles of the Spurriers on night work:

22. *Ibid.,* p. 155.

No one shall work at night, by reason that no man can work so neatly by night as by day. And many persons of the trade, who compass how to practice deception in their work, desire to work by night rather than by day; and then they introduce false iron, and iron that has been cracked, for tin, and also they put gilt on false copper, and cracked. And further, many of the trade are wandering about all day, without working at all at their trade; and then when they have become drunk and frantic, they take to their work, to the annoyance of the sick and of all their neighborhood, as well as by reason of the broils that arise between them and strange folks who are dwelling among them. And then they blow up their fires so vigorously, that their forges begin all at once to blaze, to the great perils of themselves and of all the neighborhood around. And then, too, all the neighbors are much in dread of the sparks which so vigorously issue forth in all directions from the mouths of the chimneys in their forges. By reason whereof, it seems that working by night [should be stopped] in order such false work and such perils to avoid.[23]

The guild had the power to fix wages and prices. If buyer or seller violated the fixed price, they were both subject to penalties. Likewise, if masters and workers agreed on a wage above the set pay, they could both be fined. "And if the men are rebels and contrarious, and will not work, then, the four masters shall have power to take them before the mayor and court of Gihald of the town, to be there dealt with according to law and reason."[24]

The power of guilds to discipline members was mighty, going far beyond the controls of a modern labor union over its membership. Guild ordinances could be enforced in guild or in town courts. Guild officers had the power of search into workplaces and homes; members of the craft were required to live in the same neighborhood; work hours were set up to make inspection easier; bad goods was confiscated and destroyed; penalties for violations ran from fines, to imprisonment, to expulsion—the last

23. From *Memorials of London,* cited by Davis, p. 170.
24. Gild of Fullers of Bristol from Smith, from *English Gilds,* cited by Davis, p. 174.

probably being the most severe for a man who wanted to make a living in a given craft or trade. To track down offenders, each maker had to put his mark on his goods—an early trademark or union label concept. To counterfeit a mark was a major crime.

The guilds, like other combinations of occupations, sought to make their presence known and felt in the governance of the larger community, the state. The guilds were a nation within a nation. Their territory was the craft or the trade, whose jurisdictional lines were carefully marked and defended. The place where the members of the guild worked was almost coterminous with the place where they lived. They were governed by their own laws: their rules and regulations. They had machinery to enforce these laws, with power to impose penalties and to execute them. They set up their tariffs and tolls against foreigners, a term that referred to people from other countries, cities or even other guilds. For those who wished to pursue a given craft or trade, membership in the guild-nation was compulsory: the tax had to be paid, rules had to be obeyed. Within this little nation, there were rulers and ruled, governors and governed.

As the guild-nation grew, became more stable and more complex, classes developed within the guild. Once upon a time, everyone was about equal, since every apprentice was likely to become a journeyman who, in turn, was likely to become a master. The categories were not separate classes but points of transition in a career. As time went by, the masters began to increase the number of apprentices, to lengthen their service, to hold journeymen in permanent employment. Out of the guilds developed a class of owners (masters) and a class of employees (servants). Now the masters were increasingly in control of the guilds, running it for their needs and interests.

The new class of guild rulers—the masters who composed the political bureaucracy of the guild-nation—became a new aristocracy. They insisted, for instance, in the great liveried companies of London that the rank-and-file member, who had once been compelled to wear a given costume to distinguish his guild affiliation, could now no longer wear the costume. Only the hierarchs were allowed to don the garb. In imitation of ancient custom, the new aristocracy wanted to look royal and the plain folk were ordered to look plain.

Increasingly, the new class of guild rulers came to treat the guild as if it were private property. They made the decisions; they decided who would be and who would not be admitted. Consequently, they began to peddle guild membership. As membership itself became less and less meaningful, since the dues-payer played no active role in the assemblage, the guilds allowed the idea of membership to atrophy altogether. The men who held the charter for the guild—now a mere shadow—sold licenses to enter the craft or trade. They made a great business, like royalty itself, out of absolute control over a piece of territory; namely, the occupation. (In some cases the Crown issued a guild charter to one man, some favorite to whom was given control over a sector of the economy, a kind of monopoly to issue licenses for some defined craft or trade.)

With such powers, it is not difficult to see how the guilds turned into first-rate money-making propositions. In addition, the guilds held property, some of it accumulated with a few pence or shillings a couple of centuries before. With population increasing faster than the surface of the earth, such real estate tended to rise in value steadily and over a century or two became the foundation of fortunes.

And so did it come to pass that the humble guilds rose to become mogols of the economy and potentates of politics. And then came the final irony, as the guild (so often equated with labor unions) turned into the full-fledged business corporation. When the Crown wanted men of adventure, with capital and with business sense and with derring do, it turned to the guilds.

(By now the hierarchies of the guilds, some of which had been in continuous existence since the thirteenth century, were endowed with added powers by the Crown and chartered to act as "companies.") Among the favored were the liveried companies of London, with their costumed hierarchy, lifetime office, control over the trade, political powers, and accumulated wealth. The Turkey or Levant Company was spun off the Grocers' Company. The East India Company was the Grocers' under another name. The London Company, set up to colonize Virginia, had a roster containing the names of all the important liveried companies as "adventurers." When the rebellious County of Ulster in Ireland was subdued and the lands of the rebels confiscated, James I sent out a call to organize a company to establish a new colony run by Londoners—a project he promised that was "likely to prove pleasing to Almighty God, honorable to the city, and profitable to the undertakers." In response to the invitation to serve God, city and self, the twelve great liveried companies of London responded. They organized the Irish Society, built their project around the old city of Derrie, and called it Londonderry.[25]

In one of those curious pranks of history, the guilds that so closely resembled modern unions ultimately turned out to be the parents of some of the greatest companies of England. These companies, in turn, proceeded to behave like guilds—and like the other great unions of mankind. These companies differed from other occupational groupings we have discussed in that they were created by fiat of the Crown, instead of arising as a natural association of people engaged in a common craft or trade. These "synthetic" companies were given monopoly powers to explore and develop a new sector of the economy, and as additional entrepreneurs as newcomers entered this sector, the company was authorized to govern the new field of endeavor.

25. For a fuller description of the evolution of the guild into the liveried company, see Davis, pp. 209–232.

These great companies—the Levant, East India, Hudson Bay, the African, the South Sea, and so on—all held one thing in common: they were created to develop overseas trade. They were children of the Elizabethan Age, when England became a self-conscious nation, aware of its size and importance, with a growing appetite for world trade and power. To open the earth to British goods and bottoms, the Crown created companies, endowing men of wealth and ambition with monopoly rights to probe into distant lands. These companies were truly states both inside and outside the state, with the blessing of the Crown. Any entrepreneur who wished entry into the separate realm of these companies had to join the proper company, whether it be the Turkey Company to trade in the Levant or the Hudson Bay Company. In the "little nations" governed by the company board of directors, citizenship was first exclusive and then inclusive but compulsory. The companies set down fees for membership and rules of conduct. They wandered into strange lands with their armies and navies. They were their own state department, enacting treaties with foreign nations as if the company were a sovereign state. Like later imperialist powers, the companies used their troops, their connections, and their know-how to interfere with the domestic politics of other nations, generally for a price or for a favored deal.

Thus, although these companies started as economic undertakings, they ended as political entities. They came as traders; they stayed as invaders. The companies acquired property and political rights that, in effect, made them private colonial powers. They became more than a state within a state or an arm of the state: they were private imperial powers. At the height of their influence these imperial corporations found themselves in conflict with other powers at home: with the Crown, with independent entrepreneurs, and with that universal check on undue usurpation of powers by any monopoly—outraged public opinion. Ultimately King and Parliament began to curb the companies, insisting that political and territorial rights acquired by Englishmen were the property of the state and not of the company.

These overseas companies mark a transition point in the formation of occupational groupings. Their form was taken from a previous era: the corporate form as an expression of a group engaged in a common undertaking. But the function was new, still undeveloped. Indeed, the major purpose of the corporation was to develop a fresh field of endeavor. In the case of these corporations, the idea was conceived before there was a body of practitioners, whereas in previous corporations the body preceded the form.

The overseas companies were created by the Crown as instruments with unusual delegated authority to develop a trade. They were given the political powers of government, including the right to name ambassadors on behalf of the Crown. At first, these companies were a mere handful of men, a half dozen or less. The government used them to explore and exploit a *terra incognita*, very much in the same way that the United States Government has been using the Rand Corporation and other "think tanks." After the companies laid the political basis and gathered economic know-how and wherewithal for steady trade with Turkey, Russia, Morocco, or India, new entrepreneurs entered the field. As a result of the pioneer work of the companies, a new class came into being. The latter were admitted to the companies at the insistence of the government. The exclusive corporation became an inclusive organization, with all the characteristics of a regulatory arm of the government. Ultimately, when these corporations threatened to replace the government totally in the designated realms under their exploitation, the government absorbed the functions of the corporations, rendering them obsolete.

The overseas companies were *created by the government to perform certain functions that the Crown itself was not prepared to undertake.* Viewed thus, these great companies and modern unions in the United States have more in common than is generally noted, for the labor organization of twentieth-century America is, among other things, an instrumentality for the performance of governmental functions that the government itself is either unwilling, unable, or not yet ready to perform.

Let us then turn from the universe of unions to the universe of corporations. In this investigation we may discover that unions and corporations are, in the generic sense of these concepts, ancient siblings.

4

The Political Corporation

▶   To present unions as corporations is an apparent contradiction in terms. In a word-association test, if one were asked for the opposite of *corporation,* a most common response would be *union.* The economic and political events of the past century have been deeply influenced by the battle between capital and labor, the struggle between bourgeoisie and proletariat. How then can one equate these warring parties whose conflict has so substantially shaped the contours of our times?

In the previous chapter, we have referred to the universities, the guilds, and the early regulated and joint stock companies as *unions.* With equal justification, we could have listed all of these, plus ecclesiastical orders, eleemosynary institutions, the municipalities, and the guilds, as *corporations* instead of unions. In his study of corporations, Davis does include all of these— except the labor union—as corporations. It is our intention to apply his test of corporate characteristics to the modern union, the labor organization of twentieth-century America.

In their *Conceptual Foundations of Business,* Eells and Walton stress the fact that the modern business corporation is only one of a broad category of groups. "The corporate idea, as it crystallizes in modern incorporated businesses, can be seen as one species of a genus that embraces all kinds of 'real' groups that arise from commonly recognized needs and purposes." Indeed, wherever a consciousness of common interest exists, there is "the fundamental condition for the emergence of such autonomous associations as churches, labor unions, universities, and business corporations."[1] In describing the social, warm, lifelike qualities of

1. Richard Eells and Clarence Walton, *Conceptual Foundations of Business* (Homewood, Ill.: Richard D. Irwin Inc., 1961), p. 142.

"corporate units of this kind," Hugo Krabbe cut beneath the skin of legalistic form to reveal the palpitating heart of these groups:[2]

> The group itself has ends which it pursues with more or less consistency; it has a settled policy which no individual can modify at will. Its collective character is as fixed as the character of an individual. It can assert collective rights and assume collective obligations. In short it has the same type of energy and inertia which in the individual we call will or personality.

The fact that labor unions and business corporations engage in a constant struggle over rights, prerogatives, powers, property, income and the allegiance of a body of working people does not mean that these two organizations are not of one genealogy. They are siblings, engaged in traditional sibling rivalry for the attention, the beneficence and the respect of the parent—the social order. At times, a given union and a given corporation if threatened by some outside power, will rediscover and reassert their common heritage and close ranks against the "foreign" foe.

If unions and corporations are generically one and the same, then why use two words where one will do? We do so for two reasons: (1) to break down the barrier between mass and class in the interest of our democratic ethos; (2) to break down the barrier between function and form in the interest of understanding.

In discussing corporations and unions we are the prisoners of semantics. Both words are laden with emotion. The word *corporation* conveys the idea of status already attained; *union* signifies the attaining of status. By converting corporations—universities, guilds, or modern business corporations—into unions, as organized groupings of people with a common occupational interest, we reduce the titles of these ennobled persons and the

2. Hugo Krabbe, *The Modern Idea of the State*, tr. G. H. Sabine and W. J. Shepard (New York: Appleton-Century-Crofts, 1922), p. xliv, quoted in Eells and Walton.

privileges to which they are heir to a common denominator more in keeping with the egalitarian ideals of a free society. And by discussing unions in the nomenclature of corporations, we elevate the still dubious state of labor organizations to a point nearer the democratic mean. We can then view both institutions with an equanimity free of semantic snobbery or sense of inferiority.

If the wall of words can be broken down, the society—as well as union and corporation—may be the benefactor. By discovering that they are distantly brothers under the skin, labor and capital may uncover new virtues to one another. (They already know about one another's vices.) They can then continue their eternal struggle as a family quarrel rather than as a war in which civilized gentlemen are repelling merciless barbarians. This rather simple understanding may help hold together a pluralist society with an innate impulse to fly apart.

By viewing occupational groups first through union eyes and then through the corporate lorgnette, we can study these associations in their dual role: as functional bodies and as legal forms. In discussing unions, the emphasis falls on their functions, as bodies of warm, sometimes overheated people. In discussing corporations, the emphasis falls on their legal rights and responsibilities. In the discussion of private associations (that include unions and corporations), there is an ancient running debate on whether they are "real," in the sense that they arise from the natural coming together of people for a common purpose, or whether they are "unreal," in the sense that they are a legal fantasy brought into being by the word of the state. By examining the universe of unions and then the universe of corporations, we shall discover that these private associations are both real and unreal, natural happenings imitated in unnatural inventions—a startling case of social art imitating social nature.

The debate over whether a private association is the self-generated will of a people or is the delegated will of the state is more than a piece of academic disputation. It has lasted too long to be just an intellectual plaything. It goes to the root of freedom: the relation of the individual to the state. It is a combat "in which the Sovereign State and the Sovereign Individual contended over the delimitation of the provinces assigned to them by Natural Law," as Otto von Gierke put it.

As men reach out for freedom from the Leviathan, they do so by pursuing their group interests through group organizations. The association is the handy instrument for liberation: for self-defense, self-advance, self-expression, self-respect. Such groups come into being whether authorized or unauthorized—legally, extralegally, or illegally. Those organizations that can maintain themselves usually win an ultimate legitimacy; they are tolerated by the state (or church in a church-state). At a very early time, the state, aware of the inevitability or social worth of such groups, charters these associations and endows them with purpose, privileges, powers, and responsibilities. At this point, function and form unite to blend social reality with legal fiat.

But this does not end the battle, the conflict continues at the legal level. The state—especially if it be a theocracy, an absolute monarchy, a totalitarian regime, or even a democratic republic that has granted its legal tolerance to an unpopular group—uses its charter to restrict as well as to permit. The charter is used as a strait-jacket. On the other hand, the private association seeks to defend or enlarge its area of freedom, both in practice and in law. The conflict goes into the streets, to the courts, and into academic debate.

In this conflict both sides appeal to a higher ethic, to the societal conscience and the common good. The state tolerates or legitimatizes private associations to do a work in the public interest. The association seeks to identify its goals with the highest aspirations of the greater community. And where they agree in practice, there is no friction. But sometimes, they disagree: and there's the rub. The state will claim that certain acts of corporations or unions are antisocial and will therefore seek to impose restrictions. The associations will claim that such regulation is beyond the proper powers of the state or that the government is guilty of ill will or bad judgment. As often as not, the most severe conflicts are between one association and another, each of them appealing to government to curb an opposing group—in the public interest. This polylogue—group versus group, group versus state—is not likely to end shortly. It is a prolongation of man's dilemma over freedom versus organization, an inherent problem that can never be resolved absolutely either by anarchy or tyranny.

We have already explored the universe of unions as functional assemblies arising naturally among occupational groups. Here, we will explore the universe of corporations as forms of associate activity with *legal* standing.

In a comprehensive definition of a corporation, Davis wrote:[3]

A corporation is a body of persons upon whom the state has conferred such voluntarily accepted but compulsorily maintained relations to one another and to all others that as an autonomous, self-sufficient and self-renewing body, they may determine and enforce their common will, and in the pursuit of their private interest may exercise more efficiently social functions both specially conducive to public welfare and most appropriately exercised by associated persons.

This definition is more than a simple description; it is a collection of characteristics, each of which can be used to test an organization for its right to be admitted to the fraternity of corporations. An organization that meets all these requirements belongs.

Before applying the test to unions, it should be noted that Davis' definition was derived empirically and inductively from an examination of corporations, which included ecclesiastical corporations, municipalities, guilds, educational and eleemosynary cor-

3. Davis, *op. cit.*, p. 34.

porations, regulated companies, joint stock companies, colonial companies, and modern corporations. In his study, the last of these is the least. In his search for a field theory of corporate life, Davis put modern times in its place—and he wrote before the turn of the century. But by doing so, he opened up corporate concepts before and beyond the modern business corporation and thereby invites the application of his test to the modern labor union.

A corporation is a body of persons, engaged in an associate activity. This form of activity "comprehends both the interrelations of the associated members and their relations with other organs of society."[4]

Here a labor union fits the requirement exactly. It is a form of associate activity. Indeed, it comes into being in modern times because it quite consciously recognizes that individual activity is inadequate. The union discourages individual activity in its special purpose as collective bargaining agent. The union is a body of people distinguished by their cohesive character.

The associated activities of a labor union comprehend both the "interrelations of the members and their relations with other organs of society." Internally, unions are governed by a multitude of complex relations, involving membership, dues, voting, office holding, accountability, punishments, awards. Likewise, the union has a variety of relations with other groups: corporations, associations, government, hospitals, its own employees' unions, fellow unions, central labor bodies, the AFL-CIO, the Community Chest.

In the case of both corporations and unions, there are exceptions to this rule of "associate activity" among a body of people. There is the corporation sole, where the whole corpus is one body. Likewise, there are unions that consist of one man holding a charter: a number of racket unions are nothing more than this. The corporation sole and the racket union are cases of art distorting nature, two dimensional representations of three dimensional

4. *Ibid.*, pp. 13–14.

objects. Such exceptions really flunk the test: without members they cannot have an internal set of relations; with only one person being the corporation (or union) they lose the continuing life—the ability to survive one person's lifetime—that is one of the basic traits of any true association. It is "the association of human beings, bound together in order to achieve a purpose [that provides the] fundamental and teleological basis for the coming into existence and the continuing in existence of a corporation," insisted A. S. Dewing.[5]

A second test applied by Davis is the relation of corporation to state. "The corporate form or sum of peculiar relations subsisting between the members of the corporate group and between them and other members of society is created by the state, is approved with the same legal effect as if originally created by it."[6]

Unions meet this test in a rather roundabout way. No union in America is incorporated—that is, chartered by either the state or federal government. Indeed, a modern union would vigorously resist any effort to add the legal "Inc." to its name. This is ironic in view of the fact that at an earlier time the American labor movement was eager for this status. A convention of the Industrial Brotherhood asked for incorporation of unions in their platform of 1874. At the very first meeting of the Federation of Organized Trades and Labor Unions of the U.S. and Canada (forerunner to the American Federation of Labor) held in 1881, they stated that "an organization of working men unto what is known as a Trades or Labor Union should have the right to the protection of their property in like manner as the property of all other persons and societies, and to accomplish this purpose we insist upon the passage of laws in the State Legislatures and in Congress for the incorporation of Trades Unions and similar labour organiza-

5. A. S. Dewing, *The Financial Policy of Corporations*, Vol. I, p. 4, quoted by Eells and Walton, *op. cit.*, p. 139.
6. Davis, *op. cit.*, p. 16.

tions."[7] At the 1883 convention, the Federation appointed a committee to attend the national convention of the two great political parties and there to call for three major actions: an eight-hour day, a bureau of labor statistics, and the incorporation of national trade unions. "They thought that official recognition by the U.S. would lead to recognition by employers."[8] When a law was passed in 1885 providing for incorporation of unions with headquarters in the District of Columbia or the territories, the infant AFL saw in it the "principle of the lawful character of trade unions," and regretted the fact that the law was so limited in its coverage.[9] In subsequent years, the unions reversed their position on incorporation. A charter implies the right to withdraw or not renew the corporate grant and makes possible a tight regulation of the union's internal affairs by the state—the ultimate anathema to American labor organizations.

Despite the fact that unions are not incorporated, however, they have not escaped the process of legitimatization or regulation by government. The National Labor Relations Act (Wagner Act) of 1935 stated that "employees shall have the right to self-organization, to form, join, or assist labor organizations, to bargain collectively through representatives of their own choosing, and to engage in other concerted activities for the purpose of collective bargaining or other mutual aid or protection." While this clause is not a specific charter to a specific union it is a blanket charter to any union that meets the requirements.

A key method for a union to establish itself as the authorized bargaining agent is to win an election. Such elections are far more than a private affair. They are subject to legislation and to the rules and regulations of the National Labor Relations Board.

7. Commons, *op. cit.*, Vol. II, p. 314.
8. *Ibid.*, p. 410.
9. "Proceedings of the Federation of Organized Trades and Labor Unions of the United States and Canada," 1886, p. 8, quoted in Commons, p. 410.

This government agency determines when and where elections are to take place, who may or may not vote, how and when the result is to be announced; the Board hears protests and appeals; it can nullify an election and call a new one. In sum, the Board presides over the birth of the authorized bargaining unit that is, in effect, the operative union in the instant case.

Once a union is "authorized," it has official standing in law. It has a monopoly in the bargaining unit: it and it alone has the authority to speak for the workers in the unit. It speaks not only for its members but for all. The employer must, by law, bargain with this union in good faith: failure to do so is a violation of law. Once the contract is signed, the union has the responsibility of representing all workers in the bargaining unit, whether or not they pay dues. This, too, is imposed by law. In effect, the union that wins the election is "chartered" by law to "do the business" of representing a body of workers as certainly as if the government had issued a charter of incorporation.

The Wagner Act authorized the legal existence of unions and established ground rules for the relations with employers and also with other unions where several competed to represent the same body of employees. A subsequent corpus of law and regulations, passed in 1947 as the Taft-Hartley Act and the later Landrum-Griffin amendments, then proceeded to regulate the *internal* life of unions. This Act did not authorize the government to write a union constitution, but it did lay down certain governing principles with which all union constitutions and practices had to conform.

In sum, there is now a body of legislation, amplified by Board rulings and court decisions, that prescribe the "peculiar relations subsisting between the members of the corporate group and between them and other members of society."

Although unions are cloaked with a formal authority by law, labor organizations are not a branch of government, like a Federal agency. Unions, like corporations, have wide latitude in choosing officers, setting policies, and conducting their internal and external affairs. Summarizing the status of unions vis-à-vis the state, Adolf Berle reached the following conclusions:[10]

> The National Labor Relations Act recognized the collective associations, known as labor unions, but did not undertake to settle how they should be run. It legitimatized them as bargaining agents for groups of workers and provided a method (election) by which workers could indicate that choice. It did not undertake to instruct either employers or labor unions as to bargains they could or could not make. It did insist that where workers organized, or were organized and so chose, agreements as to wages, plans, and benefits must be negotiated with the group and not with each individual.

In the case of American unions, they have traditionally been made legitimate after birth. The first labor organizations in this country were not conceived in a legal compact between government and employees, as are present day unions sanctified in an election; the first children of American unionism were born out of wedlock, sprung into being without benefit of law in some inspired or passionate moment. The legal blessing came later—slowly, painfully, bit by bit.

For many decades, there was virtually no legislation defining either the rights or responsibilities, the latitude or limits of unions. Courts made the law and in doing so there was a great inclination to turn the common law against the common man. Unionists were repeatedly found guilty of "conspiracy" for their union activities. The courts rarely held that a union per se was illegal, but they did find unions guilty of pursuing aims or using methods injurious to the public interest.

Our courts have never held directly that the simple act of workers combining to form a union was illegal. Neither have they held, since 1900, that a simple strike to improve wages, hours or working condi-

10. Adolf A. Berle, *The American Economic Republic* (New York: Harcourt, Brace and World, 1965), p. 165.

tions was illegal at common law, at least when confined to a dispute between an employer and his immediate employees. But even in such a relationship a strike was frequently held illegal when the *end or object or purpose* involved an action or result which the court disapproved on grounds of social or economic policy, e.g., the closed shop. Again, a strike against the immediate employer for a concededly legitimate objective was often held illegal because the court disapproved of the *concommitants* thereof, i.e., the *means* or *method* used to attain the end. . . . In justifying such decisions, the courts invoked legal theories of *conspiracy, just cause, malice* and *restraint of trade.*[11]

In subsequent years, the government enacted a body of law, made by the legislature and by labor boards rather than by the courts, that ultimately legitimized unions. At this point, it is sufficient to record that American unions fall into that category of corporation that "after spontaneous origin and maintenance by the force of custom is approved with the same legal effect as if originally created by it."[12] An ironic footnote: In the *Coronado* case the court "established the doctrine that a labor union, though unincorporated could be sued as an entity, and held liable for damages caused by its officers and agents."

A third test of corporations is "voluntary inception-compulsory endurance." A corporation may be initiated voluntarily. But, "after the corporate form has been assumed by a group, it is compulsory . . . upon all its members until forfeited for misuser or non-user or regularly put aside in the manner provided by the state at the time of its creation or afterwards."[13]

In a legal sense, this measure applies exactly to a union. Any labor organization may decide on a strictly voluntary basis as to whether or not it wishes to initiate proceedings to represent a group of workers. This is "voluntary inception" and can be

11. Nathan P. Feinsinger and Edwin E. Witte, "Labor Legislation and the Role of Government," *Monthly Labor Review*, July 1950, pp. 51–52.

12. *Ibid.*, p. 54.

13. Davis, *op. cit.*, pp. 19–20.

processed through an election, a card count, or the simple signing of a contract after recognition by the employer. Once the union is officially the bargaining representative, it is compelled to continue in this formal role. It must represent all in the bargaining unit; it must process their grievances; it must see that all the terms of the contract are enforced; it must act as trustee of welfare funds where the contract so declares. Having *voluntarily* undertaken to make itself the voice of labor in the workplace, it must endure *compulsorily*. If the union wishes to unload its responsibilities, it may do so "in the manner provided by the state." In the case of corporations and unions, the decision of a group of people to initiate an association is similar to the voluntary decision of parents to create a child. Once the child is born, the parents are under a set of legally established compulsions to persevere in the care of that child—even if the parents have by now decided that it was all a mistake. The child must be nurtured under parental responsibility, unless the state decides that the parent is a "misuser or a non-user" of its authority and decides, in the interest of child and community, to remove the ward from the warden. The union, like the child, is legally protected against truant parents.

In previous chapters we have explored the anthropologic roots of the congregational compulsion, a drive as common to the workplace as it is to the hunt. The decision to form a union is a voluntary, conscious act; but even in the absence of such a conscious act, there is instinctive drive toward organization among workers, in the same way that there was organization in monasteries, in universities, in the crafts before they were formally organized into corporate bodies. "The hierarchy of workers does not necessarily imply formal organizations," observes Dunlop. "They may be said to be *unorganized* in popular usage, but the fact is, that wherever they work together for any considerable period, at least an informal organization comes to be formulated among the workers with norms of conduct and attitudes toward the hierarchy of managers. In this sense workers in a continuing enterprise are *never unorganized*."[14] (Italics mine)

The element of compulsion in the inception of corporations or unions is greatest when the individual members have limited mobility. Where individuals are free to join or leave a given place—whether a job, an occupation, a monastery, or even a nation—there is a large element of voluntarism. Consider the case of a group of gentlemen getting together to form a corporation to make electronic parts: the act is purely voluntary because the investors have endless options for their involvement. As a matter of fact, the same man may simultaneously be involved in several corporations. His personal participation in the corporation is purely voluntary and, at its inception, the corporation is a purely voluntary act. How different the condition of the craftsman in the day of the guild. He had no mobility; his craft was decreed for him; he lived where he worked, and his station in life was preordained.

The modern worker is in an in-between position. He can leave his job and change his occupation. But where he settles down, he begins to organize, whether it be formally or informally, establishing a polity by rote and by writ. If he is a man of many skills who also has the special skill of landing new jobs he is in the position of the investor with many options for his capital. Indeed such a skilled man may hold down several different kinds of jobs at the same time—and many do. If, on the other hand, a man has a single skill, he is limited in his options, is frozen to occupation, place, and status; he is, therefore, under a greater cultural compulsion to form an association with those in like circumstances.

Where an individual is a transient, sojourning only briefly in any trade or place, he is not likely to develop the same sense

14. John T. Dunlop, *Industrial Relations Systems* (New York: Holt, Rinehart & Winston, 1958), in Bakke et al., *Union, Management and The Public* (New York: Harcourt, Brace and World, 1960), p. 2.

of citizenship, of group identification as a permanent resident. Such an individual is under minimum cultural compulsion to join. But where an individual is riveted down to a trade and a place, sharing this immobile fate with others in his class, he finds himself incorporated into a body politic long before it even occurs to him to ask for a charter of incorporation. (In a formal caste system, of course, there is no need for incorporation since the body politic is imposed by custom, ritual, and habit more powerful than law. Here the compulsion is absolute.)

Because the congregational compulsion is ever-present, "compulsory *endurance*" is not simply an obligation imposed by the state but is for unions an inner command as well. However a union may have come into being, once it exists as an entity it displays an inner compulsion to endure far stronger than the legal obligation to carry on its socially defined functions.

A fourth test of corporateness asserts that the "group of members within the corporation is (a) autonomous, (b) self-sufficient and (c) self renewing."[15] These three traits are grouped, as they properly should be, because all are facets of one idea: an independent life. This test applies to labor unions absolutely. Autonomy is the great boast and bane of the American trade unions. If the labor movement today resists formal incorporation, it is because of the supersensitivity of the unions about government regulation or licensing. If there is a body of law today that regulates and restricts union actions vis-à-vis both members and employers, such laws have been passed over the vigorous opposition of the movement. Even the great central organization of the American trade unions—the American Federation of Labor-Congress of Industrial Organizations—cannot challenge the autonomy of its affiliates. Any national or international union of the AFL-CIO may disaffiliate at will; many have. There are several million organized workers in the United States who have no affiliation with the AFL-CIO; they are totally autonomous, in name as well

15. Davis, *op. cit.*, p. 20.

as in fact. Within the national and international unions, there is a high degree of autonomy enjoyed by the locals. In short, to the American union autonomy is a traditional, an ideal, and, despite a body of regulatory legislation, a continuing fact. (Corporations are also regulated, but within the area of their defined purposes and prerogatives they are autonomous.)

This boast of the American unions—autonomy—is also its bane. The freedom of national and local unions to do as they please is a source of repeated embarrassment to the labor movement. Some unions are rackets; some are prejudiced; some are despotisms; some are irresponsible; some are blindly selfish; some are downright antisocial; some are Communist. Under the system of autonomy, they cannot be checked by any superior force in the labor movement. All the AFL-CIO can do is invoke the ultimate sanction of expulsion that still permits the union to go on living with even less restraint now that the family cord has been cut. The delinquent acts of some unions, though not subject to family discipline under the traditions and realities of autonomy, tend to be attributed to all unions.

Self-sufficiency is defined as a grant of powers to the corporation "sufficient to assure its existence and maintenance, and the ability to effectively exercise the particular powers granted it and the duties imposed upon it."[16] This means that the corporation—or the union—may choose its own officers, subject only to some general law that might bar office to certain categories, such as criminals and Communists. This means that the corporation or union may map its own policies, pick its own targets, set its own salaries, establish its own hierarchy. Self-sufficiency, in these senses, is an inevitable concomitant of autonomy.

A corporation must also have the power of self-renovation, the "power to renew its membership."[17] Without such power, a group dies with the death of its charter members. The power to

16. *Ibid.*, p. 22.
17. *Ibid.*, p. 23.

get new members is the source of eternal life and eternal youth to the corporation—and to the union. It ought to be noted that both corporations and unions have been known to die because they did not successfully exercise this right to renew membership rolls with fresh blood. But they did have the right, as a necessary characteristic of the corporation and the union.

A fifth test of corporateness is "compulsory unity." In considering this point, it might be desirable to quote Davis at some length:[18]

The creation of a corporation contemplated that in all its relations with other organs of society, it shall act and be acted upon as a unit. Accordingly it is provided by its charter (supplemented by its by-laws) with a means of determining the group-will of its members, with agencies through which the group-will shall be executed, and with agencies through which other social organs shall maintain their relations with it. In the element of compulsory unity, corporations are distinguished from most other associate bodies, and resemble most nearly the state itself. Blackstone very aptly called them 'little republics', though he would have been more faithful to history if he had called republics 'big corporations'. . . . Though unified in action, the corporation is none the less a group; on the contrary, its unity of action preserves it as a group; if each member persisted in following his own will in preference to finding a common ground on which a group-will might stand, the group would not act as such, but would be inactive, and lawyers would readily determine it liable to forfeit its charter for non-user.

In this quote the word *union* can be substituted for the word *corporation* consistently. The characterization applies totally. A union has "a means of determining the group-will of its officers." It holds elections for paid and unpaid officers; gathers in conventions; passes resolutions; submits contract demands to membership or representative bodies; ratifies settlements through formal vote. Indeed, it is not unfair to say that a *union is primarily an institution to formalize the group-will of a body of workers*. A union

18. *Ibid.*, pp. 24–25.

composes agencies "through which the group-will shall be executed." Shop stewards enforce contracts at the shop level; rate committees set prices on piece work; full time delegates and business agents handle grievances; pickets carry out the union will in times of industrial conflict; grievance committees penalize delinquent members. A union also composes agencies "through which other social organs shall maintain their relations with it." Bargaining committees negotiate collective agreements with employers; delegates are named to gather with other unions at the local and national level; officers and boards enter arrangements with health, insurance, burial agencies to cover union members.

In all these requests unions are, of course, unlike casual and internally undisciplined organizations such as an association of neighbors or even a political party. Unions, as union officers repeatedly tell their members, must be disciplined.

Blackstone's reference to corporations as "little republics" can be extended to unions as well. They are, indeed "little republics" within the workplace. Unions see themselves as governments over working conditions; they like to refer to their conventions as parliamentary assemblies; they conceive their elections to be a replica of local and national elections; they look upon their walking delegates and business agents as a police force, upon their grievance committees as courts, upon their strikes as wars and their settlements as peace treaties. They also see their dues as proper taxes, their control of the market as a form of tariff against dangerous foreign import, their examination of membership aspirants as citizenship tests, their union and closed shop clauses as a union version of the "republic's" prerogative to impose a burden on those who would enjoy the blessings of the society.

This concept of "compulsory unity" is closely related to the earlier concept of "compulsory endurance." To endure requires more than a resolution to continue as a fictional being. To endure requires a succession of acts performed *as a body*. This means that the association—whether it be corporation or union—must have the means to make up its mind, to enforce its will, to impose discipline within the province of its collective concern. Not to be able to live as an entity with a mind and a will and a way of its own would mean forfeiture of existence for non-use—in reality, even if some lawyer did not make the point in law.

A sixth test of corporateness is "motive in private interest."[19] This assumes that "a corporation is composed of persons having a private or particular (or local) not merely public or general interest." Does this apply to unions?

If a modern labor union is not a group of workers with a "private or particular interest," it is nothing. The interest is the basis of the union. Without some distinctive area of concern— the plant, the company, the skill, the trade, the industry—the union is not likely to come into being and if it does, is not likely to survive.

There are some highly moral and public-spirited critics of trade unions who are annoyed with the fact that labor unions are devoted to private interest. They find that unions are selfish, ego-centric, parochial. They would prefer that unions exist as instruments to promote the public and general interest rather than the particular. Some such socially motivated individuals have themselves created and run unions. But when they have, they felt compelled to recognize the private interest of the union even if they personally saw the union primarily as an instrument of general and public policy. The dreamers who wished the union to serve the societal purpose only and who ignored the private interest soon ended up with no union. The victory of the American Federation of Labor over the Knights of Labor and over the Socialist Trade and Labor Alliance is a perfect case in point. The Knights were interested in changing American society. Their dream was an economy of the self-employed. Each man should own his own tools or land. If he could not do it alone, then he should do it through a producer cooperative. If he (or they)

19. *Ibid.,* p. 27.

could not get the capital, then laws should be passed to make credit cheap. If an enterprise such as a railroad was too complex and costly for such self-ownership, then the government should take over the railroad. These ends were to be accomplished by education and elections. And because the Knights looked upon their inspired movement as the instrument to promote this ideal in the public and general interest, they structured themselves accordingly into general assemblies that either ignored or minimized the private interest.

The Knights were not without members or influence. But this happened in spite of and not because of the Knights of Labor and its philosophy. Thousands of its members, acting out the congregational compulsion of their trade or industry, rather than the social inhibitions of their leaders, organized along the lines of private interest, went on strike for their private interest, and won demands conceived in their private interest. The American Federation of Labor, on the other hand, unashamedly proclaimed its belief in workers organizing on a craft, trade, or industry basis into locals that would get more for the members in this necessarily parochial and limited environment. They were structured accordingly. Instead of general assemblies they had craft, trade or industrial locals. The separate unions were given their jurisdictions, the areas of their special or local interest. Their "turf" was the polis of the workplace and their raison d'etre was a "little republic" in that bit of territory. And where one territory impinged on another, there was jurisdictional war—as private interest of one union clashed with that of another.

In the long struggle between Knights and Federation (about which more will be said in Chapter 5) the AFL won. It also won against the Socialist Trade and Labor Alliance, a trade union federation that looked upon the union far less as a collective bargaining apparatus than as the dynamic building block of a cooperative commonwealth. According to the thought of Daniel De Leon, the inspiration and founder of the Alliance, the unions, organized along industrial lines, were one day to be the true government. The day would come when the nation would peacefully and democratically decide to meet in parliamentary session to pass a resolution proclaiming the day of Socialism, and then to adjourn permanently. Once the traditional government had committed this calm suicide, the industrial unions would one by one and jointly take over their respective sectors of the economy to become the industrial government of the United States. The Alliance was short-lived. It could attract ideologues only; it had no appeal for workers with immediate needs seeking immediate answers. These latter wanted a little something here and now, whatever it was. The ideologues of the Alliance denounced such base motives as stupid, selfish, and reactionary, for with each gain the workers would lose interest in the great ideal of Socialism. The better off they were, so much the worse for the revolution. On the other hand, the worse, the better, since hunger and want would provide the fuel for the socialist engine. Hence, petty gains like more money, greater security, and shorter work hours were denounced and disdained. The Alliance truly spat on private interest and stigmatized the leaders of the AFL as "fakirs, numbskulls, and knaves."

But it was the AFL and not the STLA that survived as a movement. Within the AFL there were social reformers and revolutionaries, most prominently the socialists. These politically oriented unionists, though dedicated to the long-range general interests of a cooperative commonwealth, knew that if they wanted a mass base among workers they would have to live in trade unions that were necessarily involved with the private, the petty, the parochial, and the personal. They understood that the trade union, like the corporation, is not just a little piece of the big society. The union has its own reason for being, a *natural reason*—the coming together of men in an occupation to relate to one another and to their surroundings.

For some socialists, this understanding came naturally; they were workers out of the workplace who needed no theories to tell them that when the boys got together they liked to talk shop, gripe about the pay, grumble about the boss, worry about the lay-off. For other socialists, the transition to unionism was difficult. To bring understanding to his comrades on the nature of unions, Adolph Strasser, a leader of the Cigar Makers, a subsequent founder of the AFL, and a spokesman for American socialism, said in 1876: "The working class pays attention primarily to those things which may be achieved immediately: provision of jobs, high wages, short working-time, support in case of unemployment and illness. . . . Those who do not pay much attention to these matters but fight primarily for the abolition of wage labor have not fully grasped the idea of modern socialism."[20] Strasser speaks as a socialist, committed to the public and general interest, who nevertheless takes a realistic view of unions as groups necessarily concerned with a private interest. In referring to those revolutionaries who ignored the realities of the labor movement—St. Simon, R. Owen, Fourier, Cabot and Wietling— he attributed the disappearance of their following to the fact that "they ignored and condemned Trade Unionism emerging from real needs and conditions. . . . The trade unions are the natural and only justified Labor Party [and they] have to struggle for the daily bread if they do not want to be doomed to death."[21]

The dilemma of Strasser has recurred for an unnumbered army of union leaders in the century since: men who came to the labor movement because they saw in it the potential to become a major force of change in the general society and who were also aware of the fact that a trade union cannot ignore and must sometimes give primacy to its private interest even over the general interest.

If unions and corporations are organizations involved with

20. *Proceedings of the Union Congress* (New York: Workingmen's Party of the U.S., 1876), cited by H. M. Gittleman, "Adolph Strasser and the Origin of Pure and Simple Unionism," *Labor History*, VI (Winter 1965), p. 75.
21. *Social-Demokrat*, September 24, 1876, cited by Gittleman, p. 78.

their private interest why should the society, through govern-ment, grant them any prerogatives, immunities, or powers? In answer, Davis provides the seventh and last test of corporateness: "functions public and appropriate for associate activity." While corporations are primarily interested in their own affairs, they also perform a public good. "The social functions performed by corporations have had two enduring qualities: they have been (a) such as were considered under succeedings sets of social con-ditions conducive to the welfare of the public and of society in general rather than to the particular welfare of the persons per-forming them, and (b) such as were more advantageously per-formed by associate than by individual activity."[22] Does this measure apply to unions?

In the preamble to the Wagner Act, Congress set forth its reasons for protecting workers in joining and forming unions of their own choosing. The government sought "the elimination of obstructions to free flow of commerce by encouraging collective bargaining." This language conceals more than it reveals: it was verbiage to justify the action of Congress under the constitutional powers endowed by the commerce clause. But this very limited reason is more a compliance with legal ritual than with economic reality. The unions served (and continue to serve) a social need and purpose going far beyond the free flow of commerce and even far above the immediate needs and aspirations of the workers involved. The Wagner Act was part of a national recovery pro-gram one of whose conceptual pillars was enlarged aggregate demand. There were three ways to boost buying power: (1) appeal to the employers to raise wages; (2) enact federal mini-mum wage laws or set all wages by law; (3) strengthen unions. The National Recovery Act, with its industry codes, was really an effort to do all three at once. Employers were assembled to get them to agree on something resembling uniform and improved standards of wages. These standards, embodied in codes, became

22. Davis, *op. cit.*, pp. 28–29.

quasi-law. Unions appeared on the scene as the official spokesmen for labor.

This "industry code" approach, depending so heavily on voluntary agreement, soon fell apart. Employers who were ready to curb their appetites when they were threatened with total destruction reverted to their private interests when the danger of revolution or bankruptcy disappeared. The power of the government to impose codes was seriously curbed when the Supreme Court declared the entire procedure unconstitutional. Some new method had to be found to lift wages as a factor in buying power. The government might have experimented with a wage law, like the old Tudor code. To have attempted it would have run counter to the spirit of a free enterprise economy and would have been impossible in terms of the magnitude and complexity of the undertaking. In such a moment, the unions were the answer. The government enacted a federal minimum wage law and the unions used that foundation on which to erect their contracts.

Unions did more than negotiate contracts to lift wage demands and the economy. They became *enforcing agencies* both for their contracts and for the federal wage and hour law. They also began to reduce the work week as a way of spreading the available work, thereby reducing the social ill of unemployment.

In this process, the unions began to perform other social functions. By relieving poverty, the unions helped retard disease, death, crime, prostitution. They lifted the living standards and social behavior of a nation. In subsequent years, unions cleared slums and built housing, opened clinics, set up hospitals, taught literacy and citizenship. They became a welfare state within the welfare state, *performing governmental functions in a specialized way and in specialized zones improper or inconvenient for the government itself to undertake.*

Needless to say, there have been constant critics of unionism and the government who question whether the unions perform any such worthy public objectives, just as there have been critics of corporations who question their social worth. Union critics do not believe that unions have encouraged the "free flow of commerce"; indeed, they argue that unions have done much to interrupt the flow. They question whether unions have raised wages, especially real wages; whether they have increased employment; whether their efforts have checked juvenile and adult delinquency; and so on. Despite these criticisms, however, the fact remains that the society, as it expresses its mind and its will through the government, has held on balance that unions do perform these worthy social functions. And where the government has not so felt—and the state is fickle—legislatures, boards, and courts have imposed restrictions on unions.

These functions that unions perform as "conducive to the public welfare" are "appropriate for associate activity." None of the above functions could be performed by individual employees, who would lack the power, the coordination, the will, or even the respect that adhere to a union.

At this point—after all seven tests have been applied—it may be appropriate to paraphrase Davis by defining a union as a body of employees upon whom the state has conferred such voluntarily accepted but compulsorily maintained relations to one another and to all others that as an autonomous, self-sufficient and self-renewing body they may determine and enforce their common will, and in the pursuit of their private interest may exercise more efficiently social functions both specifically conducive to public welfare and most appropriately exercised by associated persons.

In putting labor unions to the "corporate" test, the focus has been on form, on those classic contours that distinguish the corporate profile. Such a concentration on form is dangerous because it shifts attention away from the reality to its representation, from real beings to a fictional being. In consequence, the nature of private associations becomes distorted, turned inside out. Instead of seeing these institutions as people seeking recognition from society through a formal charter, we begin to think of these institutions as a piece of paper (the charter) to which passing people adhere, like flies to sweet sticky paper.

Confusing legal fiction with societal reality is a dangerous business because form has an oedipal relationship with content. It is true that the form arises from the content. A class arises in a society; that class begins to take shape; it formalizes its relationships internally and externally; then it seeks legitimization of its being from the society, usually in the form of a charter or, as in the case of unions, through legislation. The state issues a corporate charter and a new form is born, a fictional entity with all the legal qualities of a person. Now the form—a means to an end, a way of defining and legitimizing a going group—becomes an end in itself. The form takes on a life of its own, as the piece of paper becomes a substitute for a congregation. By the twentieth century it became possible for *one* man to become a corporation: one owner plus two dummies could apply for a corporate charter and get it. The two dummies were there to preserve the form, a kind of respectful bow to the corporate past. The dummies, of course, are just a charade played out in public in which everybody makes believe that the dummies are not dummies, that the one real owner is not the sole owner, and that the charter issued truly to one man is honestly being issued to a small congregation engaged in a common enterprise.

Why then does an entrepreneur bother to "incorporate" at all? Again the answer lies in the nonfictional past rather than in the fictional present. Out of the classic corporation, the modern corporation can draw real advantages; namely, greater power with less responsibility. The corporate form becomes a way to raise capital. Once the corporation was an aggregate of people; then its form was used to compose an aggregate of things. Instead of persons gathering in a common enterprise, they sent their symbols in the form of money. In terms of ownership, form symbolized by money killed content embodied in people. The

9 4

corporate form enables a man, or a few men, to accumulate the greater power that flows from greater capital.

The corporate form also becomes a means to limit liability. Indeed, thousands of corporations exist solely for this reason. Traditionally, this limit was a way of granting certain immunities to corporations that were, in pursuit of their private interest, nevertheless serving the greater glory of God and nation. In its purely formal state, however, the corporation continued its limited liability even though the charter was the personal property of one man interested in nothing beyond his own aggrandizement.

The corporate form, as applied in countless cases, is really in conflict with the corporate reality in its classic origin. The classic corporate body that arises in a *polis* is a real thing with live bodies honestly bound together by a common concern. The *polis*, in this sense, need not be a geographic site; it can be a trade, skill, profession, undertaking. In an archaic definition of *corporations* they were called bodies politic. In discussing labor unions as corporations, we are not referring to the corporate form (a charter held by one man or a cabal to add to power and to substract from responsibility) but to the corporate reality, the ancient bodies politic reborn in the person of unions.

"The concept of the corporation began for us with groups of men related to each other by the place they lived in and the things they did," comments Abram Chayes concerning the transformation of corporations from bodies politic into groupings of material resources. "The monastery, the town, the gild, the university were only peripherally concerned with what its members owned in common as members. The subsequent history of the corporate concept can be seen as a process by which it became progressively more formal and abstract. In particular the associative elements were refined out of it. In law it became a rubric for expressing a complicated network of relations of people to things rather than among persons. The aggregated material resources rather than the grouping of persons became the feature of the corporation."[23]

In recent years, the corporation has tended to return to its earlier character as an association of people. Immediate reasons for this reversion can be found in the necessary adjustments of the corporation to its realistic needs. A more general reason may lie in the continuing war between form and content, between means and ends, between father and son.

If the form (the ruler) is to be something more than just a museum piece, he must have a nation of people. He must make laws, set up administrative arms, reckon with the societal conscience. He must cement his people, win their loyalty, command their respect, train them for war and for peace. The form, if it is not to disappear from the face of the earth, must give birth to a progeny. The form must give life to content, the new son out to wrestle with his father. The people of the nation pass judgment on their judge. They test his laws against their needs. They find new leaders; they make new combinations; they rise in revolt. They reassert the birthright of *content* over *form* until such time, of course, as a new form is born. The ruler is reminded that the nation is people not a person; is flesh and blood and not a title.

Lest it be assumed that this war between form and content, between the ruler and the ruled, between means and ends is of recent vintage, a product of the Enlightenment or the Reformation, it might be in order to recall an ancient document on the revolt of the masses in the early times of Egypt's Old Kingdom. "Behold," wept the prophet, "a thing has been done, which never happened before. It has now come to this that the King has been taken away by Poor Man. Behold. The land is full of confederates. The Wretched now rob the Mighty of their goods."

While the ancient scribe accurately records the earthly spoils of this class struggle between the King and the Poor, the Wretched and the Mighty, there is evidence of ideologic confrontation be-

23. Davis, *op. cit.*, p. xix.

tween the people and the pharaoh. The nobility claimed immortality for men associated with the court: others were doomed to die. In effect, the rulers were gods and the people were just people. The rebels rose to put in their claim for immortality, too. And in so doing, they reminded the pharaohs that the king was, after all, just a mortal. Content had its revenge on form!

Although the reassertion of content over form is described here in the dramatic episode of a revolt against the pharaohs, the same interplay recurs in less epic and violent circumstances. Indeed, the evolution of the United States Constitution and the development of American political parties are almost perfect cases of form adjusting to content (and vice versa) with minimal armed intervention. The development of the modern corporation is another instance of a peaceful replacement of content by form, followed by an evolution of the form into a new content very much resembling the original. To do its business, the modern corporation—a charter surrounded by money and protected by limited liability—has to create a flesh and blood community within a community. It does not suffice merely to gather together a mountain of *things*. The corporation needs people and preferably people with a corporate spirit. Although these people are not the owners of the corporation, they are drawn so closely into the operations of the company as to feel the body politic become part of their own body. In some cases, they are also given shares and stock options so that they become part-owners. But even lacking that, they are turned either consciously or unconsciously into "organization men." They develop what Whyte calls the "social ethic," a concept that "could be called an organization ethic, or a bureaucratic ethic; more than anything else it rationalizes the organization's demands for fealty and gives those who offer it wholeheartedly a sense of dedication in doing so."[24]

Some of these men actually do become the corporation. These

24. William H. Whyte, Jr., *The Organization Man* (New York: Doubleday and Company, 1956), p. 6.

are the men in top managerial posts. Their "managerial revolution" is a repetition of an ancient evolution by which the technicians rule while the entitled reign. Control is divorced from ownership. The *true* corporation, especially among the great public corporations, is not the inchoate corps of multipersoned stockholders, but the corporate managers, technicians, and even blue-collar workers: in sum, those who compose the real bodies in the *polis* of the corporate operation. The "owners" are to the corporation as the ancient gods were to the state—objects of unseen worship to whom sacrifice and tribute were regularly paid and to whom the governors of the state regularly turned for legitimization of their authority. When inner political struggles broke out in olden times, the parties turned to various gods or even to the same god for support in the conflict, in very much the same way that corporate heads turn to stockholders for sanctification in a proxy fight.

The modern corporation, a live body in a living community, reassumes the original obligation of the corporation to serve a public function. This is done at multiple levels. First, the nation is led to believe that what is good for General Motors is good for the general welfare. Once this is accepted as folklore, no further justification for corporate license is required. In addition, however, the modern corporation sets up foundations for philanthropic purposes, endows education, enriches culture with museums, gifts of art, radio and television productions. In New York City, corporations have even picked up the tab for entertaining visiting dignitaries and like social functions. Not only does the modern corporation do these good deeds; it also advertises its goodness, so that the society may be aware that the corporation has an abiding concern for the public weal.

The modern worker, the lower level employee of the corporation, is very much aware that the corporation needs him and his skills to give meaningful content to the legal form. This worker is a "citizen" of the corporation within whose environment he organizes into a union: a little corporation within the larger corporation, which is, in turn, a corporation within a still larger corporation, the state.

As the modern corporation has evolved increasingly into a *community*, with its citizens, its governors, and its fiscal deities, a body of literature has begun to evolve that examines the business corporation not simply in terms of economic policy nor business management but politically, "as a social institution organizing human efforts to a common end."[25] It is in this sense that the modern union is a political corporation.

25. Peter F. Drucker, *Concept of the Corporation* (New York: John Day Company, 1946), p. 12.

5

The Ontogeny of American Labor

Ontogeny recapitulates phylogeny not only in the human fetus but also in the gestation of human institutions. The formation of an organization such as a union tends to repeat the evolution of society itself. In the previous chapter, we drew the structural parallel between the little republics of unions and the great republics of nations. In this chapter, we intend to examine the likenesses in the birth and maturation of labor organizations and human society.

Up to this point, our argument has been that man is—to quote St. Thomas Aquinas—*homo sociale et politicum*. As such, he naturally moves in groups, including occupational groups. In discussing modern unions, however, we are not discussing occupational groups, but *employee* groups. In the workplace, these employees form natural organizations, often unstructured in any formal sense. Such informal organizations are normally not called unions. The union is a formal organization, with legitimized leaders, with members who are expected to pay dues, with rules and regulations, with a charter, with the trappings of a structured institution.

At what point do such formal unions appear? The date of birth is of some significance because these dates, as in the case of human beings, tell something about the specific circumstances out of which the organism is born. In Chapter 3 it was argued that people in an occupational grouping inevitably tend to act as a group. Yet not all occupations are organized into unions, with names, local numbers, and officers. Certain crafts, trades, industries, and professions in America are organized into well-established and carefully articulated unions; others are not. What circumstances are determinant?

The question has far more than purely academic interest. In the coming years, American society will be deeply affected by the outcome of a movement to organize the unorganized sectors of the economy. In particular, this refers to the new legions in the labor force: those in service trades, in white collars, in professions, in nonprofit establishments. These relatively recent additions to the army of employees are now a majority of the nation's workers, but they are either unorganized or feebly organized. Will they organize? If so, at what point? The history of man's cultural development provides insight into man's tendency to organize.

The history of man on earth is the cyclical story of integration followed by differentiation followed by reintegration. First, man is totally integrated, unaware that he is anything but another piece of nature like a lion or a lamb, like the rock or rill. Then man begins to differentiate himself from the world around him, as he develops a sense of self-consciousness, a self-image. And finally man, conscious of his differentiated group, organizes his society into clan, tribe, city-state, nation, or whatever it may be.

Once a society is organized, the process repeats itself. At first, each member is integrated, part of an undifferentiated whole. Then differentiation—usually in the form of division of labor— sets in. Members of the larger society become aware of their new station, of their class, of the occupational tribe. They develop a sense of group being, of class consciousness. Out of this awareness arises a subsociety, a new body politic, a corporation or a union.

Needless to say, the story does not end there. The cycle continues to spiral its way across all ages, disrupting established orders, creating new establishments. The habit is so old that as America faces the future, it is reasonable to assume that we will continue in the old, refreshing, deeply embedded, revolutionary routine.

In the beginning, before man tastes the tree of knowledge, he and nature are one. Man is part of an all-inclusive collective We.

That We includes not only the animal, vegetable, and mineral kingdom but also the invisible world of the spirit, where reside dead ancestors, unborn descendants, and that other self who wanders about during the sleeping hours of night. In this view of the universe, there is no room for a man who is conscious of Self. He has an outlook but no insight. He lives, like Adam before The Fall, without shame or guilt: since he does not exist as a person, he cannot take responsibility for his acts. He need never atone for sins because his life is just one long atonement (a being at-one) with his world.

Ernest Crawley finds evidence of the self-conscious I issuing from the We in the evolution of language:

The facts of language show that the plural and all other forms of number in grammar arise not by multiplication of an original I, but by selection and gradual exclusion from an original collective We. This We represents the aggregate personality of the food-group, and therefore includes the undifferentiated I of the speaker of the time being. The procedure is from synthesis to analysis, from the group to the individual.[1]

One commentator adds that "the collective We also includes Nature, since the group includes its ancestors, who are merged with the forces of Nature."[2]

At what point in the evolution of *homo sapiens* he developed a sense of selfhood is, of course, unrecorded. But there is reason to believe that when the great event did occur, it had something to do with the invention of tools and the discovery of death.

[Somewhere between the beginning of the Pleistocene to the advance of the fourth great ice sheet] at least two kinds of human beings had long since begun to notice the world about them in a contemplative way and to express their awareness of some principle of world order in terms that have survived. *Homo sapiens* had long

1. Cited by Jack Lindsay, *A Short History of Culture* (Greenwich, Conn.: Fawcett Publications, 1966), p. 16.
2. *Ibid.*

been flaking hand axes aesthetically. Neanderthal man had learned to bury his dead, surrounding their bodies with tools and trophies of the chase to help them in the world beyond. In terms of religious interpretation, men of both species had acquired a soul. Anthropologically speaking, both had become men, not only capable of using fire and other sources of energy yet to be discovered, but also of *understanding themselves*.[3]

Of these two species—*homo sapiens* and Neanderthal—the latter disappeared after the Middle Pleistocene. The former, the inventor of the handsome hand ax, remained to become our universal ancestor.

It appears then that the "soul" begins with the ax. The tool in man's hand does something to the thoughts in his head. Technology teaches the brain.

To begin with, a man with a flint ax can begin to change his environment. He can break stones and bones; he can chop trees and tough plants; he can kill animals that are bigger and stronger than man. The ax is a tool, a weapon and, most important, the creator of a self-image. Man begins to sense mastery over his outer life; he is no longer merely the slave of circumstance: with the tool he can change the environment. Through the tool, he begins to discover order, the relationship of cause and effect. How pleased he must have been to know that, God-like, he himself could cause an effect.

Homo sapiens' self-image was a shared concept. The ax he used was also used by other vertical bipeds in his own herd. It was not used by apes, chimps, gibbons, lemurs, trees, plants, winds, or snakes. Only *homo sapiens* and his fellow workers used tools. Only they knew how to shape it, make it, employ it, and by so doing, to make the world safe for the sapient. *Homo sapiens* was not only a biologically differentiated group. He was now developing a sense of group status and role in the total scheme of things. He was developing a social consciousness.

3. Carleton S. Coon, *The Story of Man* (New York: Alfred A. Knopf, 1954), pp. 68–69.

This process must undoubtedly have been hastened when, somewhere along the way, man learned to communicate by symbols, when he developed language. Whether the first language was hand signals or glottal grunts or a mixture of both is unrecorded. Judging from current behavior, it must have been a blend, since people still talk with their hands as well as their tongues. This ancient habit has led to some theorizing about the origin of speech in the aboriginal use of the hand tool: [4]

The crucial turn in human origins must have come when the coordination of hand and brain in the making and use of tools had reached a certain point—above all when this coordination brought about the first rudiments of speech. A stable relation of cause and effect could then be grasped, and our ancestors could begin to lay hold of past and future as well as present. The activity of work (the making and use of the tool) produced a point of conscious contact between man and the world. Otherwise reasoning could never have grown beyond the elementary basis seen in apes or the elaborate but rigidly limited basis seen in insects. Now creatures were evolving who could draw themselves up out of the overwhelming succession of sensations and grasp the connections of themselves and the world. . . . They gradually became separated out from Nature by the process that was powerfully merging them with Nature and giving them power over it. . . . The concentration on the tool, on its making and use, gave men the capacity to canalise attention: to create a universe of discourse, an isolate, without which reasoning could never stably and freely arise and develop. Thus was born speech. And every step in the extension of speech intensified the power to reason, to see relationships, to make and use tools, to bind together the family or the work-group. . . . The word became the emblem of man's power to arrest and examine the flux of the world, since it made possible a conscious union in work as well as a purposive relationship to nature.

Homo sapiens then was bound together not only by the gregarious compulsions of the herd but also by a common way of work (and war) and by words. He was well on his way to be-

4. Lindsay, *op. cit.,* p. 14.

coming a culture. Indeed, if some of these popular theories about the origin of man are to be accepted, then the culture of *homo sapiens* was the first tool-makers and tool-users union. They united in a class struggle against the other forces of nature. They survived against great odds, where other species were wiped out. They improved their living standards. They followed leaders. They invented a language all their own (as most workmen in a given craft or trade have done throughout all history) not simply to communicate with one another by sound symbols but also to confirm and ratify the source of their strength and security, which was a common view of the universe.

Here then is one completed swing of the cycle: integration, differentiation, reintegration. The decisive point for forming the "union"? The time is right when the members of the differentiated group become conscious of their difference. The formal act of institutionalizing the group is synchronized with some change in the group or the environment, usually traumatic.

At each turn of the cycle there are heroes. There are the heroes of the "break-away," the nonconformists, the revolutionaries. These are the men who, having recognized the difference between themselves and the rest of the universe, want to make a declaration of independence. They want to assert themselves in terms of their new self-image. These are the differentiators, the separatists, the antiestablishment.

Then there are the heroes of the reintegration. They create a society out of their class, giving it shape, direction, moral tone. They give their lives to the service of their society: teaching, disciplining, sacrificing, dying in the name of the collective. They are the heroes of the establishment, the models of societal behavior, the paragons of virtue, the inspiration of lesser men.

Most of the great heroes of history combine both traits: they liberated their nation and founded a new nation. Consider Moses, Genghis Khan, El Cid, Washington, Bolivar, Lenin, Eamon de Valera, or David Ben-Gurion. All these heroes symbolize man's ambivalence toward himself and toward the world around him, the desire to be free and the desire to be organized—to differentiate and then reintegrate!

When men are differentiated from a larger compass and form their separate group, they do not *ipso facto* sever the umbilical cord that ties them to the great Mother Nature. There is reason to believe that the cord is never cut: it continues to run invisibly from man's soul to the primeval womb, engaging him in an eternal search for his universal relatives in the sand, the stars, the atom, or the flesh of his fellow man.

In describing an African tribe in southern Nigeria, Margaret Mead noted the oneness of the tribesman with the total universe within his ken:

A Tiv was continuous with his society and with nature. He was also a unit within himself, so that mind and body were one and thought and overt acts were equally effective. Overt acts and hostile thoughts, even when involuntary or unconscious, were equally dangerous to the community and "the land," since they were equally polluting through setting in motion forces of evil and interferences; so a man accused of killing would admit having done so. The total environment, human and non-human, with which the Tiv were continuous, was referred as "the land." Every act or thought of the Tiv went beyond the material limits of his body to the community or "the land"; and what happened within this *continuum* affected him.[5]

Although the Tiv was a differentiated group in their "land" they still were tied to the great Mother Nature as an integral part. A certain universal life force ran through the Tiv land: a positive one called *tsav* that was carried in the flesh through an amiable cannibalism and a negative force called *akombo* "based on continuity between the dead and the living and . . . effective within a continuum of man and nature."[6] Other primitive peoples have

5. Margaret Mead, *Cultural Patterns and Technical Change* (New York: New American Library, 1955), p. 113.
    6. *Ibid.*

their own *tsav*. Among Polynesians, the word *mana*, and among the Iroquois, the word *orenda* are "the best known terms for the omnipresent energy or will-power which the primitive feels to be the fundamental stuff of life."[7] Among all these people, there are practices and rites to control the original source of energy, early forerunners of man's present efforts to harness atomic power and the even more basic bits of energy that make up the life force of man, moon, or proton. Whatever the validity of other beliefs—such as pantheism or One God—they serve to retie man's umbilical attachment to the universe.

In a kind of societal return to the womb, the newly born society reintegrates itself with the older, larger and more encompassing universe from which it has liberated itself. As we shall see later, this is also an aspect of a union's ontogeny. After liberating itself from the domineering culture (company or society) it seeks reintegration with both.

Human society, like Nature itself, tends to become internally differentiated. The division, redivision, and subdivision of labor is the history of man. The more complex the divisions, the more civilized they are; the simpler, the more primitive. To a penetrating sociologist such as Durkheim, the division of labor is far, far more than some prosaic device to get on with man's work more efficiently and more economically; it is the cement of the societal structure and the heart beat of its morality.[8] If it is true to say that man divided himself from the rest of the animate universe by his capacity to invent a tool, then it is equally true to say that the progress of man in the last 40,000 years arises from the division of labor following the invention of new tools and new organization of human and inhuman energy.

Just where and when the division of labor in human society begins is another one of those endlessly challenging inquiries.

7. Lindsay, *op. cit.*, p. 26.
8. Emile Durkheim, *The Division of Labor in Society* (New York: The Free Press, 1933).

Coon suggests that there were originally only two divisions, based on sex and age. "Early man, equipped with tools and speech, divided up the tasks needed for survival, so that men hunted while women gathered and cared for the young. Where and when an abundance of food and a stability of residence permitted, old people survived long enough to serve as tutors to the young, and healers to all who needed comfort."[9] A third division of labor (or nonlabor) might have been added based on infants—the first leisure class living at the expense of the community while contributing little beyond its prized presence, a happy state to which adults have been drawn across the ages.

Durkheim suggests that the division of labor is prehistoric and of biologic origin.

The law of the division of labor applies to organisms as to societies; it can even be said that the more specialized the functions of the organism, the greater its development. This discovery has had the effect of immeasurably extending the scope of the division of labor, placing its origins in an infinitely distant past, since it comes almost contemporaneous with the coming of life into the world. It is no longer considered only a social institution that has its source in the intelligence and will of men, but is a phenomenon of general biology whose conditions must be sought in the essential properties of organized matter.[10]

When a society begins to divide up labor, then, it is social artifice imitating physical nature. The society is doing what comes naturally, what bees do, what the lone organism does within the confines of its skin, what a single molecule of water does within the variegated and populous community of impulses that compose its unbroken domain. (If we indulge in a bit of animism in these analogies by endowing an amoeba or a molecule with the capacity to create organized communities within its own being, we do so out of deference to man's sensitivity. If human

9. Coon, *op. cit.*, p. 6.
10. Durkheim, *op. cit.*, p. 4.

cultures repeat the behavior of electric charges, it is preferable to think that the inanimate world has a mind than to conclude that man is mindless.)

Whether division of labor is a rational human invention or is a nonrational universal imperative of matter, the fact remains that cultures develop internal differentiation. Men do different kinds of work; they group around their different occupations to form their different little societies; they formalize relations within the group to establish institutions. "For each type of organization that arose in addition to those of family and band, some kind of leadership, and a pattern of orderly behavior, created themselves. The shop of smiths, the crew of a boat, the members of a trading expedition, a war party, all had to have structure, with leaders, followers, and rules of procedure."[11]

This division of labor (and the organizations arising from it) is viewed by Durkheim as a driving moral force that is "more and more becoming one of the fundamental bases of the social order."[12] Whether it is moral or not, we leave to later chapters that deal with collective bargaining, with labor in politics, and with labor leadership. Here, we limit ourselves to the observation that since time immemorial there is a division of labor and that men unite within the province of their division.

It is folklore that men come together into disciplined groups in order to *war* against someone or something. Thus, for instance, unions present themselves as having been born in a moment of protest against some oppression just as nations present themselves as having arisen out of the cauldron of some revolution. There is good reason for the endurance of this half-myth. It is an analogue of man's personal trauma of birth: that shocking voyage from the warm womb to the cold, cold world. It is also a recall of man's long life as the hunter, a member of the wolf pack, united to war against other animals. It is a continuance of man's written

11. Coon, *op. cit.*, p. 7.
12. Durkheim, *op. cit.*, p. 41.

history, a repetitive recital of wars. Although these romantic versions of group origin are understandable, they are not altogether accurate; the organism precedes the trauma of birth. The embryo is formed before the baby is born; man is a group animal timidly gathering berries before he becomes the ferocious hunter; the American colonies were a people sharing a common continent and a common destiny before they struck out for independence; workers unite in common associations—formal and chartered, but sometimes informal and unchartered—for mutual aid before they go to war against the "barbarian," y-clept the boss.

The earliest craftsmen were, in effect, a family. In civilizations that were matrilineal, the mother bestowed the family name but the father bestowed the trade name. Occupations were hereditary. "Sons take the same work as their fathers before them, there being no motive sufficiently strong to induce them to relinquish it," noted Landtman. "In more developed communities . . . positive laws sometimes oblige them to follow the business of their fathers."[13] In ancient Greece, "the tradition was that a craft belonged to a family or clan. Not only do we hear of Asklepiadai (descendants or clansmen of Asklepios, who possess the art of medicine), Homeridai, who specialize in reciting the poems of Homer and the other epic poets, and actual clans such as the Iamidai, who like their ancestor Iamos, son of Apollo, were professional seers but the phrase 'children of painters' or the like is used much like 'sons of the prophets' in Hebrew to signify simply painters."[14]

Since the earliest crafts grew out of families it is little wonder that the first workmen corporations behaved like families, as mutual aid societies with family gods. Evidence runs back to the Roman Empire where workmen gathered in tight social circles. They spent their life together and spent their death together;

13. Gunnar Landtman, *The Origins of Inequality of the Social Classes* (Chicago: U. of Chicago Press, 1938), p. 88.
14. Rose, *Primitive Culture in Greece*, p. 217 ff, cited by Landtman, p. 88.

came to one another's aid in times of illness, mishap, death; formed special ideologies centered around special gods; huddled together in the here and the hereafter. "The corporations of workers were, with the Romans, far from having an occupational character as pronounced as in the Middle Ages; we find there neither regulation of methods, nor imposed apprenticeship, nor monopoly; nor was their end to unite the necessary elements to exploit an industry."[15] In short, while they were economic in *origin*, they were not primarily economic in *purpose*.

Instead these early Roman corporations of workers (the use of the term *corporation* by Waltzing and Durkheim is another reminder of the word's original meaning) emphasized the *social:*

[Although] to be sure, the association gave them more force in time of need for safeguarding their common interests. But that was not its raison d'etre, its principal function. Above all, the corporation was a religious organization. Each one had its particular god whose cult was celebrated in a special temple when the means were available. In the same way as each family had its *lar familiaris* [household god]; each city its *Genius publicus* [local diety], each organization had its protecting god, *Genius Colegii*. Naturally this occupational cult did not dispense with celebrations, with sacrifices and banquets in common. All sorts of circumstances were used as reasons for these joyful gatherings. Moreover, distribution of food-stuffs and money often took place at the community's expense. . . . The organization of workmen was, at the same time, a burial society. . . . All the fairly rich corporations had a collective columbarium where, when the organization had not the funds to buy a burial spot, there was at least the certainty that its members would have honorable burial at the expense of the common fund.[16]

Durkheim's referring to these Roman organizations as religious suggests the original meaning of the word, derived from the Latin root, *ligare*, "to tie." It is the religion that unites: it ties men

15. Waltzing, *Etude historique sur les corporations professionelles chez les Romains*, Vol. I, pp. 56–57, quoted by Durkheim, pp. 8–9.
16. Durkheim, *op. cit.*, p. 11.

together through the bond of a common belief, god, church, burial ground, rites, sacrifices, mutual aid, holy days, and holidays.

In their religious character these early Roman workmen's associations were more like the progressive than the conservative unions of America. The former pride themselves on their ideological belief in a utopian kingdom come on earth and on their pioneer work in establishing fringe benefits in the form of health and welfare, burial, and retirement funds. The progressives are more likely than the conservatives to talk of their union as a way of life. Ironically, what the progressive looks upon as the new frontier of social action for unions is actually the oldest established area of labor practice—an inspired rediscovery of the original intent and content of the worker community.

These worker-corporations first appeared in Rome whenever the economy created the necessary class, the appropriate division of labor. When the economy was no longer purely agricultural but proliferated to produce a class of craftsmen and of traders, the basis for the worker-corporation was formed. "If they seem to have been unknown in Greece, at least up to the time of the Roman conquest," speculates Durkheim, "that is because trades, being looked down upon there, were carried on almost exclusively by strangers, and for that reason found themselves outside the legal organization of the city."[17] But once Rome had its own class of traders, they formed corporations.

After a long, vigorous life, these organizations of workmen and traders were ultimately liquidated in two stages. First, they were converted into administrative arms of the state. In this respect, theirs was the same fate as the later liveried companies and the regulated stock companies of England. As adjuncts of the state, they were given duties and responsibilities so onerous that the state could only maintain them by force. "All sorts of methods were employed for preventing workmen from getting rid of the heavy obligations resulting from their occupation; they

17. *Ibid.*, p. 7.

went so far as to recruit and force enrollment."[18] Apparently what happened to these corporations at one point is what happened to labor unions under communism and fascism: they became totalitarian. Since occupational groupings, converted from free expressions of the people into oppressive instruments of the state, could only be maintained by the overwhelming power of the government, the collapse of the Roman Empire meant the collapse of these corporations. The resurgence of worker-corporations had to await a new kind of urban economy, sufficiently stable to allow craft and commerce to thrive, sufficiently decentralized to allow subgovernments to flourish. By the thirteenth century, such associations were well established: educational corporations for men practicing teaching, craft guilds for men making commodities, merchant guilds for men of commerce.

When the old order gave way to the era of enterprise, with the closed market yielding to the open, the guilds lost their original function. By that time they were just a shell of their original self. The guilds were no longer real collectives of fraternal souls; they were charters held by wealthy politicians, using the guild name to peddle licenses, to impose regulations, to establish monopolies, to serve self and state. The guilds had become what the worker-corporations had been in the latter days of Rome.

The rise and decline of worker-associations in the Roman Empire and in Western Europe testify to the fact that such organizations are not the casual by-product of some one time or place. The repetitive birth and death or transformation of worker societies is further proof of the universality of unions.

When a new social order rose later in the American colonies, it was inevitable that the ancient phenomenon should repeat itself once more, in a figure appropriate to the New World. The first occupational associations on record are gatherings of masters and journeymen to form associations for mutual aid. Although the founders of these societies probably were not Latin scholars,

18. *Ibid.,* p. 8.

they might easily have copied their pattern and practice from the worker-corporations of the Roman Empire.

In the period before the American Revolution, the worker identified himself with the economic world of his employer. Both master and journeyman worked together in serving a local market on a custom order basis. They lived in the same town. They were near equals, since the journeyman was very likely to become a master himself in due time. They had much in common: workplace, town, customers, tools, language, skill, and respect for one another.

The organizations of masters that appear in rudimentary form in the colonial period took on shape and purpose after the Articles of Confederation. These organizations, many of them incorporated before 1800 with formal charters, spoke for the whole craft or trade and hence, in some of these corporations, the journeymen were included as members. These early corporations strongly resembled the medieval guilds both in economic program and in internal social life. The resemblance, however, was far less genetic than environmental: the same conditions produced the same results.

"Buy American" was the first great demand of these societies. Like their guild forefathers, they wanted to regulate the market, primarily to close it to foreign competition. They first got state legislatures to pass tariff laws—an inadequate step since retaliatory tariffs in other states hurt their own market. Then they pressed on for a national tariff, a precondition of which was the unification of the confederated states into a United States with power to regulate commerce. Hence, they backed the Constitution, lobbied for protection, and won a tariff in 1789.

The journeyman was at one with his master in this political work, according to Commons: "In all of these movements for patronising home industry, for the adoption of a Federal constitution, and for the enactment of a national tariff, the journeymen were united with their masters.[19] The worker, as journeyman, had not yet differentiated himself from his master as a separate economic identity. Indeed, the nature of the production set-up was such that for the journeyman to have organized separately for a diverse set of economic goals was neither possible nor desirable: the class of journeymen was too fluid and the identity of interest with the master was too great.

Like the guilds, these societies tried to establish quality control over their products. They encouraged invention; they set up libraries for their journeymen and themselves; they educated apprentices; they pooled funds for these purposes. They also served as trade courts (to arbitrate disputes among their members) and as credit and mutual loan societies, using the association treasury as a local bank. They set up closed-shop provisions that forbade a member of the company to work with a nonmember on pain of expulsion. They also set up a "closed city" by getting New York to pass an ordinance (1789) barring those who were not free men of the city from trading in it except on fair days.[20] Finally, these protective societies, like the guilds, played the paternal role of uniting the fraternity of the trade into one helpful family. "Like the European guilds, the early protective organizations of this country incorporated benefit features among their activities. Sick, accident, funeral and death benefits were paid. The education and bringing up of the children of deceased members were looked after, and the widow was assisted."[21]

Once these protective associations began to accumulate money for what the modern labor union calls fringe benefits, they discovered what both the modern union and the United States Government have learned; namely, that caring for the poor, sick, and unfortunate is a big business. When the Carpenters' Company of Philadelphia, founded in 1724, discovered how rich their sym-

19. Commons, *op. cit.*, Vol. I, p. 75.
20. *Ibid.*, p. 81.
21. *Ibid.*, p. 83.

pathy for poverty had made them, they sought to protect their funds by applying for a charter of incorporation in 1792. (The fact that this society showed a record of some seven decades of existence by 1792 indicates the early beginnings and the long durability of these societies.)

The familial character of these occupational groupings is further evidenced by their involvement with the moral conduct of their members. Thus the Carpenters' Company: "Whereas this corporation is becoming more numerous, and the reputation of such institutions in a great measure depends on the morality of the individual members thereof. Therefore . . . the Company shall appoint a committee of five members whose duty it shall be to admonish such members, if any such there be, who to their knowledge shall be in the practice of any immoral conduct, and if their efforts to reclaim them shall prove ineffectual, it shall be their duty to report such members to the Company, who shall take orders thereon as to them may appear just and proper."[22]

The first separate societies of journeymen on record imitate the *familial* but not the *economic* practices of the protective associations. "On the whole, the journeymen established separate mutual aid societies. In this sense there was at this time a separation of industrial classes, but the division seems to have been more on social than economic lines."[23] The distinction between social and economic, as used here, is exemplified in the fact that the early journeymen's societies were moved by "a desire to provide for unemployment, sickness, and death, rather than a desire to regulate wages and conditions of employment."[24]

This limitation of journeymen's societies to the "benevolent" activities was partly natural and partly artificial. Mutual aid was a natural thing, another expression of the congregational com-

22. *Ibid.*, p. 82.
23. *Ibid.*, p. 85.
24. *Ibid.*, p. 87.

pulsion. The journeyman's need to extend his activities to the economic sphere was not too great since there was such a close identity of occupational interest between master and journeyman. However, when a body of journeymen did consider using their organization for economic purposes such as fixing wages, they were prevented from doing so by law. The charters of incorporation prohibited such action. The act incorporating the New York Society of Journeymen Shipwrights, for instance, stated that "the legal existence of the society ceases automatically if the funds of the society are misappropriated or if the organization is convicted of an attempt to fix scale of wages." The New York Typographical Society could not get a charter of incorporation until it was ready to accept a clause that prohibited it from passing any law or regulation "respecting the price or wages of labour or workmen, or any other articles, relating to the business which the members thereof practise or follow for a livelihood."[25]

When in due time the master and the journeymen drifted apart—the former becoming an employer and the latter becoming a wage worker—the benevolent societies of journeymen became "protective" societies as well, concerned with wages. When they did, however, they changed their character from benevolent societies to trade unions. "This was the experience of the journeymen printers of Philadelphia who were organized into a benefit society by the assistance of 'the venerable Franklin' and dissolved in 1795, only to reorganize in 1802 as a trade union with benefit features."[26]

The way in which journeymen became trade union men in early America reveals some of the details of the cycle from integration to differentiation to reintegration. It begins with the journeyman as a person integrated within the production process:

25. *Ibid.*, p. 86.
26. *Ibid.*, p. 87.

he is at one with the employer, the undertaking, his universe of work. This is certainly true when master and journeymen are one and the same person, just an independent craftsman performing services for customers when called upon to do so. As a division of labor sets in, with journeymen taking on a defined role in relation to the master, special little societies of journeymen are formed. Their first function is to be at peace with one another, to engage in mutual aid, to enjoy the body warmth and spiritual security of the herd. At this moment, they have unwittingly planted the seed of separation from their employer and the seed of reintegration as a "little republic" of their own. The moment of separation is the beginning of a new self-integration.

So long as journeymen engage only in mutual aid, their masters and society view them as benevolent. When the journeymen decide to strike out on their own for a higher wage, they are viewed as malevolent. Hence, the break-away in a combative union requires a special act of courage, a challenge to the dominant mores (and law) of the workplace and the state. To perform this act of conscience and disobedience there must be some special spur: hunger, injustice, loss of status, injured pride.

Against such oppression, there were undoubtedly many inchoate outbursts, some of which have been recorded.

John Winter, overseer on Richmond Island off the coast of Maine, began complaining as early as 1636 about workers who struck in "consortship" because he withheld a year's wages. Boston Caulkers formed some sort of combination in 1741 when they agreed among themselves not to accept paper money or due bills as wages from their employers. Some twenty tailors refused to work in New York City in 1768 because of a "late Reduction of the Wages of Journeymen Taylors," and set up their own "House of Call" to compete with their former masters. Peter Hasenclaver, eighteenth century iron monger, was constantly harassed by slowdowns among his artisans and was forced to raise wages. Carpenters at the Hibernia Iron

Works in New Jersey went on strike in 1774 because their wages were not promptly paid.[27]

But these strikes—the first sparks of a class conflagration—were not enough to make for lasting labor unions. They were just hints that some day the employees would break away to form unions to do battle with employers, not merely to gather in peace but to unite in war. Sporadic conflict was the forerunner of permanent organization: guerrilla war preceded the formation of an army.

The era of trade unionism, as distinguished from journeymen benevolent societies, came with a radical change in the nature of the economy: a revolution in merchandising. Originally the master made up things on order from a customer. Then the master stocked his store with some ready-made items for immediate sale. However, when retailing became wholesaling, which involved catering to a widespread market, a new character appeared on the scene in the merchant-capitalist who had the necessary cash, credit, and access to markets to manipulate the manufacturers of wares to his suiting. Since the merchant-capitalist sat astride the crossroads of commerce he could deny or give access to the market to those whom he chose. And, he chose those manufacturers (masters) who could give the most for the least. Under these circumstances, the masters were forced to put the pressure on their employees, the journeymen, demanding from them the best and giving them the least. The rule of the merchant-capitalist created the conditions for the revolt of the journeymen. These employees were a class, with class organizations engaged in benevolent services. Some of them had tasted blood in disjuncted rebellions. Now they found a continuing cause for discontent in the pressure of the master, himself under pressure, to squeeze the journeymen into giving more for less. The new climate turned "benevolent" societies into "malevolent" unions.

27. Joseph Rayback, *A History of American Labor* (New York: Macmillan Company, 1964), p. 17.

The precondition for a class of merchant-capitalists was established by a political act: the Constitution of the United States. Unification of the states levelled tariff barriers and opened a national market, dominated by the merchant-capitalist.

In this state, the 'manufacturer' was merely an incipient employer without capital—the "boss," the contractor—the successor of the master workman—whose function was mainly that of driving the wage bargain. The distinction between the employer and the wage-earner at the time was not so much the amount of his income or his possession of capital, as the contingent and speculative character of his income. His profit was the margin between the prices he paid for labour and the prices he received from the wholesale-merchant, or merchant-capitalist, for his product. The wage earner, on the other hand, received a stipulated income for his physical exertion. The prices received by the contractor or employer were at the mercy of the merchant-capitalist and his main source of profit was his ability to reduce the prices which he paid to labour. This "sweated" condition, produced by the widening of the labour market and seen for the first time in a few trades at the beginning of the century, but seen most clearly in the decade of the thirties, drove the wage earner as such to his first conscious union with competing labourers in defense against the master-workman who had now become the boss.[28]

The rise of the merchant-capitalist was due very largely to the use of a new "tool": improved transportation. Better roads made bigger markets, elevating wholesaler over retailer and merchant over manufacturer. In this "retooled" economy, the journeyman found himself producing for an impersonal, distant, unknown market. He was removed from consumer and from the big boss, the merchant-capitalist. The manufacturer became a straw boss, under pressure to cut wages; consequently, the journeyman was under pressure to organize a union.

Here then is the classic model of union origin. First comes a change in the economy in the form of a new tool, a new managerial arrangement, a new method of merchandising, or what-

28. Commons, *op. cit.*, p. 8.

ever. This economic change sets up new relationships within the economy, creating a new occupational grouping that organizes either formally or informally. Slowly, it develops a sense of group interest. At some point, as the group feels pressured by circumstances such as a wage cut, or loss of status, or lengthened work hours, it strikes a combative stance and becomes a union.

The original theory that the first unions in America arose directly out of the unsettling pressures of the merchant-capitalist milieu was based on a detailed study of the Cordwainers (shoemakers) conducted by Commons. However, his theory does not apply to another very early union, the Carpenters, since they could not produce a product, like a shoe, that could easily be shipped long distances and sold in stranger markets. Carpenters generally worked on buildings that could not be shipped anywhere; they produced for the local market only. Yet, in a curious way, the carpenter was also driven from benevolent society to belligerent union by the merchant-capitalist. Before America had even entered the nineteenth century, there was a class of financiers who had entered the building business. They were to the construction industry what the merchant-capitalists were in the shoe trade. These building financiers, many of whom were also the landlords, put up the money for the construction, and to get the job done most cheaply, they pitted one contractor against another. The carpenter, like the cordwainer, discovered that the big boss was the capitalist, not the master.

Thus in the building industry the menace was not the competition of workmen in neighboring cities felt because of improved transportation but the competition of fellow townsmen who through a bidding procedure cut prices and thus put downward pressure on wages. . . . Conflict between labor and capital arose from extreme competition caused by changed financial practices and not from improved transportation.[29]

29. Robert Ozanne, "The Labor History and Labor Theory of John R. Commons," in *Labor, Management and Social Policy*, Ed. Gerald Somers (Madison, Wisc.: University of Wisconsin Press, 1963), p. 27.

In the case of both cobbler and carpenter, the push to union-ize came with a change in the economy. A third group of early unionists were in the printing trades. In this skilled craft, the journeymen and masters originally felt close. The New York Typographical Society, for instance, passed a resolution in 1809 proclaiming that "between employers and employed there are mutual interests." Masters and journeymen were in one and the same society. But eight years later, the journeymen reconsidered their good will declaration after they found some employer mem-bers conspiring to break the union. This traumatic experience— the discovery of the enemy within—caused the typographers to rewrite their constitution to exclude employers and in the re-writing to state a simple verity about the human condition. "Ex-perience teaches us," they wrote, "that the actions of men are influ-enced almost wholly by their interests, and that it is almost impos-sible that a society can be regulated and useful where its members are actuated by opposite motives and separate interests. This society is a society of journeymen printers, and as the interests of the journeymen are separate and in some respects opposite to that of the employers, we deem it improper that they should have any voice or influence in our deliberations."[30]

Although the typographers had been organized for some time in benevolent societies and in associations that included their employers, it was not until this painfully discovered treachery within their organization that they finally concluded that the "interests of the journeymen are separate and in some respects opposite to that of the employers." The journeymen typographers had been in existence as a class; then they organized for mutual aid; then they developed a sense of class (actually "craft") con-sciousness; then they set up a union that excluded employers. The classic model repeated itself.

It would probably have come as a great surprise to these early

30. Cited by Philip S. Foner, *Labor Movement in the United States* (New York: International Publishers, 1947), Vol. I, p. 74.

printers to learn that in separating themselves as a group from their employers they were re-enacting the primitive drama of *homo sapiens* differentiating himself and his society from the natural world around him with which he had for eons considered himself to be coterminous. At some point, *homo sapiens* declared in his unwritten constitution that the interests of man, to paraphrase the typographers, are separate and in some respects opposite to that of the tyrannical environment. Man discovered that he was "different," as the journeymen printers discovered that they were "different." Man organized his group: family, clan, tribe, city, state, nation; the printers organized a union: local, state, national, federation.

In early America, notes Philip Taft, "the first to organize was the skilled artisan, the printer, shoemaker and building tradesman."[31] This phenomenon—the organization of the *skilled* before the unskilled—is in line with the history of social organization through the ages. Whether we examine the organization of the priesthood in the Sumerian temple-city, the organization of the nobility in the middle ages, or the organization of the typographers in the days of Benjamin Franklin, we repeatedly discover that it is not the poorest, the most illiterate, the most oppressed but the most skilled, most literate, and, in a sense, the most powerful who organize first. It may appear to be an exaggeration to describe the cordwainers, printers, and carpenters of colonial America as the "most powerful." Certainly there were more powerful men in their times—generals, governors, masters, and financiers. But these latter were already "organized," in some cases by the closest society man knows—the family. There were colonial families whose members were the landowners, financiers, generals, and governors of their day. One expanded family was a "union" of the elite. Such influential families were more powerful than the early trade unionists. But, within the class of employees

31. Philip Taft, *Organized Labor in American History* (New York: Harper and Row, 1964), p. 4.

in early America, the carpenters, cordwainers, and printers were among the most powerful. They had skills that could not easily be replaced; they were proud of their product and of themselves; they shared and protected trade mysteries; they were literate. They had a strong self-image as artisans, as patriots, as free men. When they were pushed, they pushed back.

When we speak of "power" in this context, we refer to the power of a group, such as the printers union, to change the environment. The consciously constituted union, like the consciously carved piece of flint in the hands of the primitive, becomes an instrument to affect the surroundings. Some groups in a society, when united, wield such power; others do not. The Sumerian priests had great power: they could prophecy the weather; they could bring on an eclipse; they could evoke rain and shine. Or at least they so claimed and the people so believed. The first healers could bring health to the sick. From the time of the witch doctor and medicine man to the AMA and Medicare, the social order has had to recognize their power—especially when they acted in concert. The nobility had great power: they could ward off the enemy; they could provide physical security to their dependents. At the other end of the social scale are hundreds of millions of people who are powerless: so unbelievably underfed that they do not even have the minimal body energy to feel and react to the pangs of hunger. They are without skill, without education, without physical strength, without materialistic worth to the society and, hence, without power.

"Unto everyone that hath shall be given." To those sectors of the working class where there was power more power was added in the form of unions. Where workers lacked such power (or an awareness of their power) they had to wait their turn to unionize. Some are still waiting.

From colonial America to the New Deal, the American labor movement was made up of skilled craftsmen: building and construction trades, railroads, printing, cigar-making, machinists, operating engineers. There were several seeming exceptions to this rule, among them the Knights of Labor, the miners, the needle trades workers. Yet each of these is one of those exceptions that proves the rule.

The Knights of Labor were a response to a profound and sweeping change in the American economy. Big business—industry, finance, commerce—was in the saddle following the victory of the Union troops in the Civil War. Small farmer and independent businessman were being crushed under the weight of the giants, the trusts and monopolies. The little man of the soil was losing his land; the worker in the factory was losing his hope that he could ever become an employer. The great schism between the North and South in the Civil War was followed by an even greater schism between the rich and the poor in what was to become a new kind of civil war of worker versus boss.

This was, of course, not the first time that America had experienced the simultaneous pressure of rich and poor. Class differences existed from the very beginning of our history. But the rapid rise of the capitalist oligarchy in post-Civil War America was dramatic, far-reaching, traumatic. Escape to the frontier was no longer so easy, for the West had moved farther away. Escape to the employing class seemed forbidden, since the new enterprises required massive capital. Railroads with their control over shipping, financiers with their control over credit, and merchant princes with their control over markets ruled the land as a new aristocracy of money.

The rapid advance of the Industrial Revolution in the middle of the last century convinced the more intelligent workers that their special skills would not long serve to protect their standards. Machinery, the factory, and industrial combinations, so-called monopolies, reached during and after the Civil War unheard of proportions and, by discounting craftsmanship, broke down special living standards in every direction. This bore most heavily on the shoemakers, iron and steel workers, machinists, molders, coopers and cigar makers, and it was from there that most of the labor leaders of the mid-century came.[32]

The Noble and Holy Order of the Knights of Labor was a broad movement directed against their modern mammon. Its specific program was aimed at a return to the past: the tool user would also be the tool owner. The Knights opened their doors to wage earners, farmers, small employers, and professionals. They addressed themselves, as did William Jennings Bryan, to all who labored and who were being crucified on the cross of Gold.

Although the purposes of the Knights of Labor were repeatedly spelled out in specific proposals—land, credit, currency, cooperation, nationalization, education—their philosophy is better sensed poetically rather than programmatically. In one poignant quotation, the sensitive and sympathetic historian of the Knights, Norman J. Ware, has caught the spirit:

"We are," said their great leader Terence V. Powderly, "the willing victims of an outrageous system. . . . So long as a pernicious system leaves one man at the mercy of another, so long will labor and capital be at war. . . . In what direction shall we turn? . . . . Far be it from me to say I can point out the way. . . . I can only offer a suggestion that comes to me as a result of experience. . . ." And while the General Assembly hung breathless on his words, words that should lead them out of the wilderness of "wage slavery," he suggested: "to abolish the wage system!"[33]

Powderly's proposal was not to better the wage, but to abolish wages; not a better boss but the end of bossism. To Ware, "he was a wind bag"; to his followers, he was a Moses; to employers, he was a menace—the American version of the specter of communism.

32. Norman J. Ware, *The Labor Movement in the United States, 1860–1890* (New York: Vintage Books, 1964), p. xvii.
33. *Ibid.*, p. xviii.

However hollow his words sound to some today, they rang true then. It was an appeal to a class, apparently being ground down to a least common denominator, to rise as a class against its oppressors.

It was to fight consolidated capital that the Order tried to create an integrated labor society to replace the isolated craft alliances and conventions of reformers that had preceded. . . . The solidarity of labor was fast becoming an economic reality if not a psychological fact, and it was the business of the Order to make the organization of labor fit the conditions of work. Emphasis on the principle of solidarity is the beginning of understanding of the Knights of Labor. . . . The Order tried to teach the American wage earner that he was a wage earner first and a bricklayer, carpenter, miner, shoemaker, after; that he was a wage earner first and a Catholic, Protestant, Jew, white, black, Democrat, Republican, after. This meant that the Order was teaching something that was not so in the hope that some time it would be.[34]

As in the ancient Roman workmen corporations or in the medieval guilds, so too in the assembly halls of the Order men gathered, across craft lines, to worship in the same faith and to warm each other with their own company. "The labor movement of the eighties," wrote Ware, "was not a doctrinal religion like socialism, but a vague, primitive, embryonic sentiment, a religion in the making. The local assembly was something like a congregation living in times of persecution. The early Christians had their catacombs, and it is not irreverence that suggests that the Knights had their secret sanctuaries. . . . This sanctuary became the center of the members' lives, their club, union headquarters, school, church, in one."[35] These "sanctuaries" still stand today and are called Labor Temples.

American radicals, especially those raised in the Marxist tradition, have always had a lively affection for the Knights of Labor

34. *Ibid.*, p. xxiii.
35. *Ibid.*

as contrasted with the prosaic and pedestrian American Federation of Labor. The radical feels affection for the Knights not only because the Noble Order preached an ultimate salvation somewhat akin to the socialist ideal of a cooperative commonwealth, but even more so because the Knights emphasized *class* over *craft*. The class that the Knights sought to unite in one great Order was not the proletariat of the Marxist; the class of the Knights was an almost all-inclusive community more easily defined in its scope by the few categories that were excluded as enemies of "the people." Nevertheless, the Knights tried to present a class front bent on a fundamental reorganization of society to end the rule of the plutocrat.

In this sense, the Knights were far more like the Marxist movements of Europe than like the craft unions of America. And logically so. Marx studied Western Europe in the second half of the nineteenth century. What was happening in the United States after the Civil War was also happening in Europe only more so and, from the workers point of view, more hopelessly so. The bourgeoisie was in the saddle; the artisan, the craftsman, the manual worker were being proletarianized, left without property, without tools, without workplace, left with nothing but their labor to peddle to a few buyers in an overcrowded market. From the book stacks in the British Museum, Marx looked out over Europe to see a continent in civil war, in a class war where an ever-growing proletariat engaged an ever-shrinking bourgeoisie.

Marx focused on the proletariat as a class and not on the separate trades, crafts, industries. To the extent that Marx referred to specific occupational situations in his monumental *Capital*, he did so by way of illustration to add detail to his grand presentation and denunciation of capitalism.

That both Karl Marx and the Knights of Labor should have been more obsessed with the proletariat and "the people" than with the more clearly differentiated occupations within the broad classifications was natural and understandable. The most dramatic and traumatic fact of the times was the growth, the plight, and the widely inclusive protest movement of a class: the workers dissociated from the ownership of their tools. Man the toolmaker had been torn from his tools in an age perhaps more dependent on tools than any in man's history.

Both the revolutionary Marxists and the mild-mannered Knights had a program to enable workers to repossess the means of production. The Knights planned to do it through cooperatives, cheap credit, and nationalization of the giant enterprises. The Marxists planned to do it by a revolution in which the proletariat would reclaim the means of production and exchange by socializing them. Socialists and Knights were saying almost the same thing in varying dialects.

The Knights appeared to be a very broad inclusive people's army, enlisting almost everyone from the unskilled Negro coal handler to the white Protestant storeowner and moving them into "mixed" assemblies regardless of status or skill. However, a closer look at the Noble Order reveals that this impression of a motley amalgam fused in class solidarity was an illusion, derived more from the speeches of the leaders and the resolutions of the conventions than from the practices of the membership.

The original local of the Knights of Labor, Assembly No. 1, was a craft union of garment cutters. They took in workers of other trades but only as "sojourners," who were given no voice and no vote, were charged no dues, and who were sent off after proper indoctrination by the cutters to form locals of their own craft. Not until 1878 did the idea of the "mixed" local—men of many crafts—gain ground in the Knights. These grew rapidly "in semirural districts where there were often not enough men of one trade to form a craft local." In the year of 1882, of 484 local assemblies of working men, 318 were craft and only 116 mixed. A later count, at the height of the Knights strength, showed that of 1,499 locals, 836 were trade and 625 were mixed.[36]

36. *Ibid.*, p. 158.

Even this relatively high figure of "mixed" assemblies (though still a clear minority) is deceptive. It does not represent an amalgam of the unskilled, but locals of skilled craftsmen in the newly developing West and South where there were not enough men in a given craft to compose a separate local.

The functional base of the Knights was the craft local, despite all efforts of the leaders to obscure the fact in their manifestoes. There was a "predominantly craft composition of the Order in its earlier years, and a strong trade union element throughout," notes Ware. This made it possible, despite the fact that the leaders "were not sympathetic toward trade unions either within or without," for a craft union "to establish and maintain itself within the Order, gain by its support, and at the same time lose nothing of craft autonomy. Many trades were formed and nourished behind the veil of the Knights as in a womb."[37]

The womb of the Knights, then, was the dwelling place of skilled workers drawing solace and security from the amicable *ambience* of their all embracing mother while maintaining their separate, independent identities as craft unionists. The fact that the Knights were really an assemblage of skilled craftsmen is all the more remarkable since the religion of the Holy Order wished it were otherwise.

In due time the contrast between what the local assemblies of the Order really were and what the devout leadership of the Knights wanted them to be was too great for the parent body to contain the fetuses. The craft unions left the womb. They opted for the American Federation of Labor where rhetoric matched reality.

Between 1897 and 1904, unions increased membership from 447,000 to 2,072,700. At the beginning of this period, membership was concentrated in transportation, building, metal and machinery—all skilled trades.[38] By 1900, third place went to the

37. *Ibid.*, p. 162.
38. Taft, *op. cit.*, p. 162.

miners: the next apparent exception to the rule that the most skilled are the first to organize. While there was a crust of skilled workers in the mines, most of those who descended into the bowels of the earth to dig out its riches must be counted as unskilled or, at best, only semiskilled. Yet among the miners, trade unionism has always been strong—not only in the United States but around the world. Miners lived in a kind of totalitarian society. Their employers were their landlords, their storekeepers, their credit institutions, their police force, their government. Those on top were unitary and, consequently, made the mining community a tight unit. Miners lived in a company town: they worked in the same dark pits; they lived in the same drab alleys; bought in the same store; worked for the same boss; were trapped in the same disasters. For miners, there was only one *polis*—workplace, home, government. The mining town was a model of the simple class society: a handful of rulers and a legion of ruled, separated by an unbridgeable chasm. The middle class was tiny and of no consequence in this polarized community. In such a society, there was no difference between the struggle of one occupational group and the "class struggle." In mining towns, there was only one question to ask: "Which side are you on?"

Although there were unions of coal miners as early as the 1840s, there was no permanent lasting organization until a condition appeared in the coal fields similar to that preceding the organization of the shoemakers and the carpenters. In 1848, there was a miners' union in Schuylkill County; by 1849, it was dead. The American Miners' Association was organized in 1861 in Belleville, Ill., and reached out to men in the mines over a fairly wide area; by the end of the decade, it too was dead. In the 1880s, however, a change took place in the coal industry that compelled widespread and continuing organization among the coal miners. "The 1880s witnessed the rapid growth of railroads throughout the northern coal districts. Producers from various fields started to compete for each other's markets, so that price changes tended to affect large producing areas and a greater number of producers. Interdependence of the separated coal producing areas was immediately recognized by operators and union leaders in the industry. For the union leaders, it clearly pointed to a national organization of miners working in every field regulating wages and, indirectly, influencing prices." In 1885, thirty delegates from seven states gathered in Indianapolis, to launch the National Federation of Miners and Mine Laborers. They pin-pointed the source of their difficulty with sophisticated awareness. "The increased shipping facilities of the last few years have made all coal-producing districts competitors in the markets of this country. This has led to indiscriminate cutting of market prices and unnecessary reductions in our wages."[39]

The National Federation of Miners was an "industrial union," including both skilled and unskilled in one organization. Note the name of the 1885 organization: Federation of Miners *and Mine Laborers*. The unskilled were specifically included, among whom were children laboring in the mines before their teens. The succeeding United Mine Workers was also an industrial union. Under the Knights of Labor, mixed assemblies in the mining towns included "the doctor, the grocer and the businessmen." The unitary rule of the mine boss created a unitary organization of his employees: the miners were a model and later a mentor for industrial unionism in America. It is hardly an accident that John L. Lewis, spokesman for the miners, became the inspiration and leader of workers in America's basic industries of steel, auto, rubber, and textiles when they rose in their company towns in the 1930s.

The mining milieu was not confined to the coal fields. It also left its impress on the metal miners of the mountain states. Out of the company towns resting on metal ore rose the Western Federation of Miners, an industrial union very much in the mold of the coal miners. The metal miners, however, were not just

39. Taft, *op. cit.,* p. 166.

miners; they were also Westerners. As such, their unionism had the tang of the wild. Into the mines, factories, lumber-camps, fields, and railroads of the West poured the sons of the border, the great backwash from the closing of the frontier. They came with no manners for the discipline of work under a boss. They came with the minimal respect for law and order that characterized the American frontier. They came with a quick temper and a quick gun. They came as wanderers, migrant laborers, united in the swaggering fraternity of the "free and the brave," tied to no trade, no place, no boss—tied to nobody and nothing.

American labor never produced such a romantic band of heroes. Out of the West came these rough-hewn Lochinvars, preaching "one big union," relentless war against exploitation, direct action. This was a labor movement with no place in it for dudes. This was the tough tutor of the Western Federation of Miners and the Industrial Workers of the World. It left a lasting impression on the American labor movement and an even more lasting impression on the historians, theoreticians, and song writers and folk singers of labor.

But the Western Federation and the IWW were again the exception that proved the rule: a special phenomenon arising in a special circumstance. What was the *polis* of these men, recently liberated men of the American soil intermixed with laborers imported from Greece, Italy, the Basque country, Hungary? Their *polis* was the wide-open land over which they roamed, riding the rails from camp to camp, from season to season. In this *polis*, they organized their "one big union," the "union of the wanderer."

In one sense, the IWW was like the Knights of Labor: their words outran their works. They were not really "one big union." They were many unions organized on an industrial basis. And as such, they played a double role in the ontogeny of American labor. The industrial unions of the "Wobblies" were a rational response to the great industrial combines that dominated the early exploitation of the West. Also, like the coal miners, the IWW augured the coming of the industrial unions of the 1930s, a rational response to the industrial combines of the Midwest after World War I. Although the IWW is just a bit of nostalgia for many in the labor movement of the 1960s, a fond recollection of unrealistic revolutionary romanticists, the truth is that the Wobblies actually represented a very real, albeit highly dramatic, opening act of the great industrial union drama that was to unfold in the mid-thirties. The Wobblies, like the Western Federation of Miners, proved that workers could organize on an industrial basis, but they made their point too soon.

The IWW, it should be remembered, was not a product of the nineteenth century. It was born in 1905; its strength was in the West where bigness in lumbering, mining, agriculture, transportation dominated the economy. It was destroyed during World War I and was hastened to its destruction by savage repression. Yet, many decades after its death, the spirit of the WFM and the IWW lived on in the Mine-Mill and Smelter Workers' Union—up to January 1967, when it merged with the United Steelworkers of America.

The coal miners, the Western Federation of Miners, the Industrial Workers of the World were all organizations that elevated class above craft. They all grew out of special loci—coal town, lumber camp, quarry, or metal pit—where the real *polis* was one of class not craft. In the later years of the IWW, as the transient worker began to play a lesser role, the emphasis of the Wobblies shifted from no contract toward contracts, from one big union to many separate unions (including an Italian baker's local), from class to industry. Simultaneously, the economy was becoming more "industrial." The Wobblies and the world were moving toward each other, perhaps to meet half way. But the war interrupted the meeting, turning the wrath of citizens and government against this rebel band that was apparently more interested in turning class against class than American against German. The

134

IWW was beaten to death—to be reincarnated as the CIO in 1935.

A final instructive exception to the rule that the first to organize were the skilled workers was the needle trades. In the family of unions clustered around the AFL in the twentieth century, the workers making men's and women's clothing were exceptional: they organized along industrial rather than craft lines. Among their members were many who were semiskilled and unskilled. What were the special circumstances that gave rise to these unions: the International Ladies' Garment Workers' Union that lived within the AFL continuously from 1900 and the Amalgamated Clothing Workers of America that lived off and on with the AFL and then the AFL-CIO since 1912?

Tailors were among the first of the skilled crafts to organize in America. There was an organization of journeymen tailors before 1800, the year in which the Federal and Unions Society of Journeymen Tailors in Philadelphia complained of "low wages and declared its members would not work for low standard employers."[40] As apparel manufacture moved toward mass production in the post-Civil War period, the tailor began to be displaced by the sewing machine operator, introducing a division of work into the shop. The aristocrat within this work community was the garment cutter. In 1862, a group of these cutters organized in Philadelphia to resist a wage cut: they won and they organized a benevolent society; in 1869, they reorganized to become Assembly No. I, the parent of the Knights of Labor, with garment cutter Uriah S. Stephens as their Master Workman. In the men's clothing trade, the Journeymen Tailors' National Trades Union was founded in 1865, representing highly skilled workers in the custom order business. Their top man, John B. Lennon, was treasurer of the AFL. In 1916, the Journeymen Tailors affiliated with the Amalgamated Clothing Workers of America. Throughout the history of the men and women's

40. Taft, *op. cit.*, p. 6.

apparel trades, there was always a hard core of skilled workers who, when they united with less-skilled workers, formed the firm backbone of the enlarged organizations.

As it did with the shoemakers, carpenters, and miners, the great push to organize the needle trades came as a result of a new system of production: the contracting system. The contractor—the immediate boss of the worker—was little more than a labor herder. It was not the contractor but the jobber who created the styles, bought the piece goods, merchandised the garments. The jobber was the real boss with the means to get credit, to buy raw material, to create design, to sell. This jobber, in competition with other jobbers, called upon his contractors to produce more and more for less and less. This was the infamous "sweating" system, as contractor turned to his workers to produce mightily and to be paid meanly. The result was the "sweat shop."

Where could the contractors find people for the sweat shops? They turned to the rim of the civilization, to peripheral populations. In New York City, where the contracting system leaked into the basements, hallways, bedrooms, and kitchens of the tenemented old East Side, the contractors herded their labor at the docks. The immigrant newly arrived, without money, without use of the new tongue, without knowledge of the new land, was moved into the sweat shop. At the turn of the century, the great flood of immigration into the garment factories of America's growing cities was heavily, almost exclusively, Jewish. The wandering Jew, in another one of his great tribal migrations, was momentarily coming to rest in the sweat shops. They crowded into ghettos where they looked for a place to live and a place to work. Sometimes, the home was the shop. The ghetto became a kind of company town, tied together by thread, tongue, and tightly knit living. In addition, the Jewish immigrant brought with him the portable *polis* he had invisibly packed away in his paltry baggage as he roamed across the earth for more than two thousand years.

In many ways, the conditions of the ghetto Jew in the needle trades resembled the circumstances of the worker in the British guilds. The workers shared a trade; they lived together, worked together, and lived where they worked. They gathered in religious rites; they gave to a common coffer to aid their needy; they spoke a common language. They were far more than a protective society: they were a true community, a political corporation. The needle trades unions were more than trade groups: they were communities. The community bond was great enough to overcome the normal distance and disdain between the skilled craftsmen (the cutters) and lesser crafts. The tribal tie civilized narrow self interest.

Within this ghetto community there was a group of activist-intellectuals that played a very special role in giving this natural community a sense of articulated purpose. These men of the word in search of some work drifted into the garment and clothing trades.

In this democracy of the shop, the soft-skinned intellectual learned to become a proletarian; and the tough proletarian learned to talk like an intellectual. And out of the mix issued a trade union movement that was tough and talkative, muscular and messianic. . . . The intellectual added another dimension to unionism: a view of society and the role of the working class in the shaping of this society. . . . The development of such a philosophy was hastened by the intellectual at the work bench. He knew both the shop and the world; he knew his people and he knew people; he was a tribal leader with an Oxford education.[41]

The community of the needle trade unions included the skilled, the unskilled, and the intellectual. As a result, they became political corporations with clearly articulated political programs. As practical people, however, they gave formal recognition to the status of the skilled craftsmen. The needle trades unions were

41. Gus Tyler, "The Legacy of Jewish Labor," *Midstream*, XI (March 1965), pp. 56–57.

not purely industrial in form. They were a mix of craft and industrial unionism, called "amalgamated" unionism by some. The cutters had their separate locals; so did the pressers, a more skilled craft. Sewing machine operators and other crafts also were in separate locals. These craft locals were joined in a tight confederation, called joint boards or councils. They negotiated contracts as a unit; they struck as a unit; they settled as a unit, generally speaking. Within these joint bodies, the crafts made their presence known and the more skilled crafts made their presence especially known. Indeed, it was out of these skilled crafts and out of the ranks of the proletarianized intellectuals that most of the top leaders came for the national unions.

The dominant role of the skilled craftsmen in the American labor movement of the nineteenth century and even into the first three decades of the twentieth century is a key to understanding much about skills and status in a society. Where a skill is in short supply, it soon demands a higher price, and with it, a higher standing. Where the skilled combine, they can multiply salary and status. This relationship between skill and status is as old as man on earth. *Homo sapiens* liberated himself from dependence on the whims of his environment by simple skills: tool making, domestication of animals, agriculture. Ever since then mankind has sought further independence, higher living standards, and self-respect by developing new and better skills through machinery, electricity, automation. And within the community of man—the economy and the society—individual men have sought to liberate and elevate themselves by mastering skills—especially the rare skills in high demand. And just as *homo sapiens* acted in a group to perfect his primitive skills, and just as mankind combines in organized cultures as it improves its collective skills, so too do individual craftsmen unionize to protect and promote the recognition accorded their skill.

Within social groups there is a special, rare and most desirable skill: it is the intangible called leadership. This is the ability to win power by manipulating men and their minds. This skill exists only where man is gathered in a group. And where the group is organized, leadership becomes a full-time, often well-paid profession in which the leader has the need and opportunity to perfect his natural aptitudes.

Since craft unions were the first to organize, the first leaders of American labor were craftsmen. Among the skilled manualists, they became super-skilled manipulators. They came to the general labor movement with the prestige of their craft and the power of their craftiness. The leaders of the nineteenth century were all craftsmen: Uriah Stephens, garment cutter; William Sylvis, iron molder; Terence V. Powderly, machinist; Peter J. Maguire, carpenter; Adolph Strasser and Samuel Gompers, cigar makers. The radical Eugene V. Debs was a locomotive fireman. The great and famous exceptions to this rule in the movement before the 1930s were John P. Mitchell, John L. Lewis, and William Green—all out of the miners.

The leadership of the craft-minded continued into the first quarter of the twentieth century. Samuel Gompers, who presided spiritually as well as ritually over the American Federation of Labor almost since its foundation in the 1880s, died in his chair in 1924. He was followed by William Green, a charter member of the miners' union who had served in the Ohio Senate from 1911 to 1913. Although both Gompers and Green came out of backgrounds congenial to a broad class movement, such as might be embodied in industrial unions, they both became symbols of craftism.

Samuel Gompers was a Dutch Jew who came to America as a youth perfectly miscast ever to become the leader of trade unionism in the United States. He came from the wrong religion: most unionists were Protestant or Catholic. He came from the wrong country: the unionists who were not native born came in great numbers from England, Ireland, Scotland, or Germany. He came with the wrong ideology: he looked upon himself as a Marxist, while American labor was overwhelmingly nonsocialist. But Gompers' deficits turned out to be his assets. The fact that he was Jewish made him an acceptable compromise in a movement divided between Protestants and Catholics. The fact that he was Dutch made him acceptable in a movement split along other major ethnic lines. The fact that he came of Marxist background but was no longer a socialist made him the perfect man to articulate class aspirations in a movement resting on a craft basis. Gompers was able to make an ideology out of craftism, to provide distant horizons to the here and now. He did so with a great personal earthiness, a violent vigor, a tolerant sagaciousness that made it possible to create a federation out of proud, independent autonomous, warring entities. By will and wile, he gave a common personality to idiosyncratic principalities.

Gompers was an Old World Marxist who, in the American milieu, became a New World pragmatist. He was faithful to his past—but in his own fashion. Although Gompers was not a practitioner of Judaism, all his life he wore a skull cap, the *yarmulke* of orthodox Jewry. When asked why, he is alleged to have replied that he wore the cap to keep drafts off his bald pate.

Like Gompers, William Green who followed was also the wrong man, in a sense. He was a Protestant in a movement that by the 1920s was predominantly Catholic in its leadership. He came from an industrial union in a period when craft unionism was the dominant practice. He was a politico who had held public office in Ohio, heading a movement that emphasized the non-political. Yet, in this respect too, the vices turned out to be virtues. He was a proper Protestant face for Catholic leadership; he was acceptable to the industrial unions in the AFL; his political background made him an appropriate spokesman for labor in the nation's capital. Unlike Gompers, however, Green lacked the earthiness, vigor, ideologic scope, and personal power of his predecessor. Gompers led the AFL; Green was led by the AFL.

In 1924, when Green succeeded Gompers, craft unionism in

the United States was more than a hundred years old. It was well established. The governing councils of the AFL were in the hands of men whose horizons were bounded by their job jurisdictions. The aristocracy of craft assumed that it was the whole society of labor. The craft unionism that had begun as a necessity late in the eighteenth century and had risen to an ideology under Gompers in the nineteenth century had now become a ritual under Green in the twentieth century.

This ritual was soon confronted with a triple challenge: (1) the growth of new production methods that threatened the ultimate existence of certain crafts; (2) a severe economic depression that threatened the life of existing craft unionism; (3) the rise of the union spirit among the unskilled and semiskilled that threatened the sacrosanct jurisdiction of the craft union.

Ontogeny was recapitulating again. New tools had made a new class—the mass production worker. In the new class there developed the inevitable society of the work *polis*. Then came the trauma of the Depression followed by the hope of the New Deal. The new class, like all other classes before it, organized to make its presence known. In doing so, it shook the establishment, as every emergent group reaching upward disturbs the establishment. But because the craft unions, now more than a century old, were the establishment in the society of labor, they too felt threatened. Out of this arose the battle between AFL and CIO.

6

Ontogeny Continued

In the second decade of the twentieth century, man developed a new tool, symbolized by the moving belt. It revolutionized production. Instead of the maker doing many skilled operations, he did one simple operation over and over again. The belt brought him his little task and, as it slid by, he played the role of a human cog, a bit of bone and brain moving to the rhythm of the untiring conveyor. Once more in man's history the divisions of work were multiplied, tasks were simplified, and a device was deified.

These were new times accelerated in their coming by the propulsions of a war economy. New ways of doing things; new classes to do them; new configurations and new ideas. Belt replaced bench; operative replaced craftsman; the unity of workers replaced the diversity of crafts under one roof. The time was right for a union that would tie men as tightly together as the moving belt.

The belt became the symbol because it was the hallmark of the auto industry, the infant giant of the second decade. But other industries—steel, coal, oil, chemicals, textiles—had their equivalents. They all had their methods for making man a small part of the machine in anticipation of the day when a machine could replace the man. This was the predecessor of the age of automation, a step forward in the progress of man.

The very first victims of this progress were the skilled craftsmen. Their skills were no longer needed: there was an easier, faster, cheaper way to do the job.

Old age came to craftism in the prime of its life, immediately after World War I. It was never bigger, stronger, more influential and self-confident. In 1914, when the war began, the American unions counted 2,600,000 members; by 1918, they counted almost 5,000,000—nearly doubled. Not since the beginning of the century had the labor unions grown so rapidly. (The years 1897 to 1904 were seven fat years for the unions. They multiplied membership six times over, from 400,000 to more than 2 million, from 3 to 12 per cent of the non-agricultural employees. In 1914, the unions were still on that 12 per cent plateau.)

War was good to the unions. As always, the conflict increased the demand for and reduced the supply of labor. More munitions and ammunitions and fewer men in civilian work clothes. In this tight labor market, the unions were able to organize, to make wage gains, to establish themselves firmly. The political atmosphere was congenial. President Wilson was friendly and Samuel Gompers was a friend. In the name of national unity, the government was able to prevail on many employers, especially those seeking federal contracts, to recognize the unions.

The momentum gathered during the war years continued up to 1921, by which time the unions had enrolled 19.6 per cent of the nonagricultural employees. After that year the trade union movement weakened. Many specific causes for union decline after 1921 are cited. That year saw the beginning of a recession during which there were fewer jobs and hence less bargaining power. Employers who had put up with unions during the war seized the moment to launch an open-shop campaign. They mingled their hostility toward unions with paternalism to workers. A further factor was the agricultural situation. "While retail food prices remained fairly constant . . . hourly money wages of labor rose to roughly 100 per cent above 1913 after 1926. Laboring men who secured benefits from this situation were not inclined to join unions in order to keep wages from lagging behind cost of living."[1] At the same time, new population movements were flooding traditional union towns with a labor surplus.[2]

There was a steady movement during this period from agricultural areas to the cities, and a particularly strong movement of Negroes

1. Rayback, *op. cit.*, p. 303,
2. *Ibid.*

and poorer whites from the South to the North. . . . The shifting of industry had similar effects. During the period oil wells in Ohio, Indiana, Illinois, West Virginia, Louisiana, Kansas and Wyoming; lumber camps in the Northeast, around the Great Lakes, and in the South; copper mines in northern Michigan; lead and zinc mines in the Mississippi Valley were abandoned. Textile and shoe factories in New England were moved from large to small cities. All these shifts left behind a labor supply which in some cases had been unionized but which under the stress of making a living gave up its unionism to get jobs.

Union resistance was unavailing. In 1922, the craftsmen in the railway shops struck against a second successful employer effort to cut wages. The strike was a failure; it ended with nearly half the railway shopmen returning to work in open shops. Two areas in which unionism had grown with unusual speed during the war years—shipbuilding and metal working—were particularly hard hit. The cutback in demand cut back employment— and unionism.

The leaders of labor had no ready response to the challenge of this era. Skilled jobs were withering away and so were many of the plants in which the unions had contracts. Employers were turning tough on unions and soft on workers. A labor surplus provided strike-breakers against strikes. Wages were good. After the turbulent war years, the nation wanted to return to normalcy and to keep cool with Coolidge. Many of the labor leaders also kept cool. They too were quite prepared to return to normalcy, to a membership embracing, as it had traditionally, about 12 per cent of the nonagricultural employees. It was a leadership that, according to one historian, "was content to rest upon past performances, to confine membership to the elite among workingmen, and to remain the junior partner of management in the economic system."[3]

However, even where leadership was not content, it was

3. *Ibid.*

unable to overcome the combination of worker apathy, employer resistance, and political conservatism to build on the shifting sands of a changing economy. Thus, for instance, John L. Lewis, who was soon to become the hero of the new age, was unable in the 1920s to bestir the miners or to bludgeon the employers into accepting unionism. He suffered one defeat after another in the effort to hold on to his own membership or to his hard-won pay scales. A union of 450,000 was cut down to 150,000 by 1930. Lewis was faced with internal revolt and schisms. Among thousands of miners and among "progressives" in the labor movement, John L. Lewis was a sobriquet for a "misleader," charged with "sell out," stealing elections, silencing opposition with a malevolent despotism. Yet within a decade, this same John L. Lewis became the great leonine-featured and lion-hearted leader of labor's new millions. His orotund rhetoric, granite features, uncompromising militancy, devil-may-care daring, and open defiance of the business and governmental establishment made his name a world-wide synonym for the greatness of the American worker.

It was the same Lewis—but not the same times. In the 1920s, a new class had not yet become aware of itself and its common cause or power. By the late thirties, it developed a group consciousness—after the terrible trauma of the Great Depression of 1929 to 1934.

The old craft leadership lacked an industrial tactic to deal with the economic changes of the 1920s and lacked a political program to deal with the economic collapse of the 1930s. The Great Depression bewildered the old craft leadership; it was not part of their schema; it was a forced voyage into the unknown for men who had lived in a secure little spot on earth. The secure spot was the jurisdiction and the jobs within it: on that piece of real estate the union could build. The crisis of the early '30s wiped out from one-quarter to one-third of all the jobs in the nation, leaving jurisdictions without jobs. The Great Depression was a forcible reminder that no craft is an island unto itself. Unemployment anywhere could lead to unemployment everywhere. Wage cuts made for more wage cuts. No sector of the economy could offer real security unless the economy as a whole could be made more secure.

Although it appeared to many that America was about to fall apart in the crisis years, this was truly an era of reintegration. It is true that the nation was torn with strife: demonstrations, riots, mass violence. It was class against class and man against man. Yet out of this seething social cauldron was distilled a lesson: the need for the nation to act as a nation. The great congregational compulsion reasserted itself for the greater glory of the country. The craft unionists who had spent a lifetime living almost exclusively in the confined *polis* of the jurisdiction were driven out of their caves into the greater *polis* of the nation. They had to find their way in this larger world. They had to turn to Federal action—to legislation and politics.

In Chapter 8 we will examine labor's ideologic development from "rugged individualism" to "creeping socialism," a misnomer in both cases. At this point, what is most relevant is the fact that the political as well as the economic philosophy of craftism that had once served the labor movement so well was now obsolete. The proof was in the membership rolls: by 1933 enrollment fell to the 1916 level of about 2,800,000—a mere 5.4 per cent of the civilian labor force.

The nearly total collapse of the American trade unions during the Depression years is further evidence that unions do not live by lack of bread alone. As hunger went up, unions went down. The two or three million dues-payers who clung to unionism were limited to the elite, to men with jobs and with skills that paid relatively well. The unskilled were unorganized.

The reason for this perverse phenomenon that defies the folklore of the agitator lies in the fact that a union is the organization of a *polis*. To be inclined toward unionism, a man must first have a *polis*, a place of work. In the Depression, he was either totally unemployed or wandered from job to job. He was de-politicized, a member of no one "political corporation" in the workplace. (For the relief recipient, a new kind of *polis* did develop, a place where he gathered with other jobless to get a bowl of soup or to look for work. Out of this *polis* there developed a very sizable movement of unemployed leagues, literally unions of the out-of-work, a formal structure for a formless new class.)

Labor's renascence did not begin in the Depression but in the New Deal days of national recovery. The New Deal has been described in almost as many ways as there have been commentators. It has been presented as the child of Karl Marx, of Lord Keynes, of political opportunism, of enlightened capitalism, of economic eclecticism. It has been viewed as a step toward dictatorship, toward a greater democracy; as fiscal folly, as shrewd financing. It has been analyzed in terms of personal ambitions, of mass pressures, and of the relationships between the government and the economy. Amidst these varied and seemingly contradictory notions there is an underlying congruity if one views the New Deal in the long light of man's movement to divide and then reunite, to seek independence and then organization.

The story of America is chronicled in the rubric *e pluribus unum*. We seek our freedom in the *pluribus* and our security in the *unum*. We seek our independence by going it alone, until we are forced to admit our interdependence, at which time we go it together.

In man's quest to be free, he ventures into new worlds, new lands, new enterprises, new skills. Few adjectives are more honored in America than *New*. We are proud to live in the New World. We name our states New York, New Jersey, New Mexico, New Hampshire. We name our cities New Haven, Newark, New Orleans, New Rochelle. We like new fashions, new faces, new cars, and often new wives and husbands. We are proud of our New Freedom, New Deal, and New Frontier. We are a nation of neophiliacs, driven to exploration, invention, innovation. In each new locus—geographic, social, or occupational—we compose our special new *polis*, our mark of independence.

The notion that we thus escape the rest of the world is, of course, an illusion. But it is an illusion by which men live. For generations, America felt that two great oceans isolated our fate from the fate of Europe. It took two world wars to break the illusion. For decades, the frontier was the escape from the dreary cities, until the frontier closed and the prairies became town tracts. Since World War II, millions of families have turned to the suburbs to find a New World, only to find that what was rural yesterday is urban today. The sad truth ultimately asserts itself that each step toward independence is a step toward dependence. In a complex civilization where many little groups do many little things, no one is self-sufficient. The more the work of the society is broken up into specialties, the more dependent is everybody on everybody. This is a truth that free men really resent because they spend so much time securing their own little positions of seeming independence against the rest of the society. It takes some disaster—a war or a depression—to bring the truth out.

The Great Depression was the great teacher. When the Depression came, no one was really independent. Millionaires lost their margins and threw themselves out of skyscrapers. Entrepreneurs lost their customers and were thrown out of business. Farmers lost their markets and were thrown off their land. Craft unionists lost their employers and were thrown out of work. And a President of the United States who did not quite know what to do about it all lost his voters and was thrown out of office. America needed a declaration of interdependence, a frank admission that in our search for freedom we were becoming so obsessed with our private purposes that we were forgetting our mutual dependence. When we discovered the reality, the nation was forced to reunite, to rediscover our oneness as a nation.

At first, we sought security in the ancient mold. Employers were encouraged to offer jobs even if it meant "make work." Neighborhoods were urged to offer "block aid" in the form of charitable relief organized on a street-by-street basis. We tried to solve the sickness of the whole by turning it over to the parts. Oneness was put on a divided basis.

The New Deal was an attempt to deal with national problems as a nation: to state all-inclusive goals, to reunite a people as a people. To some this was dictatorship, as any forceful assertion of the common good often appears to some who already have considerable affluence. To others, this was democracy, as it brought the "forgotten man" into the scope of public policy. To the worker who was told that he had the right to join a union of his own choosing, that he could not be discharged for union activity, and that his employer had to recognize and deal with this union, the National Recovery Act was an emancipation proclamation. To the employer who was compelled by law to surrender traditional management prerogatives, the same act was slavery. The New Deal was an effort to write a greater law to put the lesser laws of the many private governments in their proper place. Man's unity was asserting its supremacy over each man's uniqueness.

To unify a people around a policy on a national basis required action by the federal government. Economic recovery could not be achieved by any individual business decision, nor by the action of any one farmer, nor by the genius of any one financier. Washington, D.C., had to become the mind and will of the United States. Man's political animality expressed itself in the *polis* of America through the New Deal.

Among the first to recover under the National Recovery Act were the labor unions. In 1934, American unions had under 3.5

million members; by 1936, they had nearly 4 million; by 1937, 5.5 million; by 1939, 6.5 million. When America entered World War II, organized labor collected dues from one out of every five persons in nonagricultural employment.

The first recovery came among the old established unions. Union leaders who had been unable to organize new workers for almost two decades strutted their successes as new thousands joined their organizational ranks. The times made giants of all—the truly great and the truly small. Union leaders and their critics reversed roles. Leaders who had, in the past, blamed their failures on the times, now attributed union growth to their own genius. Critics who had, in the past, blamed failures on leadership, now attributed union growth to the times.

Proof that the events were children of the times could be found in the sudden rapid growth of the "federal locals" in the AFL. These grew up like mushrooms, without any outside leadership. The leaders were just workers, chosen by others in the plant to play the role of officials. These federal locals were generally industrial in form, including all the workers in the plant regardless of craft. They were attached to the AFL directly because they did not fit neatly into the jurisdictions of the various craft unions. If the latter showed any interest at all in the federal locals, it was only to tear them apart, to redistribute their members among the several crafts, to empty the content of the future into the forms of the past.

William Green, president of the AFL, realized the value of the industrial federal unions in organizing workers in mass production. The National Recovery Act had "aroused the spirit of organization . . . everywhere and came on us like a rising tide, appeals to come here, to come there. . . . We agreed that we would proceed to organize these workers [in the mass production industries] in Federal Labor Unions. . . . They are clamoring to come."[4]

4. Quoted by Taft, *op. cit.*, p. 465.

Leaders of the Metal Trades Department of the AFL were enraged with Green's permissiveness in allowing craftsmen to join federal local unions instead of being assigned to their proper jurisdiction in the separate principalities of the metal trades. Arthur O. Wharton, leader of the machinists, stated his demand bluntly:

What we want is to have positive instructions sent out by the American Federation of Labor which will prevent any poaching upon our international unions. It is true that we were informed that eventually those members of Federal Unions who properly belong to our International Union will be transferred to us, but that transfer may be postponed for a long time, for mechanics properly belonging to us who begin their trade union career on a basis of low initiation fees and low dues will not be enthusiastic over being transferred, and, in addition, under rulings which I understand have been made, it will be necessary for us to accept these members without their paying an additional initiation fee, so that our International Unions will be deprived of the necessary income through initiation.[5]

To Wharton, these new fangled unions were a direct threat not simply to his craft influence but, more painfully, to his cash income. He would have none of it.

Lest President William Green forget who was the real boss of the AFL, Wharton reminded him with characteristic clarity: "The AFL is maintained by our International Unions. It is supported by the per capita tax paid by our organizations, and it must not be permitted to interfere with our organizing campaign."[6]

Green understood Wharton's language. By January 1934, the president of the AFL was echoing his chieftains. He informed all organizers that it was "imperatively necessary that the jurisdictional rights of each national and international union affiliated with the American Federation of Labor be respected and ob-

5. *Ibid.*, p. 465.
6. *Ibid.*

served. . . . It is especially important that this rule be observed when *non-union* workers are organized into federal labor unions. . . . Special emphasis should be put upon the necessity of organizing the unorganized workers into local unions where, according to their craft and calling, they properly belong. . . . Organizers of the American Federation of Labor should not under any circumstances seek to persuade and influence workers who are eligible to membership in national and international unions to join federal labor unions."[7]

The masses were moving, but the old craft leaders were not. They had a pre-Copernican view of the universe: everything revolved around them. When Galileo held that it was the earth that revolved around the sun and not vice versa, he was threatened with death at the stake. Being a prudent man, Galileo recanted. But after his recantation, he is said to have mumbled, *eppur si muove,* "still it moves." So, too, did the old leaders insist that the labor universe revolved around the craft union, ignoring the great movement of the semiskilled and unskilled. They issued decrees to ignore this movement and to continue in the old way. As for these new masses—they continued to move.

Not all the unions in the AFL shared the official view. There was a minority composed of those unions that saw the world differently. They had seen the unskilled worker on the move in their own unions. They had been exceptions to the craft rule for many decades—industrial unions that had grown up in special circumstances and had made an ideology out of their idiosyncracy. They were ready to provide leadership, support, and a home for labor's new millions in the Committee for Industrial Organization, the CIO.

At the head of the CIO was John L. Lewis of the miners. The other union heads came from the Amalgamated Clothing Workers of America; the International Ladies' Garment Workers' Union; the United Hatters, Cap and Millinery Workers' Inter-

7. *Ibid.,* p. 467.

national Union; the United Textile Workers of America; Oil Field, Gas Well and Refinery Workers of America; the International Union of Mine, Mill and Smelter Workers; and finally, the only craft international—the International Typographical Union. When Charles P. Howard of the last named joined, he made it clear that he did so as an individual and not in the name of his organization! While each of these leaders of labor is credited with foresight, it must be recognized that much of their wisdom was derived from their own traditional ways.

The CIO burst upon America like a revolution, which indeed it was. A new class was asserting its presence, demanding a voice in the shop, in the councils of labor, in the nation. Within four years, the CIO organized several million workers in steel, auto, shipping, transport, chemical, textiles, oil, lumber, communication, utilities, electrical, and radio fabrication. Just how many million is a matter of dispute. According to the Bureau of Labor Statistics, the CIO had a membership of 4 million by 1939; according to a confidential report of Philip Murray to the CIO, there were only 1.8 million paying dues. The truth is someplace in between: the CIO probably exaggerated its report to the BLS to impress workers, the government, and especially the AFL with the newborn's strength; on the other hand, not every worker covered by a CIO contract paid dues, since their "maintenance of membership clauses" did not compel all covered workers in the bargaining unit to be a union member. A reasonable compromise is something like 3 million—a number greater than the entire AFL was able to count in 1933.

The growth of industrial unionism, however, cannot be measured by dues payments into the CIO since the AFL craft unions, always pragmatic, were swiftly converted to the logic of industrial unionism as both inevitable and desirable. During the years 1940–1949, the machinists—the proud craftsmen of Wharton—turned to industrial unionism under their new president, Harvey W. Brown. "Within a very few years," observed Mark

Perlman in *The Machinists*, "the IAM clearly ceased to be primarily a craft oriented organization. . . . The IAM had to make a choice of retaining its craft character, or expanding in the direction of industrial unionism. It resolved to expand."[8] In another craft union, the International Brotherhood of Electrical Workers, the membership rose from 56 thousand in 1935 to 125 thousand in 1939. By 1962, it counted nearly three quarters of a million members, representing as many if not more workers in industrial locals than its CIO counterpart.

The Committee for Industrial Organization, formed in 1935 as a ginger group within the AFL, changed its name to the Congress of Industrial Organizations two years later when it became a dual federation. The AFL-CIO schism continued for two decades. The dramatic split made the CIO a moment of division in the house of labor.

Underneath the organizational division, however, a profound process of unification was taking place in the world of labor. Until the mid-1930s, the craftsmen lived in their narrow little families outside the greater family of labor. They addressed the other members of their craft as "brother." It was rarely "sister" among these men who often named their organizations "brotherhoods" but never "sisterhoods." Women, the unskilled, and Negroes were generally outside the pale. Despite the efforts to prevent modernization, most of the great craft international and national unions were "industrialized" after the CIO drive. In both the AFL and CIO unions the skilled and the unskilled were being united in common organizations to a degree hitherto unknown in America. Underneath the formal split in labor between AFL and CIO, there was taking place a profound unification between the skilled and unskilled within the general labor movement. When AFL and CIO merged in the mid-1950s into the AFL-CIO, the unification of skilled and unskilled became formalized.

8. Mark Perlman, *The Machinists* (Cambridge, Mass.: Harvard University Press, 1961), p. 107.

The New Deal represented a coming together of the nation, and the organization of the mass production industries represented a coming together of the laboring man. In both cases, the essential unification was obscured by superficial conflict—liberal versus conservative in the New Deal and CIO versus AFL in the labor movement. By 1952, when for the first time in two decades a Republican was elected President of the United States, the unification that had taken place in the 1930s became apparent: the foundations of the New Deal were accepted by Republicans as well as Democrats, by conservatives as well as liberals; the concept of industrial unionism, the inclusion of the worker in mass production was accepted by the entire labor movement. In the middle of the 1950s, AFL and CIO merged.

In 1953, the year President Eisenhower took office, American trade unions were at the pinnacle of their power, representing about one worker out of every three in nonagricultural employment—32.7 per cent to be exact. The merger of AFL-CIO in 1956 was expected to give the movement new impetus. The resolution, the combined strength, the finances, the leadership were all there. But the anticipated did not happen: trade union membership began to decline steadily as a percentage in nonagricultural employment from the 32.7 per cent in 1953 to 26.7 per cent in 1962.

What happened? Labor leaders pointed to antilabor legislation (Taft-Hartley, Landrum-Griffin, state right-to-work laws) and to the apathy of workers living in relative affluence as the reasons why unionization was not making progress. Leaders said the time was not right. Labor critics pointed to the labor leaders: aged, antiquated, addle-pated. Actually, both were somewhat correct, yet fundamentally wrong. It was true that adverse legislation was a serious obstacle to organization. Yet within a year or two, despite the same obstacles, the labor movement began to grow again, especially among the most affluent sectors of the American working class. It is true that the old-timers were not natural leaders for the new labor legions. But when the new unionists were ready, they gave birth to their own leaders—as new classes have since time immemorial.

What really happened after the mid-1950s was automation. Once more man was changing his tools. And as a consequence, old classes were declining, other classes were aborning, new social institutions were in gestation.

Before examining the nature of this change in detail, let us return to our general concept of man's relationship to his tools, so we may maintain perspective both on the era in which we now live and on the flow of our integrated argument. In *The Psychology of Social Institutions*, Judd makes the simple yet significant statement that "it has been the practice of historical anthropology to designate the successive steps of civilization by the names of the materials used in making weapons and tools. Thus the earliest ages are called the stone ages; later came ages of bronze and of iron; our own age is often spoken of as the age of steel."[9] Judd was writing in 1926, when the great steel furnaces were devouring the nation's coal and iron and spitting out finished metal for the big baby of the economy, the auto. By the mid-1950s, however, it was appropriate to refer to contemporary times as the age of automation.

A change in the means of production, as Marx insisted, changes more than the movement of human hands. New tools make new classes, relationships between classes, ways of viewing the world, consciousness about self, politics, social revolutions. Changes in the structure of the economy bring on changes in the superstructure of the society, in the individual and his ideology.

As civilization develops, man becomes more and more dependent on tools. In primitive situations man can manage without railway, electricity, gas, autos, water systems, tug boats, garbage disposal, oil burners. Today, a stoppage in any of these areas

9. Charles Hubbard Judd, *The Psychology of Social Institutions* (New York: Macmillan Company, 1926), p. 5.

brought on by an act of God or of a union borders on catastrophe. "The man who lives in modern society," concluded Judd, "has to develop modes of thought and modes of action which are appropriate to a world where tools have attained an importance so superior to bodily organs that no one thinks of using his unaided strength even in satisfying the most urgent of his physical needs."[10]

In the mid-twentieth century of a sensitive American civilization, a profound change in our method of production necessarily meant a radical change in the societal super-structure. It is not our objective here to examine all the facets of a "cyberculture," only the impact of automation on the labor force and the labor movement.

Automation means that fewer men can turn out more.

The Push-Button Miner is a mechanical giant standing three stories high and weighing more than 1½ million pounds. It cuts and loads as much as 266 tons of coal an hour in one continuous operation, without drilling or blasting and with very little human intervention. The entire operation requires a crew of only three men and is performed by remote control from a panel outside of the mine shaft. . . . [In agriculture, fertilizers, chemical weed killers, insecticides and new machines have almost tripled farm output per hour since 1947.] Mechanical cotton pickers are now harvesting more than 90 per cent of Mississippi's cotton crop and doing it more cheaply than men paid as little as $6 a day.[11]

In the Pittsburgh offices of Westinghouse Electric Corporation the computer replaces a whole army of specialists.

Orders are received from district offices throughout the country by teletype. Upon receipt of an order, the computer types out an invoice containing the list price, the discount, the state sales tax and

10. *Ibid.*, p. 31.
11. *Labor Looks at Automation.* American Federation of Labor and Congress of Industrial Organizations, Washington, D.C. Publication No. 21, December 1966, p. 3.

other information. It then wires the order to the warehouse nearest the customer. There, the order comes off the teletype machine with a bill of lading, addressed carton labels and information concerning the stock bin in which the product is located. In the meantime, back in Pittsburgh, the computer adjusts its inventory record and if necessary, orders a Westinghouse manufacturing plant to replenish the warehouse stock. In this way, a process which once took three to five days is telescoped into 4½ minutes.[12]

In building and construction, a tower crane reduces crews working with concrete from twenty men to five; plaster spraying guns and pumping machines double the amount of plaster a worker can apply in one day; power nailers can drive nails three times as fast as hand hammers.

As contrasted with man, the automaton has muscles more untiring, eyes more sensitive, ears more attuned, a memory more accurate, an ability to calculate more speedy, and a capacity to make decisions more objective. It is quite a tool—one that profoundly affects our culture.

The impact of automation on the labor movement was, in the first instance, negative, wiping out jobs in industries where unions were well entrenched. Employment and union membership fell, as was recorded in the slow decline of dues-payers from 1953 on. The 1950s repeated the 1920s: the change in tools brought about a social change.

Workers who had been made sensitive to the menace of unemployment in their sad experiences of the 1930s saw in automation the coming crisis. Machines were displacing men. The unemployment of the few would breed the unemployment of the many. The economy would collapse as it had in 1929.

The day of doom, however, hesitated to dawn. The number of workers in the labor force grew steadily: 44 million in 1949; 64 million in 1954; 75 million in 1965. The percentage of the

12. *Ibid.*, p. 6.

population (above age 14) in the civilian labor force held steady: 56 per cent in 1940; 58.4 per cent in 1954; 57.5 per cent in 1965. Even the number of unemployed as a percentage of the labor force showed no dramatic rise: it revolved around 5 per cent in the 1950s and dropped to 4 per cent in 1966. The debacle did not come to the society as a whole, although it did bring disaster to many individual workers and their families, because changes in production brought changes in the superstructure—in man the consumer and in man the politician.

Automation created new divisions of labor, categories of workers, new industries. There had to be machine inventors, builders, sellers, programmers, repairers, tenders. Automation created new demands, which came from employed workers with greater leisure and greater income and from investors with bigger profits. These beneficiaries of affluence bought homes and hired gardeners, handymen, and maids; they patronized restaurants, bars, and shoeshine parlors; they visited doctors, dentists, chiropodists, beauticians, lawyers, and psychoanalysts; they crowded department stores, discount houses, and variety shops; they gave their children extended education and they went to classes for adults; they gave employment to radio and TV repairmen, auto mechanics, gas station attendants, bank clerks, insurance agents, accountants, soda jerks, car hops, and baby sitters. In their new-found affluence, this generation began to pay sizeable taxes. So they demanded services in return: hospitals and clinics, Medicare and social security, police and fire protection, low income housing and playgrounds, better parks and streets. Sensitive to the oneness of the nation, they backed programs to combat crime, illiteracy, poverty, disease. Through private spending, as individual consumers, and through public spending, as collective politicians, the people of the mid-century created a new kind of society: the service economy. As machines tended to the making of things, people tended to the servicing of people.

Sometime late in 1956, the number of workers engaged in services caught up with the number engaged in goods. By 1957, services were ahead: there were 33,807,000 in services and 32,767,000 in goods. By 1963, services had a long lead: 37,962,000 were employed in services and only 31,445,000 in goods. The race was not too difficult for services since goods has been running backward.[13]

The sector of the service economy that has grown most rapidly, according to the President's 1964 *Manpower Report*, is state and local government employment, which provided four out of ten of the "net additions to nonfarm payrolls." Between 1947 and 1957, jobs in these areas rose 4.25 per cent (185,000) a year and from 1957 to 1964, 4.75 per cent (285,000) a year.

"The growth of employment in the service trades and in government has helped change the collar of the American worker from blue to white." In addition, there has been an increase in the number and percentage of white collar *nonproduction* workers in manufacturing. In 1940, there were 44 million white-collar workers; in 1950, there were 55 million; in 1960, 61 million. As a percentage of the work force, the white-collar people were 32.9 in 1940; 37.4 in 1950; and 43.3 in 1960. "During the same period, manual workers also multiplied but not so rapidly, with the result that while there are more of them, they are shrinking as a percentage of the labor force. There were 16 million in 1940; 22 million in 1950, and 23 million in 1960. The real slowdown came between the censuses of 1950 and 1960, when the percentage of manual workers fell from 40.3 to 38.6 per cent. It was during that decade that the white collar outran the blue."[14]

In the decade of union decline (1950 to 1960), there was an increase of only one million blue-collar workers. A large part of that growth, limited as it is, came from new industries, such

13. Gus Tyler, *The Labor Revolution* (New York: Viking Press, 1967), p. 144. For a fuller discussion of this transformation of the economy, see Victor R. Fuchs, *The Growing Importance of the Service Industries*, National Bureau of Economic Research (New York: Columbia University Press, 1965).

14. *Ibid.*, p. 146.

as aerospace, where unions were obviously either very weak or nonexistent. Other blue-collar sectors declined absolutely. In 1929, there were more than a million in mining; by 1963, only 650,000; in transportation, there was a decline of half a million workers. Since mining and transportation were historic strongholds of organized labor, unions lost heavily in both these sectors. In addition, there was constant relocation of manufacturing plants out of the North and East to the West and the South, dumping old unionists in one place and employing unorganized workers in another place.

The sector of the white-collar force that grew most rapidly was among professional and technical workers. Many of these were self-employed; those who were on salary as employees had no tradition of unionism, albeit a long history of professional societies.

In sum, in those sectors of the economy where unions were strong, the base for membership was weakened. In those sectors where unions were weak—service, white-collar, government employment, and professionals—the labor force was growing. Hence, the decline in union members from 1953 to 1962.

(If one measures blue-collar employment in the United States from 1953 to 1962, there was actually an *absolute* decline. Employment of production and maintenance blue-collar workers in manufacturing fell from 14 million to less than 12.5 million. The reason? 1953 was a peak year, with the economy lashed forward by the Korean War. That year unions were at their apex, with 32.7 per cent of nonagricultural employees. By 1962, labor counted 26.7 per cent.)

The service economy is a by-product of automation. As in all previous cultures, a new tool that made man's work easier liberated people for other pursuits. In modern America, the new pursuits are services—private and social, individual and collective. Consequently, the nature of the labor force in America changed. In the new mix of employees, the ever-growing elements were white-collar, in service trades and nonprofit enterprises, especially at the professional level. The great labor question of the mid-century was would these new elements unionize?

The reply from most quarters was loud and lucid: No! The reasons given were all quite rational. The newcomers were affluent and therefore would have no *economic* reason to unionize. They identified with their employer *psychologically;* they were *sociologically* status-conscious and not class-conscious; they were *ideologically* conservative; they were *historically* individualists and not collectivists. The strongest argument was *econometric:* they were not organizing and, hence, were not organizable. All these reasons were logical—indeed, too logical. They neglected man's social instinct; namely, the congregational compulsion that underlies the universality of unions.

The refutation of the argument came from the new labor force itself—in the form of unions. Teachers and municipal employees, nurses and doctors, store clerks and building service men, musicians and chorus girls, policemen and firemen, engineers and technicians, social workers and college professors, and even a handful of Catholic priests demanded union recognition—and very militantly so. Despite the disputations of academia, the "unorganizables" instinctively and inevitably insisted on organization. History was repeating itself to the surprise of the historians, fulfilling the age-old prophecy to the dismay of the would-be prophets.

Much of the consistent error among ideologues in their forecasts on the American labor movement stemmed from a false notion about the *nature of unions.* They assumed that affluence was an automatic deterrent to unionization, although throughout all history (and surely in America) the first to organize were the most affluent. They noted that the white-collar professional identified with his employer, but without recognizing the eternal dependency circumstance of all employees until such time as they are traumatically driven to independence. They noted the search for status in the new labor sectors, but without understanding that one of the great impulses for unionism is precisely this desire to be a "somebody" instead of a "nobody." They looked upon these new elements as conservative, largely because these children of the 1950s had no interest in, or even knowledge of, the radical ideologies of the 1930s. They were utterly mistaken about the notion that the better-educated, higher-paid employee (or even self-employed) were individualists and not collectivists. Where such elements were in the labor force in earlier decades, they organized into professional societies, which, under the ripening circumstances of the 1950s, turned to unions. About one item the ideologues were right: there was little or no visible evidence of measurable organization in the new sectors. But this is one of the real deficiencies of a purely metric system for prophesying the future. The slide rule can measure what is or what has been, but it lacks the insight—the capacity to conceptualize from the past —to predict the future.

Whether or not the new sector will organize is hardly a matter for serious debate as America moves toward the last quarter of the century. Among the most rapidly growing unions in the United States are the American Federation of State, County and Municipal Workers; the American Federation of Government Employees; the Building Service Employees Union; the Retail Clerks International Association; the American Federation of Musicians; the American Federation of Teachers—in short, all those unions with the strongest direct appeals to the new labor force. A few random stories from the news columns of the middle-1960s define the trend and suggest the reasons why these employees do as their ilk has done since the beginning of the nation.

"Public employees turn increasingly militant," notes *The Wall Street Journal* (July 19, 1966). "New York City Health Department doctors strike for higher pay guarantees. Nurses in Gotham and San Francisco picket, 'resign' to win wage boosts.

Firemen in Atlanta strike over pay and hours; Kansas City firemen call in 'sick.' Social workers in Los Angeles County demand union recognition, bargaining rights. Detroit teachers threaten to strike for higher pay. New York City sanitation workers want a 15% pay increase; 'they think nothing of striking,' frets an official. . . . New state laws allowing recognition of public-employee unions feed the ferment."

The same *Journal* (August 30, 1966) notes the growing militancy of workers who once would have considered a strike unthinkable. "No-strike clauses of public employee unions come under membership fire. The fire-fighters union yields to growing rank-and-file pressure, plans a special commission to review the no-strike clause in its constitution; repeal efforts were staved off at the recent convention. The National Postal Union votes to keep its ban on strikes, but orders the union leadership to probe a constitutionality test of the law forbidding strikes by Federal employees. California nurses abandon their no-strike pledge. Public employees unable to strike grumble louder as other unions win sizable wage gains by walking out. . . . An unauthorized fire-fighters strike in Atlanta this year fueled opposition to the union's no-strike policy."

"The wholesale apparel salesman is on the threshold of unionism," notes *Women's Wear Daily* (August 4, 1966) in describing the transition of a professional society into a union seeking affiliation with the AFL-CIO. "The drive by NAWCAS (National Association of Women's and Children's Apparel Salesmen), which changed its 20-year-old association status to that of a union last December, comes at a time when organizational drives are in the air in other industries. Salesmen in other fields, and even store buyers, are talking about unions."

"Florence Nightingale all of a sudden is sounding like Samuel Gompers," reported *The Wall Street Journal* (July 13, 1966). "As a result, there are real crises at hospitals across the nation—from New York to San Francisco, and including such scattered

164

places as Oak Ridge, Tennessee and Youngstown, Ohio. Some registered nurses are on strike right now. Nurses at 30 or more West Coast hospitals are scheduled to hand in their resignations Friday and walk out later this month if their demands aren't met. . . . Only recently have they become militant. Some have elected to affiliate with established labor unions while others have organized on their own. At the same time, the American Nurses Association, a professional organization, is arming its members with economic data and bargaining techniques so they can make a strong showing in negotiations"—still another case of association going union. *The New York Times* (August 23, 1966) reported that "directors of the 13,000 member California Nurses Association have turned their backs on an antistrike policy adopted in 1950 by the American Nurses Association."

"And Now It's Doctors," groaned *The New York Times* editorially (June 27, 1966), as it pointed to "the decision of nearly 1,500 doctors to stay away from their part-time jobs in community health centers as a means of pushing the city into giving them tenure and higher pay."

The New York Times (November 4, 1966) reported that state employees in Rhode Island struck, "the first such work stoppage in the state's history"; two days earlier, policemen struck in the Detroit suburb of Pontiac; simultaneously, 700 teachers struck in the public schools of Decatur, Illinois. At West Point Military Academy, the superintendent granted recognition to a local of the American Federation of Government Employees representing the civilian employees of the institution. The same union, AFGE, reported in the Fall of 1966 that its net membership gain had been well over 5,000 a month. Deeply perturbed by the mounting militancy of public employees, *The Wall Street Journal* (October 19, 1966) described the development as "The Gray Path to Anarchy."

In March 1965, the American Federation of Casino and Gaming Employees began to organize the casino personnel of the

Carson City Nugget Casino, Inc. Within a month, the union signed up a majority of the employees and asked for formal recognition. "The mind boggles at the implications of this case," commented James P. Gannon in his imaginative column in *The Wall Street Journal* (December 2, 1966). "See some future AFL-CIO roster studded with such organizations as the International Association of Slot Machine Mechanics, the United Brotherhood of Counters and Bagmen, the Keno Runners Amalgamated Protective Society (KRAPS). If unionization of gambling houses spreads, will labor bosses demand two operators for every roulette wheel? Will blackjack dealers win hazardous-duty bonuses, early retirement? Will a shill work his way up to the presidency of the AFL-CIO? Nothing's sacred any more."

As further evidence that "nothing's sacred" came *The New York Times* report on August 2, 1966 that "the dancers of American Ballet Theater were . . . discussing strike action. . . . Dancers are quiet people. They spoke to the meeting with clarity and common sense. There was no anger, no hysteria; there were no raised voices. There was no dissent. They expressed determination to strike unless their demands were met. The debate was about when, not about if." Then from Santa Monica, Calif., came the news (also in the *Times*, October 20, 1966) that "a new labor union for Roman Catholic priests opened its national office today and announced the start of a nation-wide organizing drive. The Rev. William H. DuBay, a suspended priest who is president of the union, said that 100 priests around the country had already applied for membership, even before the start of his organizing campaign. Father DuBay emphasized that his organization, the American Federation of Priests, would be a full-fledged labor union and not a 'professional association,' such as has been formed by priests in the Chicago diocese." Simultaneously, a dispatch from Chicago announced the establishment of the Association of Chicago Priests.

On December 7, 1966, Charles Cogan, president of the

American Federation of Teachers, announced that 13 unions were setting up a Council of Professional, Scientific and Cultural Employees as part of the AFL-CIO. The unions on the steering committee were Actors' Equity, the American Federation of Teachers, the American Guild of Musical Artists, the American Federation of Musicians, the National Association of Broadcast Employees and Technicians, the American Federation of Technical Engineers, the Insurance Workers, the Air Line Pilots Association, and the American Federation of Government Employees.

In the AFL-CIO, as a whole, membership began to climb upward from the low of 12,464,000 in 1962–63. In the twelve-month period of July 1965 to June 1966, membership rose by more than one million—a high 7 per cent increase—with the highest percentage gains among public employee unions. Why has this new labor force turned to unionism? Fundamentally because unions are universal. But, immediately, because new circumstances pushed an already "organized" group (united in professional and mutual aid societies) into the militant stance of unionism.

A relevant case study is to be found among the school teachers —a large body of employees who wear a white collar, dispense a service, operate at a professional level, and are employed by government or other nonprofit institutions. Among American teachers the great organization for many decades was the National Education Association, with more than a million members oriented around a nonunion professional tradition. Competing for teacher loyalty was the American Federation of Teachers, a small ineffective outfit that had been torn internally by ideologic dissension and denigrated externally by the refusal of school authorities to pay it any mind. Then in the early 1960s, the AFT won a decisive bargaining position in New York City. From that time on, the union grew; teachers began to organize and strike all over the country; and the NEA turned more and more toward union purposes and tactics. The result was to make the American teacher a militant unionist, striking municipal school systems despite legal bans and court orders, striking Catholic colleges despite hierarchic disapproval.

In his study, *Teachers and Unions*, Michael H. Moskow assigns three reasons for the new militancy. The first reason—the growing separation between school administration and the classroom educator—very much resembles the reasons underlying the early organization of cordwainers and carpenters; namely, the cleavage between the journeymen and his real boss, the distant merchant or building contractor. "The merging of small school districts in order to obtain economics of scale has the added result of further separating the classroom teacher from the decision makers in the district," argues Moskow. "The additional layers of supervision necessitated by the increase in the size of the district most likely add to the need and to the desire of the teacher for protection by an organization specifically devoted to his interests." A second reason is the teacher's awareness of the size and strength of the public employee. "The rising percentage of our labor force working as public employees . . . has caused an over-all drive for negotiation procedures for this burgeoning group of employees." In other words, the teacher, like all other occupational groups, moves toward organization of a union as he becomes aware of his collective status as public employee and as professional. A third reason offered by Moskow is the support "the labor movement has given to the American Federation of Teachers in its drive to unionize teachers."[15]

In a study of the National Education Association, whose rubric is professional negotiation rather than the laboristic collective bargaining, six major reasons are set forth for the teacher movement.[16]

15. Michael H. Moskow, *Teachers and Unions* (Philadelphia: University of Pennsylvania, 1966), p. 4.
16. T. M. Stinnett, Jack H. Kleinmann, and Martha L. Ware, *Professional Negotiation in Public Education* (New York: Macmillan Company, 1966), p. 4 ff.

1. The mounting impatience of teachers with what they consider to be economic injustice . . . teacher salaries have historically lagged behind the returns to other comparable groups, and often behind the pay of unskilled workers.

2. As an integral part of their own search for economic justice, teachers have grown increasingly bitter at the neglect of schools by our affluent society. . . . Teachers came to the conclusion that they dared not continue the passive attitude of relying solely upon official bodies to correct these conditions; but that they must join in a vigorous effort to effect needed changes.

3. Another deeply significant psychological factor involved in the hunger for recognition by teachers is the matter of bigness—the bigness of cities and of school districts, with the resultant loss of identity of the teacher. . . . As a result, he often tends in overt ways to gain some kind of solid recognition. If he doesn't get such recognition in well planned ways, he will seek it in rebellious ways, or ways that appear to be rebellious in the light of past mores.

4. A rapid emergence of a new status for public employees in general. Greatly increased levels of preparation and of the nature of services are demanded.

5. The demand for recognition and participation in policy formation by teachers is a product of the times. The emergence of new nations as a result of the twilight of colonialism as a political philosophy—and of paternalism as its companion piece—is a part of the commitment of peoples throughout the world to a new status and dignity. Individuals, too, are caught up in this commitment, and so are teachers.

6. The dramatic push of American Negroes for human and civil rights, for elevation to first class citizenship has had great impact everywhere, especially upon the people of the United States. . . . Teachers, too, have often viewed themselves as oppressed; they have viewed their treatment by society as being far less than commensurate with the importance of their contribution to the general welfare.

In listing these reasons for teacher militancy, the authors of this study of NEA (not AFT) behavior are unwittingly recapitulating the ontogeny of occupational organizations since the earliest times.

1. An occupation passes through the trauma of mounting injustice—"salaries . . . lagged behind."

2. The personal injustice finds a moral lift by identification with the needs of the total society—"neglect of schools by our affluent society."

3. The group loses identification with the parent institution, the employing school system—"loss of identity of the teacher."

4. The group develops a collective self-consciousness—"a new status for public employees."

5. and 6. The emergent teacher draws wisdom and will from emerging nations and peoples. Since a union is a "little republic," to feel a kinship with the Congo or a march on Selma comes naturally.

As a result of the movements among the new sectors of the labor force a third dimension is being added to American trade unionism in the late '60s. To the craft and mass production workers are now added the white-collar men and women of the service economy. Although this movement was inevitable, it hit an insightless and unprepared nation with the shock of a "revolution." In all of the talk about the "non-future" of American trade unionism that was fashionable in the 1950s, one simple vital thought was neglected; namely, that the nature of unions is in the nature of man.

7

The Politics of Economics

So far, the nature of unions has been traced with minimal reference to collective bargaining—popularly considered the be-all and end-all of trade unionism. This postponed consideration of the battle in the workplace between the union and the employer should not imply that bargaining is unimportant; for most unions, it is daily fare, the bread and butter of their existence. This introduction of the bargaining function is belated for two reasons: first, to stress the fact that workers group naturally in the workplace into cultures, societies, associations *before* undertaking the formal business of bargaining; second, to underscore the noneconomic aspects of unions.

In this discussion of collective bargaining as a political process, the term *politics* is used, as defined by Harold Lasswell, as the study of "who gets what." In the world of the workplace, collective bargaining is concerned with the question of "who gets what." The union, consequently, is a *political* corporation in a double sense: (1) it is the society of the workmen arisen in the work *polis*, and (2) it engages in the *political* struggle over the division of rights and riches.

Before getting into the dynamics of this peculiar political battle within the workplace, it should be stressed that the struggle is not solely over the division of the company's income. First, there is the question of *who?* Who shall make the decisions? Who shall own the job? Who is the first fired and the first rehired or hired? Who is an apprentice and who is a journeyman? Who is classified as a skilled craftsman and who as unskilled? And then there is the question of *what*. What work conditions or work load? What work hours, holidays, vacations, promotions? What pay? The parallel with the political struggle in any organized society is patent. Who rules and who is ruled? What are the decisions and what is their impact on different people?

The Book of Exodus tells an interesting story about the political character of the first professional union—the "priestly college." When Moses returned from Mt. Sinai with the Ten Commandments, he found a dissolute people dancing around a golden calf. In rage, he smashed the tablet. And still in anger, he cried out, "Who is on the Lord's side. Let him come unto me. And all the sons of Levi gathered themselves unto him." Whereupon Moses ordered them to buckle on their swords and to "slay every man his brother, and every man his companion, and every man his neighbor." Which is precisely what the sons of Levi did, leaving three thousand dead. Whereupon Moses anointed Aaron and his sons of the House of Levi, establishing them as "an everlasting priesthood throughout their generations." And as a reward for their priestly services, it was decreed that there should be a tithe, giving the sons of Aaron "all the tenth part in Israel for an inheritance."[1]

The sons of Levi had won a decisive *political* battle. In power, they decided *who* would make the laws and *what* part of the gross national product of Israel would go to the ruling family.

Ever since then, "little republics" within great republics have engaged in political struggles over the *who* and the *what*, determining what colonies should be bestowed on what favorite lords or what natural resources should be leased, sold, or given to what oil company or what homesteader; deciding what taxes shall fall on whom and on whom not; deciding what price shall be charged or what wage paid; what tariff to levy and what enterprise to subsidize. Although these were (and are) all *economic* decisions, they are nevertheless made through a *political* process, by the

1. For a macabre and melancholy interpretation of this event, see Brooks Adams, *The Emancipation of Massachusetts* (Boston: Houghton Mifflin Company, 1887). Preface, 1919 edition.

push and pull of individuals and groups, by conquest, conspiracy, concession—by conflict within the family of man.

How far back does this struggle over the *who* and the *what* go? Apparently, it finds its origin in the origin of sin. In the first family, Cain and Abel found themselves in conflict. Whether the record of the first murder is the story of two individuals or is the symbolic representation of a conflict between keeper of the flocks and tiller of the soil, its universal quality bespeaks the ancient clash between brothers in the family of man. Between two sons of Isaac—Jacob and Esau—there likewise was no peace. The gentle-voiced youngest, Jacob, cheated the senior rough-handed Esau out of the latter's birthright. Between the two brothers who founded Rome, Romulus and Remus, strife broke out and the one slew the other. In the folklore of every people can be found the clash between brothers.

Explanations have been sought for this disquieting phenomenon in theologic, psychologic, sociologic, and biologic terms. The theologian Rheinhold Niebuhr defines original sin as man's egocentric preoccupation with himself: each soul considers itself the center of the universe. Psychoanalysis posits sibling rivalry as a primary drive. Recent ethological studies of animal behavior speak of the "territorial imperative" and "intraspecific aggression" as discernible biologic traits from which man is apparently not exempt.

Throughout history, the eternal conflict has been viewed as an evil, an immoral family quarrel that denies the fatherhood of God and the brotherhood of man. Public preachment calls for love and denounces hate, prays for peace and damns war. Yet, after millennia of suffering and civilizing, the conflict continues. Why?

Apparently, it all begins when two creatures want exclusive possession of the same thing. It occurs when two beasts want the same territory or two street gangs the same turf, when two children want the exclusive attention or love of the same parent or the same birthright, when two men (or parties) want to wear the same crown, when union and company want the same dollar, when two craftsmen want the same job, when two unions want the same jurisdiction. When brothers clash, it is precisely because they are brothers, of the same family, occupation, neighborhood, sex. In his report to America on the state of crime in 1967, President Johnson proved statistically that most crimes are intraspecific. The report of a Presidential Commission estimates that "in fully two-thirds of the cases of willful homocide and aggravated assault, the criminals and the victims are known to each other; very often they are members of the same family."[2]

Until Darwin, this intraspecific war made no sense; it appeared to be a cruel and useless way for the species to exterminate itself. And then, the great evolutionist suggested that maybe there was a divine wisdom behind this unrelenting evil. Through the conflict, the fittest would survive in a process of natural selection. When Herbert Spencer applied the Darwinian concept to human society, the theory became fashionable, especially in those upper classes who now found a scientific justification for their superior status. Might became right. What is is moral; it is heaven's way of preserving and elevating the best in mankind.

With the growth of democracy, however, the appeal of social Darwinism wore off. The whole idea was repulsive to the cry for "liberty, fraternity, and equality." As new groups began to bare their teeth—first a revolutionary bourgeoisie and then a revolutionary proletariat—the old aristocracy was not quite so sure that those who survived were truly fit to live. In intellectual circles, the rule of reason took hold, seeking engineered solutions to social problems through education and rational consensus. Even individual personalities could be made to accord with a chosen

2. A Report by the President's Commission on Law Enforcement and Administration of Justice (Washington, D.C.: U.S. Government Printing Office, February 1967), p. 3.

design by a process of conditioned reflexes, both personal and societal.

Yet, at the very moment when the Goddess of Reason proclaimed the height of her rule over the Western world, inquiring minds began to dig down into man's instincts, his unconscious, his biologic ancestors. And at the very core of these inquiries was man's conflict with his social order, his neighbor, his family, and, necessarily, himself. The conflict was all so unnecessary and irrational—but it was there.

As far back as 1893, the sociologist Émile Durkheim presented his interpretation of Darwin's findings on intraspecific warfare.

Darwin justly observed that the struggle between two organisms is as active as they are analogous. Having the same needs and pursuing the same objects, they are in rivalry everywhere. As long as they have more resources than they need, they can still live side by side, but if their number increases to such proportions that all appetites can no longer be sufficiently satisfied, war breaks out, and it is as violent as this insufficiency is more marked; that is to say, as the number in the struggle increase. It is quite otherwise if the coexisting individuals are of different species or varieties. As they do not feed in the same manner, and do not lead the same kind of life, they do not disturb each other. What is advantageous to one is without value to the others. The chances of conflict thus diminish with chances of meeting, and the more so as the species or varieties are more distant from one another.[3]

From this worrisome finding about the war among the like, Durkheim reached an optimistic conclusion. In our human society, let us multiply the "species or varieties." If men do different things, they are more likely to live in peace. They will also have to learn to cooperate with one another since they will be mutually dependent on one another's wares and services. Hence, division of labor—by spreading men out over many occupations and

3. Durkheim, *op. cit.*, p. 266.

thereby thinning the ranks of any one occupation—becomes the structural base for a moral social order:

In the same city different occupations can co-exist without being obliged mutually to destroy one another, for they pursue different objects. The soldier seeks military glory, the priest moral authority, the statesman power, the business man riches, the scholar scientific renown. Each of them can attain his end without preventing the others from attaining theirs. It is the same even when the functions are less separated from one another. The oculist does not struggle with the psychiatrist, nor the shoemaker with the hatter, nor the mason with the cabinet maker, nor the physicist with the chemist, etc. Since they perform different services, they can perform them parallelly. The closer functions come to one another, however, the more points of contact they have; the more, consequently, are they exposed to conflict.[4]

In his provocative book, *On Aggression,* written about 75 years after Durkheim's classic, Konrad Lorenz repeats and reinforces the argument, except that where the sociologist speaks of "cities" the ethologist speaks of a "coral reef." Within a cubic yard of ocean water life teems with an endless variety of fish, each species living in a different way, with each specimen keeping his fellow specimens at a proper length. Referring back to Darwin, Lorenz makes the following observation:

[Darwin] had already raised the question of the survival value of fighting, and he has given us an enlightening answer: it is always favorable to the future of a species if the stronger of two rivals takes possession either of the territory or of the desired female. As so often this truth of yesterday is not the untruth of today but only a special case; ecologists have recently demonstrated a much more essential function of aggression. Ecology—derived from the Greek *oikos,* the house—is the branch of biology that deals with the manifold reciprocal relations of the organism to its natural surroundings—its "household"—which of course includes all other animals and plants native to the environment. Unless the special interests of a

4. *Ibid.,* p. 267.

social organization demand close aggregation of its members, it is obviously most expedient to spread the individuals of an animal species as evenly as possible over the available habitat. To use a human analogy: if, in a certain area, a larger number of doctors, builders and mechanics want to exist, the representatives of these professions would do well to settle as far away from each other as possible.[5]

The battle of brothers, then, not only selects the stronger fighter to defend the turf and the more virile father to sire the young but also serves to space the specimen so the species may survive.

Lest the arguments of sociologist Durkheim and ethologist Lorenz (ethologists study animal behavior in the natural habitat) be considered an unwarranted transposition of mind-less conduct to mind-ful humans, let us consider the findings of Frances L. Ilg, M.D., and Louise Bates Ames, Ph.D., in their study, *Child Behavior*, which is based on the research of the Gesell Institute.

It may be a comfort, even though a cold comfort, to know that if your 6 or 7 or 8 or even 10 year old seems constantly to be bickering with brothers and sisters and not to be improving as you assumed he must, he is not out of the ordinary. The thing that will interest you most as parents, however, is probably not so much whether or not this is the case, as what you can do about it. We suspect and fear that there is less you can do about it than you would hope. Trying to get a rise out of siblings, teasing them, bickering with them, squabbling and wrestling with them, are probably some of the many things that increased age alone finally cures for sure.[6]

Having recorded, from voluminous scientific observation, that brotherhood and sisterhood are not friendly states in nature, the doctors propose a remedy that is not fundamentally different from that of Durkheim and Lorenz and, implicitly, Darwin; namely, *space them!*

5. Konrad Lorenz, *On Aggression* (New York: Harcourt, Brace and World, Inc., 1963), pp. 30–31.

6. Frances L. Ilg and Louise Bates Ames, *Child Behavior* (New York: Harper and Row, 1955), p. 220.

The best way we know to keep brothers and sisters from quarreling is to keep them apart as much as is necessary. Find out the customary limits of their ability to be together peacefully, and then try to separate them before those limits are reached. . . . Plan for them to be engaged in separate activities. Plan if necessary for one or the other to be out of the house. Even plan for separate mealtimes if need be. In extreme cases some parents we know even resorted to having one child spend a season in the home of some willing relative. Time and space can both be manipulated in this way. Have them do things at different times; or, if you possibly can, arrange that each has some space of his own which the others cannot invade.[7]

What the caring and thoughtful mother is advised to do in the home with her siblings, Mother Nature does for all her siblings; namely, equips them with instincts to mark off and defend a *Lebensraum*—to quote Ilg and Ames, "some space of their own which the others can not invade."

One of the prime functions of any political corporation, whether nation or union, is to mark off a "space which the others cannot invade." Whether this "space" is a claim on a continent or a job jurisdiction, each political corporation fences in a piece of the universe to distribute judiciously among its loyal members. The method for doing so can be a legal decree, the use of force, or the contract with the employer; they serve to limit the number of the same species on the limited territory.

In collective bargaining, this primeval force reasserts itself, written into the contract in the form of closed shop, apprenticeship clauses, seniority, levels of employment, and so on. At a later point, we will discuss many of the ways in which the union plays a role like that of Mother Nature, controlling either space or birth to apportion the territory. At this point, it should be noted that one of the central functions of an occupational union is to allocate "space" and that collective bargaining by the modern labor union is an attempt, in part, to do this in a civilized manner, by some rule of law and reason.

7. *Ibid.*, p. 226.

Because of a special interest in intraspecific conflict, among ethologists of the mid-1960s there is a de-emphasis of interspecific warfare, the strife between creatures of different species. Lorenz notes that the latter does not carry with it the emotional intensity of the former. "A dog about to catch a hunted rabbit has the same kind of excitedly happy expression as he has when he greets his master or awaits some longed for treat. . . . The buffalo which the lion fells provokes his aggression as little as the appetizing turkey which I have just seen hanging in the larder provokes mine." In other words, interspecific aggression stimulates appetite more than aggression.

Despite the lesser role assigned to the war between the species, mankind finds itself constantly involved in this conflict as a matter of survival. Our meals include fish, fowl, or meat—all by-products of man's interspecific war against less ingenious creatures. On summer vacations, we kill mosquitoes as if they were flies. With a swift spray of insecticide, we murder a legion of parasites in the calm of a garden greenery. With an antibiotic shot, we wage calculated warfare against armies of germs. These are all interspecific wars, between man and his closest neighbors, fought without guilt, anger, or the quickening of a heartbeat.

The difference between intraspecific and interspecific wars is not as marked among men as in the lower orders. In the animal world, the difference is easily discovered. Lion versus lion is intraspecific and lion versus buffalo is interspecific. One species is marked off from another by clearly defined anatomical traits. But, in the world of man, the difference is not so clear, because man's great evolution is cultural, rather than anatomical, and begins where biology ends. The differentiations that evolution wrought in the animal world by genetic mutations have been wrought in the human world by cultural adaptations. Hence, the conflict between man and man may be either intraspecific or interspecific. Consider the difference between war and common murder, for instance. Murder of one citizen by another is generally considered immoral. The killer is supposed to suffer remorse of conscience; his act is deplored by all good citizens; there are laws to punish him. But if the same killer slays a foreign enemy in war, his act is not immoral; he is not expected to spend sleepless nights; he is praised by the good people of his own nation; there are medals to reward him. In the way of all flesh, the killer *within* the clan is ostracised; the killer *for* the clan is proclaimed.

Within any organized society, especially one that is complex and democratic, there are many "little nations" within the nation. Hence rivalries among social, ethnic, political, and economic groups often take on the essential qualities of an interspecific conflict. In the days of the American Revolution, patriots tarred and feathered Tory sympathizers as easily as they plucked the same feathers from some butchered goose; in the Civil War, Sherman marched through Georgia with the compunction of a man squashing an ant-hill under a military boot; in Ludlow, Colorado, company thugs poured oil into a valley housing a tent colony of strikers and then exploded the oil in the manner of any hardened vermin exterminator; in the coal mines of Pennsylvania, the Molly Maguires could murder an obnoxious foreman with the icy ease of a woodsman clubbing a snake. Although these are all examples of intraspecific aggression (since all the parties are human), they carry all the traits of a war between different species, of an interspecific conflict.

Lorenz grants that there are three kinds of interspecific warfare conducted by animals that do rise to a high level of emotional intensity. There is the attack of the predator on its prey, spiritless when there is no resistance but fiercely spirited when the victim fights back. There is also the not uncommon assault of the prey on the predator. "Social animals in particular take every possible chance to attack the 'eating enemy' that threatens their safety. This process is called 'mobbing.' Crows or other birds 'mob' a cat or any other nocturnal predator, if they catch sight of it by day."[8] Finally, there is the "critical reaction" (to use the term attributed to H. Hediger) of the animal fighting like a cornered rat, the beast who would prefer to flee but no longer has the time, avenue, or asylum for flight. His fears become his weapons, as he externalizes his desperation.

All three of these forms of interspecific conflict may be found in labor-management relations, if so neutral a word may be used to describe so unneutral a confrontation. To workers, the management often appears as the predator; the union is the instrument for "mobbing" of the prey against the predator; when either side feels that its economic existence is at stake and that flight is sure death, it fights like a cornered rat. Collective bargaining is a generally polite, sometimes bloody, way of preying, "mobbing," and fierce fighting, the last of which comes into play when the bargaining touches the sensitive nerve of some "principle."

Because these interspecific wars take place in a shop, company, or industry and not in the primitive jungle, they are political struggles. They are the organization of human parties to assert their power over *who* gets *what* with the object of writing the resultant arrangement into an ever-changing piece of legislation, called the contract.

The social relation of creature to creature has become the central concern of recent ethologists. Their first cousins, the ecologists, focus on the relations between creature and environment. Ecology finds that organisms not only adapt to, but also *change* their environment. Bees build hives; birds build nests; beavers build dams; bowerbirds erect structures vertical to the rising sun; fiddler crabs dig sandy homes; termites construct long subways for their dark, damp passage. But these are all primitive builders alongside man. Beavers have been building the same dams in the same ways probably ever since the beaver discovered

8. Lorenz, *op. cit.*, p. 26.

what a marvelous trowel his tail could be. But man builds new dams in new ways because it is man's dream to be master of his "household," to be an "ecocrat," just to add another word to our ever-lengthening lexicon. And man, being a social animal, usually undertakes the assignment within his social framework.

In the factory, the worker finds himself in an environment more or less to his liking. Sooner or later, he wants to change it. He wants to change both the physical and the personal relations. He seeks what elemental trade unionists call wages, hours, and working conditions—an ecological transformation. Some industrial psychologists view this effort to change the environment as a homeostatic principle. By this theory, it is inevitable that there should be an eternal yearning for change. As one need with high priority is satisfied, a secondary need gets top rank on the human agenda. The origin of the everlasting push is possibly biochemical. "People, like all other living organisms, are in a constant state of disequilibrium," according to Stagner and Rosen in their *Psychology of Union-Management Relations.* "Such a state is inevitable. The living organism expends energy to remain alive and must replenish this energy. Behavior is constantly being initiated to satisfy the needs for survival. This attempt to balance output with input, to achieve equilibrium is called the *homeostatic principle.* It underlies all behavior and motivation."[9]

What are the various needs of man that keep him constantly off-balance as if life were a tightrope? A. H. Maslow suggests a set of priorities in his theory of human motivation in which maximum potency "goes to the *physiological* needs such as hunger and thirst; then comes *safety* needs; *belongingness* and *love* needs; *esteem* needs; and the needs for *self-actualization.*"[10]

Because these needs are so many and because the satisfaction

9. Ross Stagner and Hjalmar Rosen, *Psychology of Union-Management Relations* (Belmont, Calif.: Wadsworth Publishing Co., 1965), p. 22.
10. Cited by Stagner and Rosen, *op. cit.,* p. 25.

of one need merely unleashes others, "it is impossible to satiate all needs acting within the person. . . . This very simple characteristic is vital in explaining why—regardless of what the company provides the worker in need of fulfillment—the worker will inevitably come up with a new set of demands." And that is why, when Samuel Gompers was asked by a Congressional committee what the ultimate objectives of the American labor movement were, he answered laconically, "more"![11] The founder of the AFL was unwittingly recapitulating the long story of man's sojourn on earth.

The homeostatic principle underlying human motivation does not really reveal very much, accurate as it may be. In effect it says that equations must balance. But it does not say what ingredients go into the equation on one side or the other. The unanswered question of specific needs is answered in part by a compendium such as that of Maslow. But any such listing inevitably whets the inquiring appetite, either to lengthen the list or to distill it down to some central essence, to find a "unified field theory of human behavior."

One such attempted "unified field theory" is that of Robert Ardrey, the dramatist turned ethologist who converts lemurs into people and biology into politics. From the many worlds of animal life, he cites case after case of the creature's attachment to its territory, either individually with its family or collectively with its pack. In the quest for a unifying theory to explain this universal phenomenon—from the slime mold to man—Ardrey is embarrassed by the riches of his evidence. Unable to find any one adequate word, he offers a tripartite explanation: security, stimulation, and identity. The heart of the territory itself offers security; the periphery offers stimulation; the specific niche that the individual chooses as his very own offers a sense of identity. Here is how Ardrey richly explains his thesis:

11. *Ibid.*, p. 28.

There is the castle or nest or heartland or lair to provide *security*, and, just as important, the border region where the *fun* goes on. These are basic needs of a psychological order, for *security* and for *stimulation*, and under normal circumstances, they would conflict. The territorial principle has, however, satisfied both without loss to either. And I believe that if we elaborate [the] hypothesis with the addition of a third basic need, also satisfied by territory, we shall complete a psychological pattern common to all higher animals, and perhaps many lower animals as well.

That third need I describe as one for identity. I find it useful to define the three needs in terms of their opposites: to think of security as the opposite of anxiety, of stimulation as the opposite of boredom, of identity as the opposite of anonymity. The bird seeks his invariable branch from which to advertise his presence; it is a portion of his identity.

The animal seeks to differentiate himself from all others of his kind. As a member of a herd or flock or school or troop or *novau*, the social animal belongs to a group differentiated from all other groups; and within that group he acquires a territory or a rank of status or a perching or resting place, acknowledged as his alone, which distinguishes him from all other members of the group. He has achieved identity.[12]

In describing the animal drive to differentiate—first as a species and then within the species—Ardrey is describing the story of man. First, man differentiates himself from his environment and as *homo sapiens* from other species. Then he differentiates into clans, tribes, cities, and nations. And then within the nations, he differentiates into many communities, one of which is the community of the workplace. And then, within the workplace, for example, he differentiates himself by his earnings, his position in the company or his union. This and others of his multiple and complex social relationships provide his ecologic niche within which the *I* emerges from the *we* and the *somebody* from the *nobody*.

There are, however, significant differences between man and

12. Robert Ardrey, *The Territorial Imperative* (New York: Atheneum, 1966), p. 171.

beast. Man does more than crawl into a lair or erect a mudhut by rote; man keeps changing his environment through the miracles of invention. These man-made arrangements disrupt established relations. This is particularly true in a democracy constantly undergoing technical changes, where there is a mobility of populations and individuals in the shifting sands of a restless economy. In such a nonstatic, noncaste, nonfixed society, the threat to identity is real as the individual, losing the points of reference by which he discovers himself, lapses into a state of anomie, searching himself with the question: *what am I?*

Frank Tannenbaum has explored the role of the trade union as the re-creator of the community within which the worker discovers his identity—first, as a member of the work group and then as an individual. His emphasis is on the former—the simple re-creation of the community: "The social atomization resulting from the payment of an individual money wage was in time to be defeated by the fusing of men together functionally, and this functional coalescence became the firm foundation upon which the trade-union movement grew, and which, in fact, made it inevitable."[13]

In the world of free enterprise, where the wandering worker is just a helpless particle in a turbulent economic ocean, the union provides the community. The union establishes the *territory* in which the character of the community is defined. And it is on this bit of turf that the individual carves out his niche and establishes a sense of identity. "The trade union," argues Tannenbaum, "saved the worker his initiative and gave him an opportunity to act as a moral person. The 'society' that he needed had returned. He was a man once again, not just a cog in a machine."[14]

Although Tannenbaum wrote this view before some of the newest ruminations of the ethologists saw print, he was stating the

13. Frank Tannenbaum, *A Philosophy of Labor* (New York: Alfred A. Knopf, 1951), p. 60.
14. *Ibid.*, p. 78.

concept of "community" and "territoriality." In the language of collective bargaining, these are "the bargaining unit" and the "jurisdiction." On these bases, Tannenbaum constructed a philosophy of unionism whose "noneconomic" assumption provided the inspiration for this present book.

The union, however, provides more than a sense of security born of community. It provides Ardrey's stimulation. There is always a frontier, where the union can be restimulated to test its strength. This frontier is provided not only by changes in production methods in the plant but by the worker's rising expectations, by the new priorities that arise as old needs and goals are met.

Finally, within the circle of his intimates, the worker continues his personal battle to be a somebody. Here he is himself against all comers: against the boss, against competing crafts, against brothers at the bench, against aspirants for union office.

All these engagements contribute to the formation of his character as a person. As he scratches and is scratched, each encounter leaves furrows in his brain. Indeed, what is *character* but "scratchings" derived from the Greek "to carve, or to furrow." These and other carvings on the psyche—the complicated record of differentiations within differentiations—create an identity as distinctive as the features and furrows on the human face.

In the world of humans, these successive differentiations are a *political* process. The grouping of man in some primitive form is the instinctive expression of the political animal. The formation of churches, parties, corporations, and unions *within* the nation is the expression of the same political drive in a newly differentiated locus. The formation of groups within these groups—factions, heresies, craft divisions, subsidiaries—is a continuation of the political process. Finally, the striving of an individual to carve out his special niche—to win prestige and esteem—is the most commonly recognized form of political activity, the doings of man, the politician.

In this process, persons and groups seek esteem, a social confirmation of their individual or collective identity. The larger order around them is the mirror in which they stand reflected. The child wants love and praise from father and mother; the corporation wants legal standing before the church or the state; the politician wants election; philanthropists want hospitals erected in their name; soldiers want medals; executives want carpeted suites; workers want fancy job titles. They all want recognition. A many-sided word, *recognition* means the bestowal of esteem, as when we speak of a man seeking public recognition for his good deeds. It also means the formal act whereby one nation recognizes another or an employer recognizes a union. But the original meaning of *to recognize* is probably the fount of all these meanings; namely, to know again—*re-cognoscere.*

The stranger is faceless. The old saw about how all Chinese waiters look alike is a bad joke about a good insight. The outsider is so featureless to us that we note the species without noting the specimen. The great cry of American Negroes in mid-twentieth century has been the plaint of the faceless, of the person who is no person in the societal mirror. The act of recognition is the first step toward granting that the stranger-nobody is a social-somebody. In the one act of recognition two purposes are achieved: the outsider becomes an insider and the faceless person takes on a face. When we grant recognition to a nation, we formally state that it is no longer a nothing but a diplomatic something. When we grant recognition for a noble deed, we confirm a man in his new perch for his lofty work. When an employer recognizes a union, he admits the worker to a voice in the household and formally accepts the presence of the new somebody.

Recognition is chronologically the first and politically the prime objective of unionism. Recognition is to the worker what voting is to the citizen in a democracy: a legally admitted voice in decision-making. And just as in a democracy, the right to vote is both an ethical and structural revolution—ethically based on individual dignity and structurally based on popular rule—so, too, does recognition convey both an ethical and structural implication; namely, respect for the worker as an individual and participation of the worker in making laws for the *polis* of the workplace. As in the life of nations, the coming of recognition is the beginning of the civilized debate within the *polis*. Prior to that, as prior to democracy, the people could only intervene in public policy through demonstrations, riots, assassinations, and revolutions. Recognition of a union is the beginning of a peaceful era; the formalization of the industrial dialogue, the civilization of the politics of the workplace. But precisely because recognition represents so profound a change in relationships, it rarely comes easily. Indeed, it is this primary fight, like the historic struggles for democracy itself, that is generally accompanied by mass violence and bloodshed.

It must always be remembered [concludes Tannenbaum] that the great battle has been for recognition of the organization—that is, for the formalized 'society,' in which rules, laws, and traditions can have their acknowledged place and in which individual members can play their part in the drama. Without recognition there can be no formalized society, no accepted drama to act out, and no responsibilities for the individual or for the society to which the individual is functionally and organically related. That is why the battle for recognition of the workers' organization has been unending and why it has been resisted.

It has been resisted because a society tends to become all-embracing and a way of life.[15]

In the political game of *who* and *what*, recognition revolves around the *who;* namely, who makes the decisions. Prior to recognition, the employer is the one who decides. He rules by an implicit "divine right." He created the company; He created the jobs; He pays the wage; He owns the factory, the raw

15. *Ibid.,* p. 69.

material, and the finished product. He created this little world of the workplace as surely as God created the universe. Hence, the employer naturally and instinctively is likely to conclude that, for better or worse, he has the implicit right to rule, to determine the way of life in his petty realm. In such a closed society, the demand of his subjects to a voice in governance is a rebellion of the rabble.

Of all the trade union demands—wages, hours, job security, work conditions, holidays, vacations—recognition seems like the least. It is invisible and intangible. It hardly seems worth the pain that accompanies its birth. Weighed objectively, it is nothing; weighed subjectively, it is everything.

In 1914, a now-forgotten lady, Helen Marot, the Executive Secretary of the Women's Trade Union League of New York, captured an insight into the meaning of union recognition as the prime liberating force for workers in a forgotten book, *American Labor Unions*, addressed to the well-to-do friends of unions. In a chapter entitled "Philanthropy and Labor Unions," she delineates the difference between giving-from-above and getting-from-below. The do-gooders, she argued, want better work conditions and better wages as ways to uplift the downtrodden and, simultaneously, to lift efficiency and profits. Although the motives are noble and the end result coincides with labor's aims, there is a significant difference between the philanthropist and the unionist. The unionists have not joined with their fellow workers just to gain terms of work and existence; their union is their declaration of independence. It bears the same relation to industrial life that other declarations of independence have borne to political life:

No one doubts that measures for industrial betterment, as they are initiated by philanthropists or by capital, and administered by experts or state officials, will make large contributions toward minimizing physical waste and disease in modern industry. It is, indeed, a movement for sanitation and conservation. Its full realization would give clean homes, healthy children, and efficient workers. But class-conscious labor wants much more. It wants citizenship in industry. It is no more willing to submit to the rule of the beneficient and efficient than were the American colonists willing to submit to the rule of the British Parliament. Labor would rather be free than clean.[16]

And that is why recognition—the formalization of freedom—is a prime concern. The winning of recognition, like the winning of democracy, is quite patently a major act of politics.

Secondary to recognition, comes security—job security for the union member. In a revealing study, conducted by Robert Kahn, "*steady* work and *steady* wages" came through as the top concern of working people, with about twice as much intensity as "*high* wages."[17] To most employees, the idea of feast today and famine tomorrow is uninviting. The real love is going steady with a job. And for that reason, unions have always placed a top priority on job security. In pursuit of this policy, unions have sought (1) to abolish the employers' power to fire at will; (2) to give unions control over hiring; (3) to limit the number of workers in the job market; and, in the effort to accomplish these purposes, (4) to establish a single hegemony over the occupational jurisdiction.

Viewed *politically*, this is a battle over the question of *who owns the job*. Without a union, there is no question: the job belongs to the employer with power to hire and fire at will. With a union, job ownership is a shared concept; the worker proclaims his *right* to the job. He insists that he may not be fired without just cause, just as a citizen in a democracy may not be deprived of life, liberty, or property without due process. Every union

16. Helen Marot, *American Labor Unions* (New York: Holt, Rinehart & Winston, 1914), p. 6–10.

17. Robert Kahn, "Human Relations on the Shop Floor." In Hugh Jones, E. M. (Ed.) *Human Relations and Modern Management* (Amsterdam: Youth Holland Pub., 1958).

contract worth its salt contains a due process clause curbing the employer's power to fire.

From a purely proprietary point of view, this inhibition appears ludicrous. Since the employer created the job, it should belong to him with the right to hire and fire as he pleases. Yet this basic prerogative of management is always challenged by a union and becomes the first substantive matter in dispute. Unions offer many convincing reasons why the employer shall not have the unchecked right to fire. If he did, he would fire union activists first, weakening the organization, terrorizing union spokesmen, thereby ultimately destroying the union in the shop. He could play favorites, encouraging his pets and discouraging his "troublemakers." These are sound "institutional" reasons for the union as such that many individual workers will understand. But from the viewpoint of the ordinary rank-and-filer, the real reason is pure and simple security, a certainty that the job belongs to him. Without that sense of security, the worker is a dependent, somewhat stooped by the hat he must carry in hand. With job security, he has found his own territory, on which to stand erect.

The right-to-fire question has become exceedingly complex in modern times. Originally, the matter related to the discharge of a worker for some delinquency or other. More recently, the question has arisen as a result of a production method change in a plant that has rendered a worker's job obsolete or of a plant relocation that leaves the worker without a workplace. In these latter cases, unions have negotiated contracts that protect a worker's "territorial" rights on the job even under the unusual circumstances of job removal or abolition. Clauses call for relief, relocation, and retraining of employees, based on an internal pecking order involving seniority, standing in union, departmental attachment, and so on. This huge body of industrial "law" makes it clear that the employer may not do with the job as he pleases— he may not move, remove, alter, or abolish it without "taking the matter up" with his co-proprietor, the union.

In a summary of the worker's right to his job, the astute A. H. Raskin, after a lifetime of watching the evolution of this "ownership" in American industrial relations, concludes:

A still newer extension of the security principle carries blue-collar workers closest to the 'promised land' of lifetime job security. Put in its simplest terms, this is the principle that no regular employee will be pushed off the payroll because a machine takes his job. No matter how great the labor saving made by technological innovation, the worker is protected against unemployment. His job may go, but he stays. This is the concept known as 'attrition,' and it is becoming widely accepted as the most socially responsible method that collective bargaining can devise for meeting the problems of technological displacement. In effect, it provides for drawing a circle around the existing work force in a plant, enterprise, or industry and giving assurance that nobody inside that circle will be fired because of automation or other changes made in the interest of increased efficiency. The workers remain employed until they die, retire, or leave of their own accord.[17]

The bargaining battle over the right to fire is a political struggle over a piece of territory and the title thereto: who owns the job? The same battle over the same question continues over the right to hire: who owns the job?

Not all unions raise this question at the bargaining table. Most of them are quite content to allow the employer to hire whom he pleases, provided the new worker joins the union after some stipulated brief period. These latter unions generally are factory- or office-based; the members are attached to a given employer doing a given job; so long as the worker is with that firm, his job is secured by the contract.

In other unions, however, the right-to-hire is as vital as the right-to-fire in providing job security for the worker. These are the unions that operate in the so-called journeymen trades, where

17. A. H. Raskin, "Recent Developments in the Strength and Philosophy of American Labor," in *Labor in a Changing America*, ed. William Haber (New York: Basic Books, 1966), p. 314.

a worker puts in a brief stint on one job and then moves on to another—such as a musician playing one-night stands or an electrician wiring some new building in one-week installation jobs. After the one night or the one week, the musician or the electrician is out of a job: he turns to the union for security. The craft unions in the journeymen trades provide job security by establishing a *collective ownership* over the job. The union marks off its territory in terms of craft and geography. This boundary is termed the *jurisdiction*, another one of those revealing words whose Latin origins add up to the concept of "speaking in the name of the law." By the "divine right" of self-preservation, the union makes it a law that it owns all within its jurisdiction and that no one dare cross that line. When an employer wants a new worker, he hires that worker through the union. Hence, no one may enter this sacred land unless he be an initiated and admitted communicant.

In the language of collective bargaining, this arrangement is called the closed shop. It is different from the union shop of the factory or office-based union in one basic respect. In the latter, the worker need not be a member of the union before his hiring; in effect, the employer may hire whom he pleases. In the former case—the closed shop—the worker must be a union member before hiring; he is usually hired through the union hiring hall that controls its lists according to its own rules and regulations. In the case of the union shop, the job belongs to the individual worker; in the case of the closed shop, the jobs belong to the *collective* union.

The closed shop serves a double purpose. First, it gives the individual worker job security. When he finishes one job, he can report to his union hall, reasonably certain that if there is work in the trade, he will be on a new job shortly. He need not fear that the new job will be filled by some nonunion newcomer or by some craftsman of another union: the jurisdictional frontier will exclude all such marauders. Second, the closed shop permits the union to "space," to balance the number of workers in the craft and town with the number of available jobs, to keep labor supply and demand in equilibrium. By limiting admissions to the union and by reserving all jobs in its jurisdiction to members of the union only, the organization is able to see to it that the work population on this bit of occupational terrain does not become overcrowded. The concept of "spacing" whose virtues Darwin formulated for the preservation of the species, and Durkheim for the preservation of a society, and Drs. Ilg and Ames for the preservation of the family, is applied by the craft unions in the journeymen trades for the preservation of its occupational species. The union controls its own population explosion: it marks off its land and limits the inhabitants thereon.

In America, the closed shop has been illegal ever since the passage of the Taft-Hartley Law. It was made illegal after evidence that the union's power under the closed shop was often abused. To get a job, a man had to join the union; to join the union, a man often had to kick-back to the union chieftain. In possession of a realm, the king of the land used his power over entry to enrich himself.

Although the closed shop is illegal, it is not extinct. It continues to be the way of life where it always flourished. Employers turn to the union hiring hall for help. The union operates as always—complying with the law to the extent of entering the names of nonunion members on their rolls for job assignment. The modified system operates smoothly so long as jobs are plentiful and the hiring rolls can accommodate a couple of strays. Should the terrain get crowded, however, the "strangers" would soon find out whether they were "one of the boys" or not—without any official intervention of the union. Quiet "mobbing" would guarantee "spacing."

The union stoutly defends its jurisdictional borders, not only in bargaining with the boss but also when butting up against other unions. There is no better evidence that a union is a "little nation" than the jurisdictional war between two unions. Two unions will engage in bloody battle over a handful of jobs. In more recent times, these disputes are handled at a higher diplomatic level before the internal disputes courts of the AFL-CIO, in the manner of quarreling nations bringing their problem before the U.N.

Jurisdictional warfare is also political warfare. The union negotiates with the employer to define the bargaining unit, the territory over which the union shall have some say, fights off other unions that seek to invade this territory, and limits admissions to the territory. These are all traditional political acts. The union also levies taxes, as any organized society does. This tax is known as dues. And because the union is a "nation," it insists upon a compulsory tax. The compulsion is simple and direct: to be a union member, a worker must pay dues, otherwise he is not a member of the union and, under the "union shop" clause, is dropped from the job, is exiled from the "nation."

The union shop clause has been assailed repeatedly in America as *compulsory unionism*. In the early 1920s, American employers sought to abolish the union shop with their open shop campaign. In mid-century, the same effort was renewed through right-to-work laws making the union shop clause illegal in almost half the states. The central theme is that union membership should not be made a condition of work. Since federal law allows the separate states, under Section 14B of the Labor-Management Act, to pass right-to-work laws, the American labor movement has made repeal of 14B a top priority issue. In state after state, right-to-work laws have been subjects of state-wide referendums in legislative and gubernatorial elections. The issue is one of the oldest unresolved questions in labor-management relations.

The union shop is not equivalent with compulsory unionism. No worker in the United States is compelled to join a union, as workers are in some countries where the law makes it mandatory for any individual pursuing a given craft or trade to affiliate with an authorized union in that jurisdiction. The union shop clause makes it compulsory for a worker to join a union only if he holds employment in a plant and in a bargaining unit that is covered by a union shop contract. Put differently, when a worker wishes to live in the territory where the union contract prevails he must become a citizen of the union, including the payment of dues. The issue here is not financial, although it would be quite impossible for a union to operate efficiently without income. The issue is not even that of the "free-rider," the worker who gets the blessings of unionism without carrying the burden. The real issue is the nature of unions as natural societies within the greater society. As such, it is not possible for a union to exist without the union shop.

Modern unions give very modern reasons for the union shop. Under the Federal Labor-Management Act, the authorized union must represent all workers in the bargaining unit, must process all grievances, must service all employees whether they are members or not. Is it just, asks the union, for the organization to provide all these services to persons who refuse to pay the fare? In reply to this argument, some Congressmen propose to amend the federal law to exempt unions from representing or servicing nonmembers. The union would not have to care for these nonmembers and the latter, as a consequence, would not have to join the union. No union is likely to accept these terms, for then the word *union* is no different from the word *disunion*. A union if it is not a *oneness*—an exact translation of the word *union*—is nothing. A union that bargains for some in a craft, trade, or industry and not for others doing like work can only engage in noncollective bargaining, an inchoate horde confronting the well-ordered hosts of the overlord. The union is obliged to speak for one and all not simply by law but by the laws of its own being.

The modern union can also argue that the union shop is democratic, with majority rule in the shop community. This, indeed, comes much closer to the concept of the union as the worker government in the *polis* of the workplace. In this community rules are made, officers elected, and taxes levied. Membership and dues are as compulsory as is citizenship.

While all these arguments carry merit—no free-riders, union responsibilities under law, democratic decision in the workplace—they are of more recent vintage than the union shop, and the closed shop as well.

The roots of the union shop run back to ancient Greek and Roman practices: no man could practice the mystery unless he be an initiate in the proper family or corporation. The format is repeated in the guilds of medieval Europe. In colonial America, the iron law of the union shop recurs—sometimes in the most unlikely places. "It existed," notes Rev. Jerome L. Toner, "long before the great struggles concerning the 'open' and 'closed' shop began in the United States in 1903. It was present even before the American Revolution. In all probability, it animated the tailors in their strike of 1768 and the printers in their strike of 1778. When the rope-makers organized at Philadelphia in 1698, the closed shop principle may well have furnished the inspiration of their proclaimed motto: 'May the production of our trade be the neck-cloth of him who attempts to untwist the political rope of our Union.' It came to our shores with the settlers from Britain."[18]

In 1648, shoemakers and coopers were given authority by the Bay Colony to control their trade, "to make orders for the well governings of their company, in the managing of their trade and all the affaires thereunto belonging," and to summon before the court anyone who dared "to use the art or trade—not being approved." In 1675, a group of carpenters gave a nonmember a ride out of town on a rail. They argued in court that "he was an interloper and had never served his time in the trade of a Ship carpenter and now came to worke in theire yard and they understood such things were usuall in England." What was "usuall"

18. Rev. Jerome L. Toner, *The Closed Shop* (Washington, D.C.: American Council on Public Affairs, 1942), p. 6.

was not to have an interloper work but to have him "mobbed" out. In 1667, the carters of New York City petitioned the City for a contract that would give them, as it had given the weigh-house workers, the exclusive right to cart "in their actual present number and no more." This was a closed shop agreement with the municipal government, providing for a closed membership as well.[19]

The inevitable jurisdictional problem inherent in the union or closed shop concept is described by Toner from the *Minutes of the Mayor's Court,* December 1, 1674. "When, in 1674, the 'Corne Porters and the wyne Porters' protested against the em-ployment of laborers by brewers, bakers and other tradesmen to carry their products, a colonial court ordered the brewers to employ the vine porters 'to carry-out their Beere as formerly was accustomed and the Bakers are not to hyor or permitt any Corne to be carried up or brought downe in their Houses or Garretts, by any other persons than their owne Servants, or the Corne Porters.' "[20]

Although the spelling of the court's finding is ancient, the practice is modern. The origin of present usage is not to be found in imitation of the past but in a recurrence of the nature of unions.

In their study of British unionism in 1897, Sidney and Beatrice Webb spoke of the "silent and unseen, but absolutely complete compulsion of membership" which is "coeval with trade unionism itself."[21] This comment is all the more remarkable be-cause many British trade unions do not have a union or closed shop clause in their contracts. This is because in England, where class solidarity is far more traditional than in the highly mobile

19. *Ibid.,* p. 59.
20. *Ibid.,* p. 61.
21. Sidney and Beatrice Webb, *Industrial Democracy* (London, 1897), Vol. I, p. 214. Cited in Toner's little goldmine on the closed shop, p. 21.

America, custom makes a union shop clause unnecessary. "The enforcement of the closed shop in England," argues Toner, "does not depend upon its formal inclusion in the collective agreement. That is no more essential for the effectual execution of a cooperative closed shop understanding between employers and organized workers than is the writing of a constitution necessary for the political functioning of the English people."[22] In Britain, the union shop is part of their unwritten constitution in the work *polis*.

The union shop is really a union's way of establishing itself as a polity in the shop, with its political leaders, its defined policy, its own police force. The union shop is the government that rises on the foundation of recognition, seeking security for the worker as an individual and for the union as a corporate entity. The union shop is the formalization of the union as a political corporation.

Because the union shop is the personification of the worker presence in the plant, in the same way that a government is the personification of a nation, employer assault upon unionism strikes centrally at the union shop. To enfeeble a union in this sector is far more meaningful than to cut a wage or lengthen the work week, both of which are more likely to strengthen than weaken the union. In 1903, John E. Edgerton, President of the National Association of Manufacturers, stressed the key issue of the union shop. "It was not until . . . the annual convention of 1903," he recorded, "that formal cognizance was taken of the increasing aggressiveness of organized labor. At that convention our first labor principles were adopted, and the *open shop* was first proclaimed by a representative national body as the *sine qua non* of our industrial safety, advancement and supremacy."[23]

To Edgerton, the open shop was a *sine qua non* of industrial

22. *Ibid.*, p. 22.
23. Quoted by Toner, pp. 8–9.

existence; to Gompers, the union shop was a *sine qua non* of labor's existence. The clash over the issue is a continuing battle ground, a political struggle over who governs in that bit of territory known as the jurisdiction.

The evolving effort of unions to control the work domain in order to establish job security and to enforce the contract inevitably raises the question of management prerogatives. This goes far beyond the simple question of the employer's prerogatives over hiring, firing, lay-off, work distribution, plant removal, or production changes. To secure jobs and to enforce contracts, unions have written contracts to examine employers books, to regulate contracting, to establish the responsibility of one employer for another employer, to freeze work rules, and so on.

An instructive example of a union's need to extend its controls into traditional areas of management prerogative in order to put flesh and blood on the contractual skeleton is to be found in the dress industry in the United States. The union signs its key contract with the *jobber*, the king pin of the dress industry who designs, sells, finances, and puts together an integrated production process in which he also contracts out work to *contractors* who do the sewing and sometimes the cutting and pressing of the dress as well. The union negotiates a contract to protect the jobs and to advance the standards of the *employees* of this jobber. But who are his employees? Only five per cent of those engaged in the manufacture of his garments may be on his premises or directly on his payroll; the other ninety-five per cent may be employed by *contractors* and appear on the latter's payroll. Hence, to write a meaningful contract, the union stipulates conditions that apply to the *indirect* employees of the jobber. The contract provides that the jobber may not contract out work unless it be to a union shop, affiliated with the mother union, the International Ladies' Garment Workers' Union. The contract stipulates that the jobber shall pay to the contractor such sums as will permit the latter to live up to the union agreement. The jobber must register his contractors with the union, so that the union may check up on him to make certain that he is not using nonunion contractors and also that he is not offering work to twice as many contractors as he can supply just to turn them against each other to beat down prices. The union has the power to limit the number of contractors—to "space" the available work so that the contractor and his workers may earn a living. If a jobber needs additional contractors because his business has expanded, he must so notify the union and get the union's permission to add new contractors on either a temporary or a permanent basis. And finally, just to make certain that the jobber is not cheating on all these arrangements, the union has the right to examine the company books.

A jobber, of course, has reason to complain that he has lost his management prerogatives. He may *not* send his work to any contractor he pleases, to as many as he pleases, or even to consider such matters as purely privy. He must share this decision-making with the union. Because production in the dress industry is an integrated operation stretching from jobber to contractor, the union must confront the employer over the total terrain, writing an agreement that legislates for the process in a unified way. In doing so, the union inevitably revolutionizes the concept of "management prerogatives."

In four basic areas of collective bargaining then, the issue is not *what* but *who:* recognition, or *who* speaks for the workers; job security, or *who* owns the job; union shop, or *who* governs the work *polis*; management prerogatives, or *who* makes decisions in business areas that affect labor conditions. The *what* of the political process in the workplace, more commonly known, deals with wages, hours, holidays, vacations, and medical and retirement plans. Although secondary in the life of a union, these measurable matters get primary play. Nevertheless, under the

Lasswellian concept that politics addresses itself to the question of "who gets what," these tangible topics are also political in character.

The wage question, moreover, is more than a matter of money. There are employers who are quite prepared to pay their workers the union wage and *more*, but who will refuse to sign a contract with a union. What is involved here is not money but power. *Who* is the boss? To maintain his bosshood, an employer will in many instances pay more, in the same way that some workers will make endless sacrifice, including their own lives, to win union recognition. Power—meaning management prerogatives to the employer and union recognition to the worker—is to some more important than money.

The distribution of company income between employer and employees is so gross an act that it overshadows a much subtler political process; namely, the distribution of the income among the *crafts*. This intraspecific struggle among the workers in the plant, often members of the same union, goes almost unnoticed, not because it does not exist but because the pecking order of crafts is so established that it appears to be as just as it is inevitable. The intralabor conflict comes to public attention only on those rare occasions when a craft within an industrial union will suddenly strike out on its own, demanding special status, consideration, and contract provisions. When such a craft, usually the most skilled, differentiates itself from the mass union, it does so to win *recognition* for its *special group identity*—still another example of a group differentiating itself from the larger group.

When a union is first organized, although it may revolutionize all arrangements in the relations between employer and employees, it hardly ever, if ever, upsets the basic relations among the crafts. The top craft remains top and the bottom craft remains bottom. They may all move up; the gap from craft to craft may narrow; but the basic relationship remains and, if the gap between top and bottom gets too close, the top will *organize* and revolt. The craft status relationships go on undisturbed or, if disturbed, meet stiff resistance.

What is the reason for pre-union status levels, generally reinforced by union scales? In part, it is skill, although there are so many exceptions to this rule as to make the rule itself questionable. In part, it is scarcity, although very often such scarcity is artificially created by restricted apprenticeship, the traditional practice of a group protecting its status by maximum exclusion and minimum inclusion. Very largely, however, the standing of the craft is traditional, inheriting its aura or denigration from a long-forgotten past, preserved through pretense and prejudice. "With the division of labor and trades," comments Landtman in examining the origins of "inequality" in social classes, "varying degrees of social estimation are assigned to the different groups of workers. One craft is valued more highly than another, and in consequence, the man working at that craft enjoys greater consideration, while the contrary is the case with other trades. Although in this matter, personal conditions play an important part, certain crafts are intrinsically calculated to win esteem or to be but slightly regarded."[24]

Thus, work associated with pigs, butchery, or leather work are traditionally of low esteem. Work traditionally associated with women, such as sewing, cooking, and even agriculture in some civilizations is low on the scale. But the traditional male work—killing wild animals and strange men—is high. Those who practice the mental vocations predominate over those who are trapped in the manual pursuits. Those who derive income from nonwork stand above those who must work. Whatever the origins, there is a political protocol in the workplace (and the economy) as severe as that in an embassy. It is a political fact of life that no collective bargaining ever dare ignore.

In recent years, the problem of craft status has posed dif-

24. Landtman, *op. cit.*, p. 81.

ficult problems for several industrial unions that were busy practicing what they preached in terms of egalitarian democracy. One of these was the Transport Workers' Union in New York City whose leader, Michael Quill, over three decades had been engaged in raising the standards of the lowest earners in the union at a rate more rapid than that of the top earners. Porters were going up faster than motormen. Vexed by their loss of relative status, as well as by their grinding work in a lonely subway box, the proud motormen revolted: organized a separate society and ran a wildcat strike. The TWU had to grant them special status to hold on to them. The highly idealistic United Auto Workers ran into an almost identical situation with their skilled craftsmen, who demanded special consideration and noised threats of separate organization. Thus, within the political corporation of the union there are political corporations of the crafts. They are "little republics" within "little republics" engaged in endless conflict within the brotherhood for special standing, privileges, wages.

As in any political process there are in labor-management relations the inevitable moments of stark confrontation between union and employer. The two most common acts of dramatic conflict in the politics of the workplace are the picket line and crisis bargaining. Both seem to defy reason, especially after a union and an employer have lived through or lived down their original encounter.

The rationale for the picket line is usually presented in economic terms. The worker who has only one thing to sell in the free market—his labor—withholds his labor jointly with his co-workers. In union, they withdraw their vital product from the reach of their employer who must then bargain with them to come to terms. In pure economic language, this is simply a matter of supply and demand in which a strike is a way of shutting off the supply to jack up the price of the desired labor.

The strike, however, is more than the withholding of work. With it goes the picket line—an unusual political experience similar to the birth of a nation. On a picket line, workers who were solidified by their shop condition express their solidarity outside the shop. They leave their native hearth of factory or office. They sever the umbilical cord. They walk on strange ground, drawing courage for their act of daring from the presence of their brothers. To one another, they are proving that the tribe can survive way from the old sod and away from the old padrone provided it holds together. The worker who has walked the picket line—especially if it was bitter and bloody—never forgets. It was here he won his red badge of courage, his manhood.

In the birth of nations, the long march—the historic equivalent of the picket line—plays a symbolic, sometimes mythical, almost mystical role. There is Moses leading his people across the desert; Genghis Khan mastering a Mongol migration across two continents; many Mayflowers carrying the seeds of a nation across the ocean; and many covered wagons wheeling across mountains and prairies; the Acadians wandering from Canada to the Mississippi delta; A. Philip Randolph leading a march on Washington and Martin Luther King leading a march on Selma; Mexican farm workers serpenting their way across Texas; Mao Tse-tung marshalling the Eighth Route Army across the breadth of China.

A strike is more than a reasoned method to halt work, to stop scabs, or to display strength. Like a revolution for national independence, the strike transforms the people who walk the picket line. They become patriots, founders of a nation who established the borders of their own "land." After the "long march," the worker is not simply *in* the union; the union is *in* the worker. The strike is the politics of the workplace conducted at the level of a war, arousing all the moral cohesion and immoral hostility of open conflict.

Crisis bargaining offers all the emotional and social satisfactions of such warfare—often without the war itself. The expiration of a contract is a crucial moment in the life of a union and its members. It is the hour of trial: the testing of strength, the clash of values, the assertion of greater purpose. Such a confrontation has psychic as well as pecuniary content for the worker.

Rationally, whatever could be worked out at the last moment could have been worked out before. Emotionally, however, it is the crisis that provides the occasion for workers to show their independence, to fly their flag, to defy the old tyranny, to close ranks—to unleash the atavistic man in the cage of collective bargaining.

Long and close observers of certain collective bargaining sessions have recorded the similarities with a ritual dance: precise steps stomped out to primitive percussion. To the strange civilized eye, this ritual is without reasonable purpose, like the war dance of some elemental tribe. To the social psychologist, who has probed into man's aboriginal roots and the role of ritual in nourishing these roots, the contortions of crisis bargaining take on profound meaning: a sort of socialized way to play at war without going to war. Many a trade union leader who did not understand the role of properly choreographed crises in building a union has come to grief. He brought bread to a people who also craved bravado: the bread could fill their physical but not their spiritual hunger. The very fact that the dollar gains came so easily caused distrust. The members somehow felt cheated out of something. Actually, they were being cheated out of their primitive impulse for strife: to strut and to strike. Out of such frustration, the members turned to anger against their leader who failed to provide the primitive pleasures of the hunt.

The ritualization of conflict is a life-saver for any species. Without it, every specimen might devour his brother and neighbor. As Ardrey notes, in the lower orders such ritual is almost universal. Consider the case of the stickleback, a fish that in-

206

habits sandy bottoms. He stakes out his bit of territory for himself and his family. "When two male sticklebacks, proprietors of adjoining properties, get into a border uproar and pursue one another back and forth, now on one property, now on the other, to wind up facing each other at the invisible wall bubbling rage and frustrated fury, both will . . . up-end to a vertical position and while goggling at each other in loathing stand on their heads and dig holes in the sand." Or the case of the herring gulls who confront one another on a grassy turf. "There will be threats, and heads will be lifted high and wings readied for beating. Since they face each other not two feet apart yet both are still gripped by ferocity's storm, any observer will predict instant battle. But there will be no battle. Both gulls instead will suddenly, murderously, start pulling up grass."[25]

The ruff, the stickleback, the herring gull have their own ways of "blowing off steam," of "getting it out of their system," of ritualizing conflict. We call the ritual *politics*. In the politics of the work *polis*, it is called collective bargaining; its most creatively cathartic act is possibly the carefully controlled crisis.

Sometimes, the ritual runs riot. Men go to war, make violent revolution, strike and seize plants. The same happens in the lower orders. The creatures that usually respect one another's persons and properties, working out their hostilities in games of fight and flight, will devour one another if the space gets too cramped and crowded.

The degree of ritual in collective bargaining is a measure of its sophistication. In the early stages of unionism, the conflict is real—an interspecific war between two alien "nations," the workers versus the bosses. It is only with time that both labor and management discover their symbiotic dependence and instinctively begin to evolve a ritual of hot rhetoric and cool riot to define their mutual need.

For many unionists, this transition of the labor movement

25. Ardrey, *op. cit.*, pp. 87–88.

from class struggle to class collaboration is an unbearably painful trauma. To begin with the assumption that it is the prime mission of a union to work out an accommodation with the "system" is betrayal. To put the accommodation down on paper, to sign it as a contract that is enforceable in the courts is a double betrayal. And then, shame of shames, to work out a prearrangement with the employer and then to lead unsuspecting workers through a ritual war dance to win the prearranged demands is total proletarian depravity. Yet this stage of sophistication or cynicism in trade unionism is as logical as it is inevitable. Unless workers intend to oust the employer they must learn to live with him. In doing so, they must re-establish the unity that was disrupted with the first fight.

Again, let us revert to our recurrent theme about the nature of the political animal. In the beginning, man is a lump of an undifferentiated mass, of nature. Then he differentiates himself as man. This man lives in some tribe, within which he is again an undifferentiated being. "Tribal man is hardly a personal *self* in our modern sense of the word," concludes Harvey Cox in *The Secular City*. "He does not so much live in a tribe; the tribe lives in him."[26] In due time men differentiate themselves from the tribe (or nation) to form their "corporations" or "unions." But even as this process of differentiation goes forward it is paralleled by a process of unification. Man never severs the umbilical cord: the child eventually comes back to the parent. For instance, urban man runs away from the tyranny of nature, only to discover that in so doing he is poisoning the air, polluting the waters, choking the highways, shattering his identity. Man cries out that the "world is too much with us, late and soon, getting and spending, we lay waste our powers," and man prays that he may be "a pagan suckled in a creed outworn," that he might once more lay his feverish head on the cool breast of nature. Within a nation,

26. Harvey Cox, *The Secular City* (New York: Macmillan Company, 1965), p. 10.

there is a constantly proliferating division of work as each person seeks his own niche within the economy, establishing some private occupational preserve. And yet each becomes more dependent on the other and on the economy as a whole. Likewise within the company, trade, or industry, the union marks a differentiation, followed by a reunification which is formally expressed in the contract and in all the relatives surrounding the contract, such as collective bargaining.

The simple act of recognition is both differentiation and unification. The union is recognized as a differentiated body. But simultaneously, the employer is recognized as the party with the power to extend such recognition, an implicit unification of the union to the company. The relationships become more apparent when made analogous to corporation and state. The corporation is a private association, a differentiated entity, but as it seeks formal *recognition* from the state through a charter, it officially recognizes the authority of the society.

In its revolutionary hey-day, the Industrial Workers of the World refused to ask for union recognition "because it wanted no recognition from employers whose rights it refuses to recognize in the ownership or administration of wealth and its production."[27] Unions that seek recognition, unlike the IWW, do implicitly recognize the employer's rights, his title and power. Hence, recognition, extended by the employer and accepted by the union is a form of reunification; the acceptance of mutual interest provides a unity that recognizes diversity.

Job security, a second basic of union life, is also a two-sided phenomenon. The job becomes the "property" of the worker or the union—but only in a limited sense. If the employer goes out of business, the job is lost. Hence to hold on to the job, the workers and the union have an active interest in maintaining the employer, making certain that he does not go bankrupt.

The highly elaborate system of arbitration in industrial rela-

27. Marot, *op. cit.*, p. 122.

tions rests on the "dear enemy" entente between union and management. The mature union writes a contract that turns unresolved grievances over to a common court of appeals: the arbitrator. His decision is binding, precluding strikes and lockouts. He does more than keep the peace; he elaborates a body of law for the *polis* of the workplace. The acceptance of this "law" that stands above both parties—labor and management—is the kind of unspoken compact that holds diverse social orders together as political units.

The development of the fringe-benefit system is still another striking example of the unification of employer and worker through collective bargaining. What is now called fringe benefits were once called mutual aids, which worker associations set up to protect their members against the hazards of accident, death, and illness. For the earliest unions in America, these "mutual aids" were the most solid and continuing base of the organization. Even into the twentieth century there were giant unions, such as the railroad brotherhoods, where the insurance features were the most attractive aspect of the labor association. "The large membership of the brotherhoods," noted Helen Marot in 1914, "is unquestionably due to the insurance features of the organization, rather than to the collective bargaining or the 'protective feature,' as they call their trade agreements."[28] The old craft unions accumulated huge sums to assist members when out of work, in retirement, or ill. These funds were all contributed by the members and were for the members.

Some employers set up similar systems to care for their employees when in need. Such employer plans were strictly paternalistic—managed by the employers alone and generally financed by them alone. As often as not, such a paternalistic plan was a device to block unionization.

Today, the efforts of union and management to provide fringe

28. *Ibid.*, p. 34.

benefits are merged in almost every collective agreement in America. By contract, funds are established to provide a wide variety of benefits—optical care, medicine, hospitals, burials, retirement, supplementary unemployment benefits, maternity and even paternity payments. These are handled in one of two general ways. In some cases, the employer obligates himself by the agreement to provide or purchase the services. In other cases, a fund is established through employer contributions to act as the insurer or the purchaser of the insurance. On the board of such funds employer and union representatives sit as trustees jointly administering offices, listening to claims and appeals, writing rules and regulations, and, in a new development of finance capitalism, deciding how to invest their multi-billion dollar treasuries.

What was once the union's exclusive and sometimes only role as the community chest in the work *polis* or the employer's righteous paternalistic pride has now become the joint responsibility of both parties.

The most subtle tie between union and company can be found in the *structure* and *functioning* of unions. The worker-corporation invariably imitates the employer-corporation, both of them risen from a common matrix; namely, the nature of their sector of the economy. Local unions sufficed in a day when local businesses dominated the economy. But as corporations became national in nature, unions became national in nature. Whereas at one time in American labor the local central labor body—a federation of unions in some town or city—was the core of trade unionism, at a later time the national union became the operative center. In great oligopic industries, such as auto and steel, bargaining is done on a national basis because the ownership operates on a national basis. Each great owner has plants in many states operating as part of a great central design. Hence, the union writes a contract covering all these states with an agreement of relatively uniform design. In the garment industry, the vital center is New York; so the national headquarters of the union is in New York. The steel union is in Pittsburgh; the auto union in Detroit; the rubber workers in Akron. The teamsters had two headquarters: an official one in Washington, D.C., and an unofficial one in the central states conference of teamsters that lay astride all the major over-the-roads traffic from coast to coast.

In corporations that deal with many different unions, the unions have had to restructure, forming a council of unions to bargain with the employers. Similar councils have existed for many years in the building and printing trades. When American corporations, especially in the automotive industries, became international enterprises, the United Auto Workers took the first step to form an international conference of unions so that like might confront like.

One of the most curious examples of cross culturation between corporation and union took place in an industry it would be discreet not to name, except to say that it was heavily involved in getting government contracts. The top men in the company were politically minded gentlemen, who knew how to land contracts. On the supervisory staff were many lesser executives who were likewise highly political, having in many cases gained posts either because they were soulmates of the employer or playmates of other politicians. Since the contracts were negotiated on a cost plus percentage basis, the company felt little incentive to run an efficient plant: the greater the cost, the greater the profit. Within the union sector of the company, there grew up an army of full-time men to handle shop grievances. The company paid them for time lost and again the company did not object because the contract called for cost plus. These full-time stewards became full-time politicians, digging up grievances, walking the aisles, electioneering for office. For the proletarianized intellectual—the college graduate who had joined the ranks of the workers—this company was a paradise: a place to move masses of workers while liberated from the bench. The plant became a pulpit. Factions multiplied: socialists, Stalinists, Trot-skyites, Schachtmanites, Cannonites, and anti-ismites. The union child—fierce enemy of the company—was unwittingly imitating the hated parent.

The process of collective bargaining, like the union itself, is a political process in which the union differentiates itself from and then unites with the company. It is a marriage of two political corporations, engaged in the unending politics of the work *polis*.

8

Polis and Cosmopolis

▶ Among the several significant derivatives of the word *polis* is *cosmopolitan*, an adjective that refers to the greater city of man. Each man who lives in a *polis* (union, corporation, university, or hamlet) also lives in a cosmopolis. In modern societies, the cosmopolis is the nation. In the minds of some men, the cosmopolis is the world or even the universe.

Within the cosmopolis, organized forces are arrayed in conflict and coalition. When the force is one nation vis-à-vis another, the interaction is diplomacy, pacts, wars. When the force is one interest group versus another, the process is politics, which in a democracy is conducted through elections.

A union is the organized force of workers in the work *polis*. As such, it inevitably seeks to affect the policies of the cosmopolis —city, state, nation, and sometimes the world. This is the role of unions in politics.

The reason why unions go into politics might be derived from the following excerpt from *The Federalist:*

The most common and durable source of factions has been the various and unequal distribution of property. Those who hold and those who are without property have ever formed distinct interests in society. Those who are creditors and those who are debtors fall under a like discrimination. A landed interest, a manufacturing interest, a mercantile interest, a moneyed interest, with many lesser interests, grow up of necessity in civilized nations, and divide them into different classes, activated by different sentiments and views. The regulation of these various and interfering interests forms the principal task of modern legislation, and involves the spirit of party and faction in the necessary and ordinary operations of government.[1]

1. Alexander Hamilton, John Jay, and James Madison, *The Federalist*, No. X (Colonial Press, 1901), p. 46.

The authors of the Federalist Papers, although stressing the politics of economics, did not imagine that man is so narrow in his interest that there would not be any factions unless there were property differences. They had learned from history that men like to vex one another and, if they cannot fight over property, they will fight anyhow:

> The latent causes of faction are . . . sown in the *nature of man.*
> . . . A zeal for different opinions concerning religion, concerning government and many other points, as well of speculation as of practice; an attachment to different leaders ambitiously contending for preeminence and power, or to persons of other descriptions whose fortunes have been interesting to the human passions, have, in turn, divided mankind into parties, inflamed them with mutual animosities, and rendered them much more disposed to vex and oppress each other, than to cooperate for their common good. So strong is this propensity of mankind to fall into mutual animosities, that where no substantial occasion presents itself, the most frivolous and fanciful distinctions have been sufficient to kindle their unfriendly passions and excite their most violent conflicts.[2]

Why do men inevitably vex one another with their partisan wars? According to the Federalist view of human nature, man is fallible, egotistic, and the product of his *polis:*

> As long as the reason of man is fallible . . . different opinions will be formed. As long as the connection subsists between his reason and his self-love, his opinions and his passions will have a reciprocal influence on each other. . . . From the possession of different degrees and kinds of property . . . and the influence of these on the sentiments and views of the respective proprietors ensues a division of the society into different interests and parties.[3]

This unsentimental view of politics hardly squares with the pious maxims of public utterances. The high-minded statesman

2. *Ibid.*
3. *Ibid.*, p. 45.

prefers to "talk sense," with the faith that reason knows right from wrong. He counsels against a policy that is merely the passionate extension of his self-love. In the public interest he eschews the special interest. All this he does with minimal self-awareness that reason is the handmaid of the ego and the ego is the child of the *polis*.

For this reason, the tough-minded often look upon the high-minded as hypocrites, although they are not necessarily so. They are human, confusing good reasons with real reasons, the urge with the urgent, and the self with the society. They appear to be hypocrites precisely because they are moral men seeking to give eternal and general truth to their passing and parochial passion.

In a brilliant theologic critique of Karl Marx, Reinhold Niebuhr lays bare man's "inevitable dishonesty" in equating his *polis* with the *cosmos*, and his rationale with eternal truth:

[Marx contends] that men do seek the good but that they define the good in terms of their own interest. He thus recognizes, as no hedonist can, the profound paradox of human spirituality and morality: that the interests of the self cannot be followed if the self cannot obscure these interests behind a façade of general interest and universal values. This fact, which in Christian theology is regarded as the element of inevitable dishonesty in original sin, becomes in Marxism a tool of class conflict. It is used to transvalue the values of the dominant class and destroy their prestige. Marxism thus tentatively discovers and finally dissipates a value insight into human nature. It dissipates the insight because it fails to recognize that there is an ideological element in all human rational processes which reveals itself not only in the spirituality of the dominant bourgeois class, and not only in the rationalization of economic interest; but which expresses itself in all classes and uses every circumstance, geographic, economic and political, as an occasion for man's assertion of universal significance for his particular values. This defect in human life is too constitutional to be eliminated by a reorganization

216

of society; a fact which constitutes the basic refutation of the utopian dreams of Marxism.[4]

While Marx sought to enthrone the proletariat in order to remake the world in its (or Marx's) image, others have sought to enthrone other classes. Plato would have a republic run by the philosopher king; Massachusetts was run by the theocrat. Charles Wilson insisted that "what is good for General Motors is good for America." Each class elevates its finite understanding to eternal truth. It is this inherent contradiction that makes politics so mean and so moral: often the more moral, the meaner.

The concept of politics expressed in the Federalist Papers makes short shrift of self-righteousness. In recognizing the necessarily partisan and limited nature of political truth, it denies to any man or faction a monopoly over the business of politics. The Federalist view is inherently pluralistic, envisioning a society where diverse elements clash in an atmosphere of tolerance.

Labor is *one* of these plural forces. Within the labor movement there has been a running debate between the revolutionary and the reformer, between those who saw the proletariat as *the* force and those who saw the unions as *a* force, between the chiliast and the pragmatist. Before examining the nature of this debate and its outcome let us continue just one step further into the origins of pluralism—once more from the theologic approach.

In *The Secular City*, Harvey Cox provocatively uncovers the roots of a free society in a kind of triple revolution, in which man liberated himself from the divinity of (1) nature; (2) the state; (3) himself. Cox associates each of these breakthroughs with a section of the Old Testament: Genesis depicts a cosmogony that liberates man from the tyranny of nature; Exodus celebrates the revolt against the tyranny of the state; the Covenant on Mt. Sinai pledges man not to play God by setting up his own

4. Reinhold Niebuhr, *The Nature and Destiny of Man* (New York: Charles Scribner's Sons, 1964), Vol. I, p. 35.

tyranny. By positing one great God above nature, the state, and man, the Bible strips all earth things of their divine right to rule.

Two of the continuing concepts of this book and a third, which is a central theme of this chapter, might be viewed as parallel to these three phases of liberation. Earlier, we sketched man's laborious efforts to liberate himself from the tyranny of a Mother Nature. Yet for centuries after man learned he could effect changes in his physical environment, he continued to worship the sun, the moon, the stars, rocks, rills, cows, birds, and snakes. In Genesis, God makes it clear that he is placing the sun, moon and stars in the heavens to light man's way by day and by night, and that all living things on this earth are here to serve man—and not vice versa. The Biblical story of creation is, to use Cox's phrase, the "disenchantment of nature," the acceptance of Mother Nature as she is and not as some divine being.

We also sketched man's inevitable tendency to organize private associations within the state, to form political corporations within the total body politic, and to use these "little nations" within the "nation" to challenge the divine right of kings. In Exodus is related the story of a people who challenged the sacred character of the Pharaohs, a major historical event in what Cox calls the "desacralization of politics." He notes the parallel between man's liberation from nature and his liberation from the state. "Just as nature is perceived by tribal man both as a part of his family and as the locus of religious energy, so the political power structure is accepted as an extension of familial authority and as the unequivocal will of the gods. The identification of the political with the religious order, whether in a primitive tribe where the chief is also the sorcerer, or in the Roman Empire where the emperor is both political ruler and pontifex maximus, betrays the same sacral legitimization of political power."[5] Exodus represents a break-away from the sacred state. Cox describes the walk-out of the Hebrews as an act of "civil disobedience . . . an

5. Cox, *op. cit.,* p. 25.

act of insurrection against a duly constituted monarch, a pharaoh whose relationship to the sun god reconstituted his claim to political sovereignty."[6] In the long struggle to liberate himself from divine nature and the sacred state, man moves toward freedom in organized groups, through the *polis* and the political groups within the *polis*. These very groups, however, once they dethrone nature and the state from their heavenly seats, tend to capture the high chair for themselves as the self-appointed and self-anointed new gods for new times. Man (or, better, his tribe) fashions a fresh shiny deity—first familial and then universal— and demands obeisance before this man-made idol, the god created in man's image.

In the Ten Commandments, man is warned against fashioning such new gods, against making graven images to worship. If the idol is the "work of man's hands," then it is no more than the "collective representation" of man's values in a given place at a given time. Hence, it is forbidden that such a household god masquerade as the eternal ruler of the universe. This view, argues Cox, is "the recognition that since everyone's perspective is limited and conditioned, no one has the right to inflict his values on anyone else. In political terms, a certain degree of healthy relativism provides the philosophical basis for pluralism."[7] (And, it might be added, such pluralism provides the basic condition of a free society.) This relativism is named the "desanctification of values."

This triple liberation from the demons of the earth, the demon of the state, and the demon within leaves man in a lonely and burdened state. He is nailed to the cross of his own freedom: a crucifix he must shape and carry through his life until the hour the way of his life becomes the way of his death. Man's separation from authority is also his separation from his environmental beginnings. Consequently, he is seized by an anomie, a sense of

6. *Ibid.*, pp. 25–26.
7. *Ibid.*, p. 31.

desertion by his ancient parents. Man becomes alien to nature, society, and self.

In search of the lost values, man reaches out for the old certainties. He seeks to reunite himself with nature by walks in the country, by sun worship, by orgies, by philosophies or by suckling at some creed outworn. He recurrently demands an authoritarian state: a charismatic leader who will command the society to adhere to itself by obeying his will. Repeatedly, groups of men have seen in their momentary predilections the will of God—a manifest destiny—to govern the universe.

To return to Federalist Paper No. X, here was a document that argued for a coming together of the colonies in a tighter union, while simultaneously arguing the positive values of clashing concepts and plural politics. It sought a unity resting on diversity.

Teilhard de Chardin sees in this interplay between unification and differentiation, an eternal force of nature. "This dramatic and perpetual opposition between the one born of the many and the many constantly born of the one runs right through evolution."[8] In man's political behavior, this antithesis between the one and the many is repeatedly found in man's yearning for freedom and for organization, for autonomy and for authority.

In the long debate among American trade unionists on their relationship with politics (using the term to refer to participation in elections and legislation), the central problem has been how the one (the union) should relate to the many (the total society). Put differently, how a force in the *polis* should relate to the forces in the *cosmopolis*.

The dominant dialogue can best be described by stating the theoretical extremes. At one end have been those who believe that a union's function begins and ends in the workplace; at the other end have been those who believe that a union's mission begins

8. Pierre Teilhard de Chardin, *The Phenomenon of Man* (New York: Harper and Row, 1959), p. 111.

and ends in the total society. The former seeks to transform life in the work *polis* through shop reform; the latter seeks to transform the cosmopolis through social revolution. The former wants to stand *outside* the political system; the latter wants to *take over* the political reins. The one is parochial, partial, and economic; the other is catholic, total, and political.

These theoretical extremes hardly ever existed in practice in American trade unionism. In practice, the pure-and-simple business trade unionist with his prime focus on the shop or trade inevitably entered politics; likewise, the social reform unionist with his prime focus on politics inevitably became concerned with the shop and the trade. The great argument in the realm of action was not really about whether unions were purely economic or purely political, since all unions are by nature both, but about objectives, methods, and emphasis. The prime objective of the pure-and-simple unionist in politics was to protect the union's right to live and act; the method was nonpartisan pressure politics to reward friends and punish enemies, the emphasis was economic action first and political action second. The prime objective of the social unionist was a basic reorganization of the social system; the method was a political party of the working class; the emphasis was political first and economic second.

The dialogue continued for almost two centuries, until the last half of the twentieth century when a near consensus was reached. The pure-and-simple trade unionist has conceded that political action on behalf of broad social programs is necessary and desirable; the social unionist has conceded that reform of the present system has made "revolution" either unnecessary or postponable. The pure-and-simple trade unionist has agreed to establish a permanent organization of labor voters, a kind of nonformal "party," while the social unionist has agreed to use this nonparty, endorsing Democrats, Republicans, or others on a programmatic but nonpartisan basis. They have both agreed that as discrete *unions* they are compelled to give first heed to economic matters but that as a *labor movement* they should give prime time to political action.

What is it that moves unions into political action? The same factors that dominate the union's thinking when it engages in collective bargaining: recognition, job security, union shop, wages, hours, working conditions, fringe benefits. And just as the first two of these—recognition and job security—predominate at the bargaining table so, too, have they historically predominated in the legislative halls. Indeed, for most of the unions in the years before 1934, politics revolved around recognition and job security. These same unions actively *opposed* governmental action to enact minimum wage, maximum hour, unemployment insurance, social security, full employment laws. These latter categories were deemed the exclusive territory of the unions over which their private governments would preside. It was not until the Rooseveltian revolution that a majority of the unions carried their *economic* demands to Congress.

Among the first moves for legal recognition was a petition of New York City mechanics in 1785 asking the legislature for incorporation. At that time, incorporation meant social acceptance, a grant of special rights, a legal being—a formal and traditional way to get autonomy through authority. The Senate rejected the petition on the ground that it would give the mechanics "too much political importance." In retaliation, the mechanics turned to politics. They nominated their own "assembly ticket and in the following campaign elected all but two of their candidates—including a blacksmith and a shoemaker."[9]

In the first two decades of the nineteenth century, unions found their right to survive and to live as unions seriously challenged by the courts. In six cases, the cordwainers were charged with conspiracy and their existence or their methods declared outlaw.

In the Philadelphia case (1806) the court held that "a com-

9. Rayback, *op. cit.*, p. 61.

222

bination of workmen to raise their wages may be considered in a two-fold point of view; one is to benefit themselves; . . . the other is to injure those who do not join the society. The rule of law condemns both." This flat illegalization of a union's right to raise wages was furiously assailed by the shoemakers, by other worker associations, and, significantly, by the Jeffersonian press. The outcry was not without results. In the next case (New York, 1809) the court shifted its ground. It did not hold against the union because it was a combination to raise wages, but because it used methods "of a nature too arbitrary and coercive," that deprived their fellow citizens of rights "as precious as any they contend for."

In the Pittsburgh case (1815), the arbitrary and coercive means were spelled out. It was illegal to "confederate together to impoverish or prejudice a third person, or to do acts prejudicial to the community; . . . to compel an employer to hire certain descriptions of persons; . . . to prevent a man from freely exercising his trade in a particular place; . . . to compel men to become members of a particular society, or to contribute toward it; . . . to compel men to work at certain prices."[10]

In sum, by 1815 the court held that a union had the right to exist but could do none of the things it thought it had to do in order to live. The courts legalized a bald Samson.

The combined impact of these decisions and the depression after the War of 1812 wiped out existing unions: they enjoyed neither recognition nor job security. When in the 1820s unions revived, they were once more assailed by the courts as conspiracies. The most notable cases were the New York Hatters (1823), the Philadelphia Tailors (1827), and the Philadelphia Spinners (1829). In all these cases, the court found that the means employed by unions were those of an illegal conspiracy.

By the late 1820s, however, the American worker had picked up a new weapon: the right to vote. In the years after 1812, the

10. *Ibid.,* p. 57.

suffrage had been extended to include men with little or no property. With their economic right arm tied behind their back by the courts, the workers began to swing with their political left: the ballot.

In 1828, the Mechanics Union of Philadelphia reconstituted itself as the Republican Political Association of the Workingmen of the City of Philadelphia. (It must be remembered that the first "Republicans," the followers of Jefferson, were really the first "Democrats," the later followers of Jackson.) In 1829, a Workies Party was set up in New York. In a few short years similar parties sprang up in sixty-one cities. The ballot made its proletarian debut. These parties were given further push by the depression of late 1828. "Thousands of industrious mechanics who never before solicited alms were brought to the humiliating condition of applying for assistance," reported *The New York Times*.[11]

The Philadelphia party was the first labor party in the world: two decades before Marx wrote *The Communist Manifesto* and three generations before the British unions organized their Labor Party. The Philadelphia party and its sixty brother parties were not imitators of any European model; they came into being *ab origine*, from the nature of their political being.

These first workingmen's parties foreshadowed the problems and prospects of the larger later movement. In the 1820s, as later, the unions entered politics to win secure jobs and secure unions. In doing so, they devised broader social programs going beyond purely union needs. In shaping these programs, the movement developed many attitudes, from slowly evolutionary to rapidly revolutionary. In the pluralist culture of America, no matter how these movements started, they invariably came to the point of playing pressure politics.

The workingmen's parties came into being during a depres-

11. *Ibid.*, p. 67.

sion. This turn to politics in economic adversity was to become a model for the next century. When the business cycle dipped, the trade unions were also depressed. They could not prosper unless the hated boss prospered. Out of work, unions were out of luck: no boss to fight, no bargain to press, no help wanted. They turned to politics to remake the economy. This was to happen again in the 1840s, when labor turned to free land and flirted with utopian colonies. The Knights of Labor turned to educational politics largely in reaction to the repeated destruction of trade unions after the panics of 1859 and 1873. The great appeal of the socialists in the opening decades of the twentieth century rested on their conviction that the little depressions that were endemic to capitalism would one day become a cataclysmic crisis: hence political action was the only answer. When American labor finally went political in a serious way after the great crisis (1929 to 1934), the central reason was "recovery" and then full employment.

"Full employment" is really little more than a societal paraphrase for "job security." Political action to secure full employment is as natural as economic action to secure the job. There is one great difference, however. To understand how a ballot makes for greater employment is somewhat more difficult than to understand how a union contract provides fixed employment for an individual. Job security written into a contract is simple, direct, and personal; full employment obtained through legislation is complex, indirect, and impersonal. The former appeals to immediate self-interest; the latter to ultimate enlightened self-interest. But, since enlightenment requires experience and education, it comes more slowly than the instinctive reaction, in the same way that civilization trails slowly after primordial response.

Even when labor does turn to politics to protect the job, its instinctive reaction is to fasten on to some narrow simplistic device, born out of immediate circumstances and momentary experience. For instance, the workingmen's parties of the 1820s and 1830s made much of outlawing convict labor. A contractor could hire prisoners at a very low wage.

In the same vein, to make their jobs more secure, the Typographical Society objected at the beginning of the nineteenth century to the hire of "two-thirders," workmen who had not completed their apprenticeship and who worked below scale. In subsequent years, unions sought legislation on apprenticeship and licensing.

Unions sought to bar women from their trades. The female was a job competitor whose presence was bad for male morale and for female morals. A committee of the National Trades' Union in 1836 reported: "The physical organization, the natural responsibilities and the moral sensibility of woman, prove conclusively that her labors should be of a domestic nature." With such noble sentiments and pompous prose did self-respecting workingmen protect their jobs against the sweet marauder.

Unions instinctively moved against foreign competition: import of foreign goods and foreign labor. Both were threats to employment and job security. In the mid-1830s, the cordwainers passed a resolution against importation of foreign boots and shoes as destructive to the interests of journeymen engaged in their manufacture at home.[12] In later years, during the hey-day of protectionism, high tariff Republicans were repeatedly successful in their appeals to workingmen to vote for import barriers. As early as 1802, the typographical unions of New York and Philadelphia petitioned for an increased duty on books from abroad. A century and a half later, some of America's most progressive unions in textiles and clothing were petitioning for restrictions on foreign imports of competing products.

Even more fierce has been the opposition of many unions, especially the oldest and best established, to import of contract labor and to immigration in general. The reason was very clear

12. Taft, *op. cit.*, p. 29.

to unionists in the early nineteenth century: employers who barred foreign goods to boost their profits were busy importing foreign labor to beat down wages. Unionists looked on immigration—especially in the form of contract labor—as an antilabor instrument.

The Know-Nothing Party, with its nativist appeal, proved attractive to many workingmen. The Order of United Americans proposed to protect its members against immigrant competition. Where simple protectionism ended and prejudice began among the nativists is hard to say, for where a nation closes ranks against the foe, the will to live and the need to hate often become one.

On the West Coast, unions demanded laws excluding Chinese. In the old South, unions simply excluded Negroes. And in the years after World War I, the AFL placed the pennant of immigration restriction at the top of its political flagpole.

These are all examples, some of them shockingly antisocial by mid-twentieth century standards, of unions turning to legislation to "secure the job." Labor's full employment program of the post-New Deal years—with its concept of a constantly expanding economy to provide more and more jobs for more and more people—is a sophisticated version of a primitive urge for steady work.

A second objective of early unions was political action to win recognition: the legal right to live and to *act alive*. By ballot, they hoped to change courts and law to turn an illegal "conspiracy" into a legal association.

From the 1820s to the 1960s, American unions have been repeatedly propelled into political action to defend their institutional integrity, their scope of action. In the first decade of the twentieth century, Samuel Gompers led the AFL on a political course to save the unions from the Sherman Act. In 1947, the same AFL created its first permanent political organization—Labor's League for Political Education—to save organized labor from the Taft-Hartley Act. During the decade of the 1960s, in one state after another, labor was aroused to intense political action to battle state right-to-work laws. These were all campaigns to win legal recognition for labor's right to unionize and to function effectively as a union.

In a curiously ironic way, the early political crusade for legalization of labor unions became enmeshed with another one of the Workies' first demands: the prohibition of chartered monopolies. Over many decades, unions joined politically in popular movements to "bust the trusts," to break the monopolies. They cheered Andrew Jackson because he assailed the banks. They joined hands with the Greenback and Anti-Monopoly Parties. They sympathized with the Populist assault on "bigness." And, finally, these enemies of the business Goliaths were successful: Congress passed the Sherman Anti-Trust Act. But, irony of ironies, within a few short years, the courts turned the Act against the unions, charging that combinations of working people were conspiracies in restraint of trade. When the Danbury Hatters' Union tried to boycott the nonunion product of one of their employers, the union was found guilty of violating the Antitrust Act and fines were imposed on the union, its officers and its members. Labor was about to be hoisted on its own petard. The antimonopolists were to be executed as monopolists, a grim bit of poetic injustice.

The AFL took action:

[The Sherman Anti-Trust Act] as now interpreted and applied, constitutes the most serious menace to the labor movement. That law, which was intended to benefit human beings, to prevent or check monopoly and absolute control over the products of labor and of the soil, to assure to the people the necessities of life at reasonable prices, has proved useless in establishing control or regulation over the trusts and monopolies. In a spirit of ironic glee these same monopolies, trusts, and corporations, unharmed by the law which was to have regulated them, now turn this law against the human beings who were to have been protected. Is the conscience of the American people so dead, is their sense of justice so dormant, that they will tolerate that horses, wheat, hay, sugar, hogs shall be placed on equality before the law with human beings?[13]

To amend the Act—to win recognition for unions as associations of persons and not aggregates of pigs—Samuel Gompers led a crusade to certify that labor was not a commodity. This desired declaration was inscribed in the Clayton Act, which specified in Section 6 that "the labor of a human being is not a commodity or article of commerce."

Nothing contained in the antitrust laws shall be construed to forbid the existence or operation of labor . . . organizations, instituted for the purposes of mutual help, and not having capital stock or conducted for profits, or to forbid or restrain individual members of such organizations from lawfully carrying out the legitimate objects thereof; nor shall such organizations, or the members thereof, be held or construed to be illegal combinations or conspiracies in restraint of trade under the antitrust laws.

Section 20 of the same Act barred the issuance of federal court injunctions prohibiting activities such as strikes, boycotts, or picketing "in any case between an employer and employees, or between employers and employees, or between employees, or between persons employed and persons seeking employment, involving, or growing out of, a dispute concerning terms or conditions of employment."

Although this exemption of unions from the Sherman Anti-Trust Act appeared to be all-inclusive, it was not comprehensive enough. In the *Duplex* and *Bedford Cut Stone* cases, the court found that forms of secondary boycott were illegal. To restore to the Clayton Act the full force of its original intent, Congress

13. Samuel Gompers, Newsletter, January 10, 1914, cited by Marot, *op. cit.*, pp. 167–168.

passed the Norris-La Guardia Act in 1932, defining a labor dispute as "any controversy concerning terms or conditions of employment . . . *regardless of whether or not the disputants stand in the proximate relations of employer and employee.*" (Italics added)

Labor's real Magna Charta, however, was still to come in the form of Section 7a of the NRA (National Recovery Act). Here workers were told that they could have unions of their own choosing and employers were told that they were under legal obligation to bargain with such unions. Unions had finally won the true legal recognition they had sought—but not for long.

In 1947, the National Labor Relations Act was amended through provisions sponsored by Senator Taft and Congressman Hartley to remove some of the exemptions unions had won under the Clayton Act. In addition, the Taft-Hartley Act moved quite consciously to tip the scales toward employers on the theory that the unions had grown too powerful. In response to the new law, stigmatized by the AFL as a "slave labor Act," the AFL set up its Labor's League for Political Education. Into the LLPE came unions that had, in the past, either rejected political action at the Federal level as a matter of principle or had ignored such action in practice. The passage of further "restrictive" amendments in the 1950s (Landrum-Griffin Act) and the enactment of state right-to-work laws further spurred unions into politics—the politics of survival.

The new wave of unionism among government employees revived debate on union rights. In the Spring of 1967, firemen in New York City prepared to strike. Why not? If transit employees, social workers, teachers, doctors, and dentists could strike, then why not members of the Uniformed Firemen's Association? Who shall decide that question? The answer, of course, is the government. But in a democracy, who is the government? The answer is the people, including the fearless firemen and the

230

hundreds of thousands of other city employees and their fellow unionists and their families.

In short, the question of what rights the government employees shall enjoy is a *political* question, battled in the political arena, with the civil service unions prominently a participant.

The New York mechanics who went into politics in 1785 to fight for "incorporation" and New York firemen who went into politics in 1967 are of the same genre. They are fighting for their "rights." In both cases, there are those who believe that these *rights* are *wrongs*, that to "incorporate" the mechanics would give them "too much political importance," to yield to the threat of a firemen's strike is to invite a tyranny of the uniformed services. In theory, the debate becomes a matter of right and wrong. In reality, the outcome is almost always an inevitable compromise between need of the *polis* (in this case, the firemen) for freedom and the need of the cosmopolis (in this case, the metropolis) for organization. Boundaries are drawn to mark off areas of regulated freedom—a formula whose success depends on the readiness of the free to accept regulation and of the regulators to tolerate freedom.

Job security and recognition are political expressions of typical trade union demands from 1785 to 1965. Labor politics, however, has always included other planks of a nonunion character. Typical of such proposals among Workie parties of the 1820s were abolition of the militia system, a mechanic's lien law, no imprisonment for debt, and universal free public education. The reasons for these planks were obvious at the time. Under the militia, everyone had to appear at drills, with fines for those unable to come. The rich paid the fines with pleasure; the poor paid their fines with pain or served. A mechanic's lien law was needed to protect employees whose employer would hold back pay for weeks or months and then go bankrupt. The employees wanted to be privileged creditors. Imprisonment for debt made poverty a crime. Universal education meant learning for better earning and fuller citizenship.

No one of these demands arises from the *institutional* needs of unions as unions. They arise from the class needs of workers as workers, as individuals with a common caste and complaint in the society. Such demands come to the fore when unionists meet in assemblies greater than their local union—as in central bodies, political parties, or federation conventions. In the shop, workers "talk shop." In the big conclaves, they "talk big." Hence, whenever labor goes into politics, it inevitably discovers its *class*—as well as *craft*—character.

In an old dialogue on whether unionists are craft or class conscious, there has been a constant emphasis on the one versus the other. In fact, unionists are both: sharing with their fellow craftsmen what is common to the craft and sharing with their fellow workers what is common to the class. What they do not have in common, they do not share. This is most apparent at the political level, where unionists have for nearly two centuries in America been pushing for legislation that is craft *and* class based, that is both institutional and personal, self-centered and socially oriented.

Craft-based legislation has been one of the oldest products of labor politics, embedded in decades of state statutes. Although each item looks like a petty pebble alongside the great boulders of America's legislative landmarks, the accumulated body of "craft" law is mountainous. Its variety is as great as its details are minute: to require catch platforms on the netting of all multiple-tiered buildings; to require protective netting and lifeboats under bridges; to require bidders on public contracts to have safety programs; to require first aid stations on the job; to put headlights on locomotives; to put frost glasses on locomotives and heating in the vestibules of street cars; to outlaw power-activated tools in certain jobs or spray guns in others; to put blowers on polishing machines; to specify the width of pipe or the thickness of railings.[14]

In contrast with these craft-conceived measures are the broader societal programs common to broader political movements of labor. Thus, for instance, in the three decades after 1936, the political program of the American unions called for ever higher Federal minimum wages, a body of legislation applicable chiefly to workers who were not members of any unions; for expanded coverage of the minimum wage law, applicable almost exclusively to nonmembers; for a social security system that began by providing pensions for those over 65 and was then expanded to provide pensions to those disabled at any age, survivor's insurance to spouse and children, hospital care for the aged, medical care for the indigent; for civil rights legislation; for consumer protection; for low-income housing; for quality integrated education; for a full employment act; for progressive income taxes; for antipoverty legislation in the form of Job Corps, Teachers' Corps, Vista, vocational training, area rehabilitation.

The programs of the first workingmen's parties were far less ambitious, but at that time they looked very big, with the goal no less than *equality*. If the rich could escape the militia, why not the poor? If the money-lenders could rescue some dollars from a bankruptcy, why not the workers, who needed the few dollars more than the bankers did? If the rich did not go to jail for impoverishing the poor, why should the poor go to jail because they could not repay the rich? Above all—and this was the crux of the matter—why should not the children of the poor know how to read and to write so that they, like their overlords, might get good jobs and run for public office. Democracy in learning became the high road to an economic and political democracy.

The idea of equality came easily in 1830, not because it was present but because it was promised. The memory of the Ameri-

14. For a fuller account, see Tyler, *The Labor Resolution*, pp. 60–61.

can Revolution was still fresh: no man had the divine right to rule the land or the workplace. All men are created free and equal. "The objects we have in view," said one of the Workie parties, "are hallowed by the sympathy of patriotism—it is the finish of the glorious work of the Revolution."[15] The French Revolution in 1789 and a Second French Revolution in 1830 rekindled the American dream. A Chartist movement in Britain in the 1830s and continental revolutions in 1848 fanned the fire. From 1776 to 1876, new layers of the American population caught the spark to make our relatively short history the story of a permanent and unfinished revolution.

Although the meager program of the early workingmen's parties hardly looks like the expression of an ideology, it was the ideology of the Declaration of Independence spoken in the language of pidgin politics. Over several generations, this language developed a lexicon, a grammar, and a rhetoric. It developed words like insurance, rights, coverage, security, and community. It developed structured thoughts to put these separate "legislative" words into meaningful sentences that added up to societal programs. It adapted a rhetoric that rang with Square Deal, New Deal, Fair Deal, New Frontier, Great Society. This is the way an ideology grows—haltingly, painfully, unwittingly—among the nonideologues of the work *polis*.

Ideologies, however, attract ideologues—even when the ideology is not put in so many words—especially if the ideologues are authors in search of actors. Hence, many men of ideas have been drawn to the American labor movement, sometimes from afar and sometimes from the ranks. Such ideologues play a double and contradictory role. They unify by verbalizing the unspoken and conceptualizing the common, but they also divide by creating doctrinal differences of no immediate meaning. They elevate and inspire by seeing beyond today to the more distant horizon and

15. Philip S. Foner, *History of the Labor Movement in the United States* (New York: International Publishers, 1947), Vol. I, p. 127.

by giving labor a sense of mission. But they also depress and narrow by using the ultimate goal to denigrate the present gain and by turning away from external action to internal debate. Caught in this paradox, the effective ideologue in labor politics must learn the political role—to become a man of many seasons who knows when it is time to stand like a rock, to roll like a log, to sow the seeds of revolution, and to harvest the fruits of reform.

In the first workingmen's parties there were ideologues: Frances Wright, Robert Owen, George Henry Evans, and Thomas Skidmore. To them, the Workies Party was an instrument not merely to patch up a piece of society but to remake the society. Of these, the most colorful was Fanny Wright—feminist, abolitionist, politico, educator, gadfly, libertarian, and libertine. She abhorred the corsets of society, preferring to wear life like a loose raiment. In the rising labor movement of the 1830s, she saw the elemental explosion that would liberate. She saw in the unions "the only large mass among the heterogeneous fragments of society" whose interests "more nearly approached to the great natural interests of man, and incline, therefore, more immediately to wholesale reforms and general union."[16]

Almost two decades before *The Communist Manifesto*, she penned a piece for the *Free Enquirer* (November 27, 1830) from which Karl Marx may well have plagiarized: "What distinguished the present from every other struggle in which the human race has been engaged is that the present is, evidently, openly and acknowledgedly, a war of class, and that this was is universal. . . . It is labor rising up against idleness, industry against money; justice against law and privilege."

The revolutionary tone of Fanny's writing resounded through the proclamations of the other leaders of the workingmen's party, one of the most articulate of whom was Thomas Skidmore, a self-educated machinist who in his spare time wrote a book entitled, *The Rights of Man to Property: Being a Proposition to*

16. Frances Wright, *Address to the Industrious Classes.*

*Make it Equal among the Adults of the Present Generations; and
to Provide for Its Equal Transmission to Every Individual of
Each Succeeding Generation, on Arriving at the Age of Maturity.*
The Skidmore Plan—popularly called agrarianism—called for
every young man on his twenty-first birthday to get 160 acres
of land, which he could hold forever so long as he worked it. He
could not sell it or rent it. Men who held huge estates would not
be able to pass their holdings on beyond death. The property
would be seized by the state and distributed according to the
160-acre formula. Thus, at the end of one generation, property
inequality would be ended. The proposal was utterly rational,
possibly too rational for the human animal. In Skidmore's perfect
society, there would be no discrimination because of race, religion, or sex.

This levelling proposal of Skidmore's caused the Workies
considerable embarrassment politically. Enemies of the party
seized upon this thoroughgoing bit of egalitarianism to charge
the Workies with seeking to destroy every proper pillar of social
order. Within the party arose a demand to drop agrarianism from
the platform. Skidmore argued that without his plank the platform would lose its main meaning, since all the other points—
debtor's prison, militia calls, convict labor, and so on—were petty
and passing. Intent on his panacea, he broke with his confreres;
organized his own Poor Man's Party, set up his own paper, the
Friend of Equal Rights, and went to work attacking the Workies
Party. The idealist had become a moralist; the mass leader had
become a sectarian. "Whatever be his motives," wrote the *Daily
Sentinel,* "he is doing what in him lies to divide our party. . . .
If he were suborned by the aristocratical party, and kept in their
pay for the express purpose of sowing dissension where nothing
but dissension can produce defeat . . . he could not do their
bidding more effectively than he does now."[17] In differing with
Skidmore, Robert Owen, another of the party intellectuals, warned

17. Foner, *op. cit.,* p. 135.

2 3 6

that "reform ought never to travel faster than the public mind."

Within one year, however, the same Robert Owen joined with Fanny Wright and led a movement to split the party again. Their plan was to set up a system of free universal education (to which the party did not object) under state guardianship (to which the party did object). Under the guardianship plan, "children would be taken from their parents at an early age and placed in state boarding schools until they reached maturity. They would wear the same clothing, experience the same treatment, and be taught in the same branches of learning. There would be no room for religious instruction; only knowledge based on the experience of the senses would be in the curriculum." To protect the children against the corruptions of the parental past, parents would have limited visiting rights.

Guardianship, like agrarianism, looked most rational: it was an early device to solve mid-twentieth century problems, a way to liberate the poor from the web of poverty and the rich from the prejudices of pride, and to put them all into quality integrated education in an objective egalitarian system. This brainchild of the Goddess of Reason almost destroyed the Workies. The enemy press charged the party with atheism and family destruction. Within the party, there was a demand to withdraw guardianship from the platform. Owen insisted that his idea was "the grand design of our party. With this Great Measure, we will stand or fall."[18] The party fell!

Wright and Owen, like Skidmore before them, lost faith in the narrow-minded workers who did not recognize the messiah when he came. Although the prophets of guardianship were kindly, knowledgeable folk who had liberated themselves from the divinity of potentates and priests, they were unable to liberate themselves from the deification of their own notions.

Having failed to create the perfect society in New York through the Working Man's Party, Owen decided to continue his

18. *Ibid.*, p. 138.

social experiment elsewhere. He became leader in the movement to establish utopian colonies in America. This great dream of model communities built on American soil by people of good will caught up many: St. Simon, François Fourier, Horace Greeley, Albert Brisbane, Nathaniel Hawthorne. Land was available; good will was plentiful; and ideas were abundant. But the movement failed. To start his colonies, Owen was able to get many people out of society, but he was quite unable to get society out of the people. They could bid goodbye to the old sod but not to the old ego nor the cultures in which their ego had evolved.

The most realistic of the intellectuals in the first working-man's party, it turned out, was George Henry Evans, who had edited the *Working Man's Advocate* and *The Man*. In the mid-1830s, he left his editing work because of poor health to live in upstate New York. After recuperation, he returned to the pen to advocate land reform. His simple plan was to distribute the public domain to people who would work it. In these new areas, settlers would establish Rural Republican Townships, where each producer would double as farmer-artisan, and would exchange his wares in direct barter with his neighbors. The movement into these new lands would relieve the pressure in the cities. Many would settle on the public domain to start a new and better life. Those left in the cities as workers would command a better wage because of the labor scarcity. The entire nation would be richer, happier, and freer as the lands of the West were made available to the people.

The Evans' plan was an interesting mixture of Skidmore's agrarianism, Owen's utopianism, and a pure-and-simple trade unionism that appreciated the value of "spacing." By redistributing the working population Evans found a simple and natural way to redistribute the wealth. His movement found its practical application in the Homestead Act, a quiet revolution that laid the foundations for a free American yeomanry.

In Evans' own mind, his proposal was to solve both the economic and political problems of America: an answer to the still incipient sickness of the cities. He worked out a timetable for perfection. By 1850, general prosperity would prevail and peoples from all over the world would pour into America; by 1860, wages would leap upwards and city rents would fall; by 1870, no man or woman in the United States would "beg leave to toil"; by 1880, free soil Republics would spring up all over South America and Europe; by 1890, almost every family in America would own its own home and employment would be plentiful; by 1900, Evans prophesied, "the United States is now a Nation of Freeholders. The doctrine of the Declaration of 1776 is fully recognized and practiced. . . . Men wonder why their fathers tolerated Land Monopoly . . . and whether the Millenium has arrived."[19]

By 1900, of course, America was crossing the great divide from rural to urban civilization and the problems of city living that had repelled and inspired Evans in the 1840s were now becoming national problems. Sensitive souls looked back on antebellum America, debating whether that had not been the Millennium.

In the many decades and many debates following the first workingmen's parties there have been many plans for the basic and radical reorganization of the social order. To the end of the century, the "great designs" were all based on the assumption that "God gave the land to the people." In the tradition of Skidmore and Evans and the Homesteaders, Henry George continued with his single-tax proposal to end human exploitation by taking the profits out of land ownership. The George movement was the last dying gasp of the land-based revolutionaries, the prophets raised in a rural America.

To millions of Americans, Henry George was much more than the author of the single-tax idea. His book *Progress and*

19. Cited by Foner, *ibid.*, p. 186.

Poverty (1879) was read by hordes of laborers who had never before looked between the two covers of an economic book. He was a brilliant lecturer, prolific writer, and good politician; he was popular with religious Irish Democrats, atheistic German Socialists, and reform-minded Protestant Republicans. In 1886, he ran for Mayor of New York City with labor backing and polled 31 per cent of the vote; the winner polled 41 per cent; the man who ran third with 27 per cent of the vote was a Republican, Theodore Roosevelt. George insisted, perhaps accurately, that he had been counted out.

Not all those who backed George believed in single-tax; especially was this true of the socialists. They did not believe in his program; but they did believe in the *movement*. They favored independent political action by the masses of workers, and if Henry George was the way to get the masses moving, then the socialists would join in with enthusiasm.

The unions were propelled into this campaign by much more than George. Like the unionists of the late 1820s, they were enraged by a court decision that placed the life of unions in jeopardy. It all started in the saloon of George Theiss that provided music with its beer. The musician's union lost a strike and declared a boycott; the waiter's union joined in; the Central Labor Union made the boycott general. The case came to court, where the District Attorney demanded that "this boycott business . . . be annihilated and stopped." The jury, limited in its panel to men of property worth at least $250, found the defendants guilty and sentenced them to State Prison at hard labor. As in 1828, and again in 1947, labor turned to the ballot box as its best court of appeal.

The George campaign was a *movement*. The unions stood behind him solidly. Both Samuel Gompers, for the AFL, and Terence Powderly, for the K of L, endorsed George, albeit reluctantly. The *Irish World* and the *Yiddische Volkszeitung* backed him. It was toward this movement that the socialists responded, while rejecting the George program.

Viewing the campaign from afar and after it was over, Friedrich Engels, close coworker of Karl Marx, set forth the socialist attitude toward movements: "That the first program of this party is still confused and extremely deficient, that it has raised the banner of Henry George, these are unavoidable evils but also merely transitory ones. The masses must have time and opportunity to develop, and they can have the opportunity only when they have a movement of their own—no matter in what form so long as it is their own movement—in which they are driven further by their own mistakes and learn through their mistakes."[20]

To Engels, the program of the party and the structure of the party were purely matters of form and therefore of passing and secondary importance. The enduring content was the *movement* itself, the coming together of workers for political action in a broadly class conscious direction. The dogma was secondary; the deed was primary. The end goal was of less importance than the immediate action.

This emphasis on the movement made it possible for American socialists, who had their own concept of the proper social order, to make greater direct contributions to the evolution of the American trade unions than many of the other structured ideologies. The Marxist idea that one step forward in the movement is more important than a hundred programs made it possible for the socialists to participate in unions whose philosophy they disagreed with and in political movements whose means and ends they disagreed with. Their faith in the movement saved them from alienation.

Among the many doctrinal debates of American radicals none has been more decisive than the argument over relations with trade unions. In the campaign of 1886, while the socialists were

20. Letter to F. A. Sorge, three weeks after the election of 1886.

backing Henry George, the anarchists denounced the move. "A man who desires to bring about an improvement," they said, "must proclaim the overthrow of all existing laws, and not promise to carry them out as George has done. . . . Only look at the gang who are supporting him: social quacks, K. of L., Trade Unionists, school teachers, priests."[21] The anarchists would settle for nothing less than total anarchy in the society—and in the movement.

The debate between those who placed *movement* first and those who placed *program* first broke out again before the end of the century between the followers of Daniel De Leon and his opponents. De Leon was a lecturer in international law at Columbia University. After joining the Socialist Labor Party in 1890 he took the leadership by storm, armed with a brilliant and biting tongue and pen, endless energy, and unbridled will. He believed in socialism intensely—and in nothing else. The work of the trade unions was a colossal fake. They could win little for workers (compared with the fruits of socialism) and what they could get could only dampen the workers' zeal for the cooperative commonwealth. Being something of a pragmatist, De Leon conceded the need for unions, but only his kind of unions. He called on his followers to set up a new federation, the Socialist Trade and Labor Alliance, whose affiliates would be pledged to his brand of socialism. At some future appropriate time, Congress would declare socialism officially established and would adjourn permanently and the unions—that is, De Leon's unions—would take over the economy and run it through an industrial parliament.

De Leon's sectarianism split the party; he continued to hold the official name of the party (Socialist Labor Party), and his opponents set up a new party (The Social Democratic Party). Within a few short years, it became apparent that De Leon held

21. Foner, *op. cit.*, p. 120.

the form and the Social-Democrats held the content. The SLP turned into a withered fossil; the Social-Democrats (later transformed into the Socialist Party) gained members, took over leadership in unions, captured municipal governments, elected state legislators and congressmen.

After the First World War, a new schism appeared in the American Socialist Party between Communists and Socialists. Although the division was brought on by the Bolshevik Revolution, the hidden and subtle difference between the "left" and "right" was less the question of attitude toward the Bolsheviks or toward violent revolution than the matter of man's role—particularly the workingman's role—in the society. The real debate was over democracy and dictatorship. It was a debate that had to proceed out of theory before the world had been exposed to the one-man rule of Joseph Stalin.

To the Communists, the road to power was clear. The proletariat would take over power and establish its dictatorship, shattering all existing governmental forms and resting its rule on its own structure—the soviet. Within the proletarian dictatorship, leadership would go to the Communist Party as the only party truly representing the faith. Within the party, power would be centralized not only within one country but internationally with head and headquarters in the Soviet Union—the fatherland of the proletariat.

To Socialists, the road to power was much muddier. They had many paths to socialism: consumer cooperatives, producer cooperatives, municipal ownership, nationalization. They favored formation of Socialist Parties, Labor Parties, Farmer Labor Parties, People's Parties. Above all else, however, they favored democracy —minority rights and majority rule.

In a decade, the Communists, like De Leon, set up their own trade union federation in the United States (Trade Union Unity League) affiliated with the Red International of Labor Unions.

The Socialist Party continued to work in the drab, dull, senescent AFL.

This review of the factional struggles within the American radical community, especially as they related to unions, is an oversimplification of a complex development. But at its roots was the problem of relativism versus absolutism, of pluralism versus totalitarianism: a difference in theologic and political concepts.

The Socialist Party opted for relativism and pluralism, which made it possible for them to accept the traditional forms of the American labor movement and American politics while infusing both with some of the content of socialist programs.

Although the Socialist Party was shattered during World War I and never recovered, the influence of the Socialist ideology has continued into the present. The Socialists argued that it was the responsibility of government to play a creative and central role in the economy. While the Socialists would have turned over all the major means of production, distribution, and exchange to the co-operative commonwealth, a much more limited use of the govern-mental power in the economy has become a reality of American life. The Socialists set forth detailed programs for the here and now, advocating old-age, health, and unemployment insurance, minimum-wage and maximum-hour legislation, abolition of child labor—most of which have since become law. The Socialists believed that both their immediate and ultimate goals could be obtained through use of the ballot by education of the voter. Socialists counted on the wage earner, through his union, to be the mass base of the movement toward an industrial and social democracy. Socialists insisted that a political party should have character, that it should be an expression of ideology committed to enact and enforce a platform rather than a loose collection of individual politicians and political machines. Above all else, the Socialists believed that they were moving with history, that their agitators were the chosen people, that any sacrifice of self would ultimately be rewarded in the realization of the good society. This last conviction among Socialists produced doers—dedicated, selfless, indefatigable, and self-assured—decade after decade and generation after generation. Socialist influence, which started as a separate stream of action and ideas in the last half of the nineteenth century, became a current in the political mainstream by the middle of the twentieth.[22]

The pas de deux between socialists and trade unionists in America resembles a ballet in which two dancers arise from the same spot, dash to opposite corners of the stage, and ultimately reunite after many gyrations of approach and rejection. Both socialists and trade unionists arose from the milieu of the industrial proletariat in revolt against the brutalities of capitalism. The socialists, however, rose against the *system*, whereas the trade unionists rose against the *boss*. For the socialists, the area of action was the social order, the cosmopolis; to the trade unionists, the area was the "jurisdiction," the work polis. Socialists talked about the cooperative commonwealth; trade unionists about the contract. Socialists concentrated on the voting line; trade unionists on the picket line. Yet, despite these deep differences, socialists and pure-and-simple trade unionists in America merged, arriving at similar conclusions through opposite approaches.

Socialist ideology rests on an inherent duality: a simultaneous commitment to *collectivism* and to *individualism*. Structurally, socialists believe in collectivism; ethically, they believe in individualism. The model of a socialist society calls for collective ownership; the ideal of a socialist society calls for individual freedom.

Modern Communist Parties have seized upon the collectivist aspect of socialism to impose dictatorships on millions of people. The Socialist Parties have rejected the Communist solution because it denies the freedom of the individual. Laissez-faire capitalism proposed to build a society on rugged individualism, with minimal social ownership, regulation, or restraint. Socialists reject this capitalist solution because it allows individuals and corporations to exploit workers who compose the great mass of society.

22. Tyler, *The Labor Revolution*, p. 34.

The socialist paradox is man's oldest dilemma: freedom versus organization, autonomy versus authority, individualism versus collectivism. Because socialists find themselves totally committed to both sides, they generally end up with a middle mood that eschews absolutes. Hence, socialist practice in America has been less involved with ultimate goal than movement, less with dogma and more with deed. This "secular" attitude made it possible for the American Socialist Party to reach a *modus vivendi* with the trade unions and a *modus operandi* within the political system.

The pure-and-simple trade unionists were caught in the same dilemma. By nature, the union local is individualist in outlook. Unions wish to stand on their own feet, unregulated by government, unaided by socioeconomic legislation, uninvolved with big "isms" and national political parties. Unions in America prefer to be autonomous. But, despite themselves, they ultimately develop a societal point of view. In a complex society, the unions cannot be an island unto themselves. They turn to politics, to government, for the bigger solutions of the bigger problems with which the small local cannot grapple.

The presence of the socialist ideologue in American labor undoubtedly hastened the political maturation of trade unionism in the United States, providing articulation for actions, legislation for needs, electoral know-how for politics. The pas de deux between the unionist and the intellectual has not come to an end, however. The early separations of Frances Wright, Robert Owen, and Thomas Skidmore from the workers are repeated regularly. For most radical intellectuals, the unions are too parochial and prurient. For most unionists, the intelligentsia is too opinionated and puritan. The conflict between the two is recurrent.

To a sophisticated sector of American unionism and intellectual progressivism the solution for this conflict lies in a liberal-labor coalition. The concept of coalition politics is a continuing theme in American politics. It is foreshadowed in the Federalist Papers, with its assumption of majority governments arising from minority interests. The first national coalition took form in the Presidential election of 1800, when the Tidewater planter Jefferson composed an alliance with his backwoods Virginians and then with New York's Tammany Hall to win his way into the White House. The coalition was realigned in the formation of the Republican Party, a complex and contradictory coalescence of Wall Street financiers and Midwest farmers, Know-Nothing Wasps and newly liberated Negroes, grasping robber barons and exploited proletarians. The present "lib-lab" alliance was shaped in the complicated Rooseveltian years as a coalition of Southern Democrats, aspiring Negroes, Protestant reformers, Catholic politicians, Jewish radicals, industrialists, unionists, Columbia University intellectuals, and Jersey City ward leaders.

The way of American labor in politics has been the way of coalition—even when labor has had its own independent party. Again, the Workingmen's Parties of 1828–1830 are the seminal model. The Philadelphia Party, in its very first campaign, named a mixed ticket, composed of men running on the Workingmen's Party line alone and of Federalists and Jacksonians who were also endorsed by the Workies. In the election of 1829, the Workies named full slates in city and county, seeking Jacksonian and Federalist endorsements in both areas. In New York City and elsewhere, the party of the workingmen pursued a similar course, using its independent strength to bargain for coalition candidates. Sometimes, the Workies endorsed Jacksonians or Federalists; sometimes, Jacksonians or Federalists endorsed Workies; sometimes, they clashed head on in tricornered battles. The basic strategy remained unchanged: to promote the workingmen's program by playing a balance-of-power game.

When the American Labor Party of New York was formed more than one hundred years later, it pursued exactly the same tactic. This party, founded in the mid-1930s, was composed of socialists, communists, and progressive trade unionists who wished to give their backing to the New Deal Democrat, Franklin D.

Roosevelt, for President; the ALP became the device to do so, a means to merge in a coalition. The same ALP gave its support to the reform-minded Republican, Fiorello La Guardia, for Mayor of New York City. In short, the Labor Party sought effective coalitions with either Democrats or Republicans, in addition to running its own candidates. When the Liberal Party was organized in New York in 1944 (as successor to the ALP) it continued the strategy of coalition, backing Republicans such as Newbold Morris, Democrats such as Robert Wagner, and its own Liberal Party candidate, Rudolph Halley, for Mayor in various years.

Throughout most of the history of unions in American politics, labor has not operated through any party at all. The traditional policy has been nonpartisan: "Reward friends and punish enemies." Since the New Deal, when unions developed a continuing concern about social legislation enacted at the Federal level, American labor has put together a standing political machine that acts as an independent force without being an independent party. Its formal origin is in the CIO's PAC (Congress of Industrial Organizations—Political Action Committee) formed in the early '40s, in the AFL Labor's League for Political Education formed in the late '40s, and in the merger of these two into the AFL-CIO Committee on Political Education (COPE) in 1956.

This nonpartisan strategy is not peculiar to labor in America. Every pressure group has used the same method, backing candidates who are friendly and opposing candidates who are inimical, regardless of party. The method has been used by women suffragettes, corporations, farmers, doctors, Negroes, Catholics, antivivisectionists, and prohibitionists. The idea is to organize a bloc of votes into a club to exert pressure. Instead of organizing separate and multiple parties, Americans organize pressure groups.

American parties have responded to these pressures by adapting their programs to popular demand. In this way, both the Jacksonians and the Federalists swallowed up the Workies; the Republicans ingested the free-soilers; the Democrats merged with the Populists; the post-Rooseveltian Democrats devoured the Socialists. The two great national parties—the Democrats since Jackson and the Republicans since Lincoln—have shown a remarkably omnivorous appetite for gobbling up new programs and powers.

As a consequence, both our great parties are coalitions of conflicting and complementary social forces. They both seek to mirror the entire nation with mixed success. Within each party may be found the liberals and conservatives, the isolationists and internationalists, the intolerant and tolerant, the rich and the poor, the plebians and the patricians. While neither party is dedicated to the classless society, each is committed to the classless party.

American party structure reflects this lack of definite ideology. The national committees of both parties are powerless, without standing in law since the parties are legal entities only at the state level and not at the federal, without power to discipline elected officials, without any consistent programmatic commitment. The great nominating conventions are a feudal council, with each state bringing its special view and with different views within delegations from the same state. The Presidential nominee represents a majority of the delegates but his platform is not binding on candidates for Congress who will run on the same ticket. The nominee for a seat in the House of Representatives or the Senate is under no obligation to follow the line of his national party, since he owes his nomination and election to the people in his district or his state and not to the national convention or committee. Once elected, he may act as a liberal or conservative, a communist or fascist, without any fear of the "party" so long as the active voters in his bailiwick give him the nomination in the primary and victory on Election Day.

This system of choosing candidates either directly or indirectly through the primary has, for many decades, been a structural guarantee that the national parties would be, as they are, loose congeries of local personalities, organizations, pressure groups, needs, and ideas. This is in sharp contrast to the European parties that rest on some set ideology based on some definable social class.

Tactically, unions in the United States see in the American system three distinct opportunities to influence the selection and election of a candidate. First, the unions can bargain collectively with parties to have a friendly candidate nominated. Second, unions can enter primaries to win the nomination for a candidate. Third, unions can give their endorsement to a candidate in the final election.

Behind this tactic is the perennial push of the unions to form a more consistent voting bloc out of their members. To do so, the unions formulate broad political programs, as broad as those of any political party. Labor then tries to get its members to back these programs with their money and their votes. Unions then keep the score on candidates for office so that members may measure the candidate by the record, test promise against performance.

The labor vote, however, cannot by itself elect any significant number of candidates in the United States. At no time have unions represented more than 30 per cent of the labor force. Furthermore, not all union members can be expected to vote as the union proposes, nor can all unions be expected to agree on platform or candidates. Hence, unions enter coalitions on behalf of candidates or programs. The longest continuing coalition of labor in twentieth century America has been a political alliance with the liberal intellectuals, the programmers of the New Deal, Fair Deal, New Frontier, Great Society. The unions also find themselves in various standing alliances, such as that expressed in the Civil Liberties Clearing House or the Civil Rights Leadership Conference. Labor lobbyists and voters also find themselves in alliance with forces advocating rural electrification, cooperatives, public power, consumer protection, low income housing, improved education, and so on. The basic strategy of labor politics is to form coalitions around candidates and concepts on an *ad hoc* basis—but not to form a separate party.

The nonexistence of a significant labor, socialist, or communist party in the United States is seen by many European working class leaders as evidence that the American unions are politically either impotent or immature. They assume that if there is no independent *party* there is no independent *force*. They read the American legend through European glasses.

The difference between European and American political forms arises from the differences between historic experiences. European parties, by and large, are tightly disciplined organizations, wed to a fairly well-defined ideology, resting on some recognizable social grouping. The party begins with the social class, whose struggle against other social classes in the society probably pre-dates the right to vote. Indeed, the right to vote is commonly the product of some democratic revolution. The parties that arise after the "liberation" reflect the social divisions of the nation—divisions that remain fixed and frozen even in some of the most democratic and enlightened nations of the Old World.

The American experience, on the other hand, has been marked by a mobility and a diversity that made it almost impossible to construct well-knit political parties resting on fixed social classes. Social lines in America have been continually smeared and blurred, even if not erased. There are classes in America, but individuals and families are constantly moving across class lines. They also move from one geographic area to another. Out of this going and coming from here to there and from down to up have arisen a multiplicity of social groups and organizations with a constantly shifting membership. To compose majorities of these many minorities requires coalition parties.

Despite the differences between the European and American party systems, there is a hidden resemblance. In the European nations with multiparty systems it is not uncommon for no party to win a straight majority. In order to govern, the parties form a coalition in the parliament on which to rest a cabinet. This is the form of coalition politics in Europe. In the United States, the two major parties form their coalition at the national nominating conventions where candidates for President and Vice President are chosen by delegates representing a multiplicity of views. This coalition—whether it be the Democratic or Republican Party—agrees on the national leader before the election. The difference, then, between European and American methods lies in the fact that in the Old World the coalition is formed *after* the election and in the United States the coalition is formed *before* the election.

It is significant that the orthodox socialist parties of Europe rejected the concept of coalition governments as a form of treacherous class collaboration with the bourgeoisie. For a Marxist to enter a cabinet with the hated class enemy was anathema. Yet, today, there is hardly a Marxist party in Europe, including and especially the Communists, that does not think in terms of coalition cabinets.

The reason for the *volte face* in the thinking of European socialism lies in the changed status of the European working class. So long as the proletariat was an alienated class in the economy—vegetating in economic misery, ruthlessly oppressed, without a voice in either industry or government—the parties of labor viewed the entire state apparatus as an instrument of the ruling class. But, once the European worker began to rise in living standards, in human rights, in political prestige, he wished to share in the governance of the society, to enter the cabinet, to make a coalition.

The American worker, on the contrary, developed a sense of belonging to the society at a much earlier time. Wages were relatively high. Economic, social, and geographical mobility liberated the laborer from his caste. The right to vote came early. American labor parties came generations before like parties in Europe. Indeed, they were effectively in existence *before* either the Democratic or Republican parties were formal national organizations and, therefore, had to be reckoned with from the beginning. As a consequence of this inclusion of the worker in American civilization, the concept of a separate class party of the proletariat has never taken deep root in the United States. But the idea of an independent force, acting in alliance with other social forces, did take hold at a very early time and, in a changing variety and mix of forms, continues to be the dominant way of labor in American politics.

The labor movement itself, by its accomplishments in American society, has contributed to this integration of the worker into the civilization. Unions have abated hunger among the poor and tamed arrogance among the rich. As a consequence, social strife has not been so heated as to dissolve the social fabric. The unions have pushed universal free education. As a consequence, each generation is more literate, more hopeful, and more able to attain a measure of its hope. Mounting literacy has made better producers and, more relevantly here, better citizens. Participation in both extended education and "politicking" has been increased by labor's drive for leisure, whether it be the shorter work day or the shorter work life. The growth of unions has regularized industrial relations through contracts, arbitration, grievance procedures, and so on. As a consequence, conflict is channeled through due process rather than exploded through guerrilla war. The end result is a labor movement that does not act as a force *outside* the civilization, impatiently waiting for the ultimate crisis, but as a contributing element *within* the civilization, working to avoid a crisis.

While the politics of American labor is a form of *differentiation* from the American society, since the unions are an independent bloc, the same political action is a form of *integration* with the society, since labor operates within the coalition concept of the civilization. Where unions feel alien to the society, they do tend to pull out of or stay away from the traditional political system in the United States. The Industrial Workers of the World, for instance, easily adopted anarchist views on the nature of politics. The only kind of "politics" they ever accepted was direct action, a hopefully constructive destructiveness by which the ruling class would be terrorized into good behavior or swift abdication. The early Socialists, although they opposed anarchist nihilism in politics, viewed both the Democratic and Republican Parties as the arms of the bourgeoisie and created a separate party outside the coalition system. This party was most successful in the pre-Wilsonian period when neither of the two national parties had yet developed a program that had any appeal for the numerous class of industrial workers that had been burgeoning since the end of the Civil War. The Socialists, however, were unable to maintain a mass party in the post-Wilson and, especially, in the post-Roosevelt era. The great mass of workers, acting politically through trade unions, opted for social integration rather than separation.

The development of American trade unions and American society, then, does not augur a proletariat party intent on taking class power to institute a classless society—or some other Erehwon. Indeed, the evolution has been to the contrary. Labor in politics is itself an internal coalition, with various unions emphasizing varying planks, with action loosely federated. This labor coalition acts in alliance with other liberal forces, on tenuous and tentative bases. This broader coalition finds alliances with political men and machines in nonpartisan and nonlasting compacts. The programs that issue from such combinations arise more from the dynamics of the coalition than from the dogma of the class.

Because the trade unions in politics follow the coalition concept, they have unconsciously adopted the philosophy of *political pluralism* and *ideologic relativism*. Pluralism is imbedded in their daily deeds. The AFL-CIO is, first of all, a *federation* that assumes an internal heterogeneity. The labor-liberal coalition is based on the realization that a progressive-minded majority must be composed of diverse minorities. In brief, federation and coalition preposit a politics of pluralism.

By the same token, their pluralism rests on an acceptance of ideologic relativism. Within the AFL-CIO, different unions have different political commitments because they live in different places. Where they stand depends on where they sit. Within the labor-liberal coalition, various elements have their own agenda of priorities—each according to his own light.

American labor has come to these views in the way of most mass movements: by experience. Where labor has tried politically to "go it alone," it has suffered defeats. Hence labor seeks the common ground to unite itself and to unite it with other social forces.

It is in this process that trade unions, like other political corporations, develop a *conscience*. The definition of this much abused word is generally limited to an inner rectitude arising within an individual in conflict with the forces of evil around him. Actually, the conscience is born in the collective and not in the person. The individual internalizes the concept of the community, its rights and wrongs; its commandments become his compulsions. The very word *conscience* means knowing together, a reference to the shared tradition, taboos, or teachings of the group.

In a pluralist society, the individual can be plural, the carrier of more than one conscience. As a union man, he may share the conscience of his labor community—a conscience derived from the *polis* of the work place; its exigencies and its edicts. As part of a labor federation, he may have a broader conscience—a class conscience that may, on occasion, conflict with the narrow conscience of craft or personal interest. As a participant in a broader political coalition, he may develop an even broader conscience as he ponders the more inclusive problems of the total society. In sum, coalition broadens not only contacts but also conscience.

The role of labor in American politics evidences the inevitability of political corporations imitating the political society. The point is dramatized in the comparative politics of Russian, British, and American workers.

Pre-Revolutionary Russia was a Czarist tyranny within which trade unions lived only a semilegal existence. When the Bolsheviks took over they did so with a party dedicated to dictatorship of the proletariat. The result was the downfall of Czarism and suppression of trade unions.

Britain raised its workers under a constitutional monarchy, resting on popular rule, with a vigorous trade union movement based on a society with traditionally fixed classes lacking real mobility. When the British Labor Party took power, it continued the traditions: it did not depose the King or Queen; it did not abolish democracy; it did not abolish classes; it had to contend with a vigorous trade union movement.

In the United States, workers were raised in a pluralist democracy that eschewed class parties and class power even while a multiplicity of classes sought power through coalitions around parties. As the union twig was bent, so grew the tree of labor politics in America.

In his theological discourse on man's relationship with his community, Cox sees in relativism the "desanctification of values." No man's invention is divine law. Human values are, at best, human valuations.

By an inevitable political irony, the extended participation of trade unions in the national electoral process carries with it such a "desanctification of values." In the limited *polis* of the workplace, unions develop simple values born out of the elemental struggle of worker against boss. Where the struggle is fierce and emotional, there arise movements with absolutist goals of a messianic character. Lifted to the political plane, such goals are nothing short of cataclysmic revolution, usually resulting in the death of the old values and the birth of new ones. But, as unions reach into the general political process as an enfranchised group, seeking alliances, winning reforms, they invariably discover other views with which they seek accommodations and which they affect.

9

The Dilemmas of Leadership

The union leader, like the priest in Sumer, is part of a class—a class within the "little republic" called a union. His *polis* is the organization; his occupation is leadership. He performs his job through the exercise of many mysteries: bargaining skills, organizing talent, oratory, threats, favors, pretentions, and imagery. Indeed, his resemblance to the original priesthood is striking: leader of a city-state arisen from the economic wilderness, he exerts spiritual, economic, and political power.

The fact that union leaders are elected and are removed does not make this "priestly college" less a class. While in office, the labor leader, like a man on any job, is part of an occupational category, in the same way as a congressman or a college president. In static societies, position is inherited; in democratic societies, position is earned. But those who hold a common post and posture belong to a common category, at least while they are in that particular niche.

This does not mean that a labor leader is a different kind of animal from his rank-and-filers, anymore than a congressman is a different kind of creature from his constituents. Elected officials in both cases arise from their like. But once they have risen, they must learn a new role as leaders in a structured culture of the governing elite.

In an earlier chapter on the universality of unions, we described traits that are typical of an occupational organization, of the political corporation. It is our contention that labor leadership is a political entity in the same way that a union is. To delineate the anatomy of labor leadership, let us begin with an application of these universal tests.

First, all members of the college have a common occupation. This is patently applicable to union leaders, of whom a high percentage hold the same or a similar post for most of their days after their first elevation. The object of the profession is governance of the union; its practitioners are the governors. They associate with one another, develop a common attitude, think of themselves as men with certain prerogatives and responsibilities, wielding power and commanding fealty and respect.

Second, they are organized into a polity, a highly structured group. Protocol in most unions is as precise as in church, state, business corporation, or university. The pecking order is scrupulously followed in the listing of speakers, on official stationery, in platform seating, in salutations, in posing for pictures, in the greeting of dignitaries, and, above all, in the fixing of fault and the taking of credit. Many constitutions specify how long a man must serve at a lower level before he may advance to a higher level. Salaries reflect status, as do expense accounts, cars, carpeting, and office space. The status is so much a part of the office that it is also transferred to wives of office holders, as in army or university.

Third, the college controls admission to its own ranks, imposing long apprenticeships, vows of loyalty, careful screening. It is not easy to become a union leader, especially where both the union and the leadership are well established. An aspirant is expected to prove that he is worthy as evidenced by waiting, fealty, discipline, service. As in any political structure, this may be modified by nepotism, favoritism, internal pressures, ethnic considerations, or the demands of an opposition. Leaders groom successors, often in twos and threes to make sure that the succession shall not be too logical. The unauthorized attempt of any group to oust the "ins" is treated as heresy, as lese majesty or an assault on "the union." The monopoly can be broken, as it is repeatedly, but only by invitation or insurrection.

Fourth, the college seeks monopoly control over its calling. Union constitutions spell out discrete powers. A shop steward may do so much and no more; a delegate or agent may do other things but may not do everything. The union manager or president has still other powers. These various jurisdictions apply to the running of the union and to the relations with employers. Should any outside group step in to play the role of any of the authorized parties, such interference would be resented and halted. Indeed, even when the government seeks to intervene—to regulate the internal life of the union, to compel a contract settlement, to review grievance handling—labor leadership is reflexively resentful. The government of unions is considered the domain of the union, that is, of its duly authorized spokesmen. Outsiders are to stay outside.

Fifth, the college develops an economic point of view and a means to assure steady income from the office. Since the union treasury is the source of income, union leaders seek adequate coffers. The union shop and maintenance-of-membership clauses are helpful in supplying an even and fairly predictable flow of funds. The "check off" regularizes collection. While some leaders prefer high salaries and other leaders preach poverty, in the final analysis they must all be concerned with dues and investments to obtain a livelihood, in the same way that a pastor caring for his flock, no matter his dedication to the other world, must somehow find a way to live in this one.

Sixth, the internal relations of the college are evolved in a complicated political game. Union leaders are children of the Medici and Tammany, the smoke-filled room and the convention hall, the street brawl and the Byzantine court. The Machiavellian maneuvers of union leaders as they hug and tug, compete and combine are on a par with those in church, state, business corporations, and academia. The game is further complicated by the active presence of "the people," whose assent or dissent may be the crucial force.

Seventh, the college reaches out for political power in the larger society outside the precinct of the faithful tithepaying parishioners. A local leader will reach out for influence in his national union; then, he will try to make his presence known in the federation; and then he will enter the political game in city, state and nation—acting either for himself, his "boys," or his membership. If he develops some social ideology, he will also envision himself as acting on behalf of all mankind.

The formation of a union elite is but another chapter in the endless story of cultures within cultures. *Homo sapiens*, the political animal, forms tribes and nations. Within these societies, *homo faber*, man the tool maker and tool user, forms occupational groups, of which one type is the labor union. The union engages in political struggles within the *polis* of the workplace and in the cosmopolis of nation and world. And, finally, within the union, *homo politicus*, the very special politically minded man, forms an elite.

Man's eternal tendency to differentiate does not run contrary to an equally lengthy history of integration. Paradoxically, the two trends reinforce each other. When *homo sapiens* differentiates himself from nature by the formation of civilized societies, he does not sever his relations with his physical environment, although he is no longer totally at the mercy of nature's whim. He can now begin to shape nature to meet man's needs. He is no longer the helpless object of his surroundings but is now a conscious force in affecting the outer world, able to play a role as an actively integrated element in the cosmos. Similarly, when workers form a union, they differentiate themselves from the complex called the company. But they do not sever relations with the company. The union rescues workers from merely being the object of the company's whims. Now workers can affect their surroundings, by assuming a distinct role in the integrated work *polis*. And when unions enter politics as an independent force they differentiate themselves from the other competing and coalescing political elements. But this does not mean that the unions sever their relations with the political process. Indeed, quite the reverse: the participation of unions in politics is an act of integration, of participatory citizenship. When an elite arises in a union as a differentiated entity, this leadership does not sever itself from the membership. The elite becomes more closely integrated with the body of duespayers. An individual rank-and-filer is normally and instinctively inclined to think in terms of his or her immediate situation: the particular shop, job, or pay envelope. Vision tends to be circumscribed by circumstance. But, when this same man leaves the work bench and seats himself at the union desk, he is compelled to think more broadly, to generalize about his role and identity. As rank-and-filer, he thinks personally; as union officer, he thinks institutionally. His vision is widened by his wider world. The leadership becomes the formalized instrument for *integrating* the union—in the same way that the President and Congress of the United States become the structured means for *integrating* the will and way of fifty states.

In the formation of an elite, the form emerges from the amorphous. Labor leadership is not structured from the day a union is born. The first days are chaotic; then out of the chaos comes contour—in this case, the union hierarchy. The early hours of a union, like the first waking hours of most social movements, are characterized by uninhibited action, undefined ideologies, and untested leadership. Whether the movement is the birth of a nation (like the United States), or of a federation (like the CIO), or of an ethnic assertion (like the civil rights uprising), the awakening is tumultuous. In this crucible, leadership is refined through a process of natural selection.

The uninhibited action of unions in their first days is the instinctive reflex of the young as they flex their muscles. The "old man" must be denounced; old gods smashed; old tyrants toppled. "No more tradition's chains shall bind us, we have been nought, we shall be all." To this eternal conflict between the makers of tomorrow and those of yesterday—whether it be a class, generational, national or ethnic struggle—must be added the impact of the accumulated resentments of the liberation armies who have been gathering their wrath as a bursting reservoir gathers angry waters. Although not all the grievances are real, in the absence of some legitimized device for ventilation, every complaint becomes a case compounded into a cause. When the dam breaks under pressure, the flood of feeling rushes fiercely. Bastille is stormed; guillotine is erected; and there is dancing in the streets under the heady wine of new-found freedom.

Constant companion of such rebellion is violence—as in the American Revolution of 1776, the railroad strikes of 1877, or the racial riots of 1967. Such violence is rarely one-sided. The desire of the "new" to run loose is matched by the determination of the "old" not to let loose. The past denies the present, whether it be by Hessians holding flintlocks, Pinkertons firing sawed-off shotguns, or sheriffs poking cattle prods. To those who have governed long in their own image what is at stake is not simply self and pelf, but a way of life, a cultural complex, a "religion." Likewise, to those who have long been governed, the struggle is more than an animal urge for "more"; it is an assertion of manhood, of a new self-image. The combat becomes a moral confrontation— and the more moral it appears to the combatants, the more immoral and uninhibited are the forms of struggle.

Out of the cauldron of uninhibited action are distilled both good and bad—and leaders who are either or both. Class conflict creates dedicated unionists who have passed through the baptism of fire, gathering psychic toughness to match their physical scars. For decades, these veterans of the class war will recall their finest hour of courage, repeating the story in embroidered detail to inspire some generations, to bore other generations, but always to recollect the self-image of the moral man who suffered for the cause. The ancient deed makes for lasting dedication.

In the same crucible will be fired the prime amalgam of unionism: solidarity. In the hand-to-hand combat, men learn the brotherhood of the barricades. Come what may in the years ahead, the leader and his men who stood shoulder to shoulder and—more significantly—back to back on the firing line are not likely to forget their loyalties to one another. The solidarity of soldiery gives a union an instinctive fusion against the days of later confusion.

Out of the bodily battle, however, comes an exaggerated notion of the role of the brute in history. Like linesmen in a football team, many social rebels who have used their heads primarily as a battering ram into a closed society tend to believe that there is a muscular solution to all problems. Their thinking is not unlike that of the jingoist who assumes there is a military solution to all international problems, or of the plutocrat who believes there is a pecuniary solution to all interpersonal relations. Faith in physical force creates the impression that a punch in the nose is the best way to see eye-to-eye, a somatic solution for all psychic problems.

Out of the same seething cauldron arise the vapors of extremism. Violence produces bodily juices stirring emotions that pundits seek to intellectualize. Dogmas are woven out of glandular secretions. These doctrines tend to be extremist not simply because they are highly charged with passion but because they are built on non-relations. In the absence of defined relationships between combatants, the prevailing relationship is mutual murder. The war is total; the terms of peace are unconditional surrender; the ultimate moral purpose is the seizure of power by the new class and the liquidation of the old.

The violence that marks American social movements in their youth gives the impression that they are "revolutionary." In a way, they are: they break laws, threaten to turn things topsy-turvy, dramatically confront underdog and topdog. In addition, the call to combat will be embodied in resolutions dreamed up and drafted by ideologues who will be articulating their own wishes with the conviction that they are merely giving conscious expression to the unconscious strivings of "the people." Hence, when the historian looks back on these events, he will read news-

paper accounts about the deeds of warriors and he will read the
resolutions of the chiliasts to conclude that these conflicts were
revolutionary struggles for revolutionary ends. The impression
is reinforced by the knowledge that in some countries these, or
similar upheavals, did result in revolution.

Yet, in most cases of American trade unionism, the notion
that militancy means revolution is to confuse the *id* with the *idea*.
Mass anger is generally mass id unleashed. It is a form of free-
floating hostility that can attach itself to many momentary moods—
communist or fascist, KKK or black power, union recognition or
social revolution. In and of itself, it is not a program: it is the
raucous voice of the rebel without a cause, muscle minus mind.
To the revolutionary ideologue who is directly involved in such
a struggle, however, this unleashed action appears to be the instinctive identification of the masses with his social ideal. Indeed,
he is likely to view it as the instrument of his invention and the
means to his millennium, as midwife to the utopia he conceived.
When the revolution does not come to pass, the ideologue often
feels betrayed by the masses. In those countries where the revolution did come to pass, the masses have just as often felt betrayed
by their leaders, as the liberators turned dictators.

In the crucible of the formative years, however, a variety of
ideas and ids are fused in the heat of social friction. The differences
do not become apparent until the struggle for leadership sets in.

A perfect case in point is the formative years of the CIO.
No sooner had the great industrial unions completed their initial
break-through but that the ideologic struggle began. A union had
been formed and almost simultaneously a cadre of leaders began
to form. Socialists, Communists, Lovestoneites, Trotskyites,
Wobblies, Anarchists organized their separate and combined
caucuses to take the leadership. John L. Lewis had consciously
encouraged many of the "leftists" to take over major posts in
the CIO because he felt he could harness their idealism. He soon
found that they had ideas of their own. Each of the "isms" had

its own multiple factions—always highly principled and somehow always named after some person—that believed seriously that no matter how small, their one and only true banner would someday become the rallying point of the "revolutionary masses."

Yet, at the very hour of maximum radical influence, the *members* of these selfsame unions were voting Republican and Democratic or—even more symptomatic of their political apathy —were not voting at all. The largely inarticulate mass had its own ideology, which was far less millennial than that of their leaders. It was an ideology unspoken but not unfelt. It may have looked revolutionary in the light of the pyrotechnics but it was fundamentally conservative, instinctively seeking a reintegration into the *polis* of the workplace and the cosmopolis of American society.

This period of uninhibited action and undefined ideology is also the period of untested leadership. The crucible of conflict is the initial stage in a time of testing followed by further stages of natural selection as the union develops.

Three types of leaders come to the surface in the troublous times: the demagogue, the militant, and the sectarian. The demagogue wins quick acceptance since he need not prove that he can deliver on his promises. He can always promise more; he can ride the waves of anger; he can denounce all compromise; he can inflate the ego of the mass with hot air. His hour of trial comes with his success, with the day he is acclaimed and then must redeem his promises. As often as not, his day of doing is his day of undoing. The militant is admired and followed as is any brave fighter in any war. He is shield and sword to his comrades. He thrives on strife. When the struggle subsides, he becomes uneasy, especially if he has no greater purpose than the fighting itself. He seeks solace in recall of the old days with old buddies, an outlet in personal brawls, and hope in struggles he sees ahead. The sectarian is very often the public face of the union or a significant part of it. He verbalizes purpose and hence is likely to be quoted. He is a "party" man who starts with a hard-core cadre whose dedication and determination are invaluable in intraunion combat. His time of tribulation comes when he, as leader, tries to stuff the mass into his mold. The more unyielding he is in his mission, the less likely is he to survive with his members.

The formative years of unionism are an awkward age, like those of a youth whose discomfort is marked by rapid physical growth, by mixed moods, and by a yearning to out-talk and out-fight papa. This is the syndrome of adolescense as expressed by the dependent youth now making his declaration of independence.

Who then arises as the mature leader from this crucible? The model would be a man who would use the flame of his oratory to keep aglow a hot spirit, from which he would try to draw more light than heat. He would flex his muscles but not use them except as a last resort. He would hold to his grand design but would scientifically lay down a foundation and then proceed to place brick on brick.

Are there such men? In his *Power in America—The Politics of the New Class*, David Bazelon says, No. "I take as the starting point for a discussion of American politics that intellectuals favor ideals too much, and our more practical men lack both the ideals and the ideas that may lead to a new American realism. So the persistent effort underlying the pages of this book is to imagine— he must be imagined; he does not exist—a person with the virtues of each and the faults of neither."[1]

A similar dichotomy is set up by Hans Morgenthau in an essay on American foreign policy in which he posits that intellectuals are interested in *truth* and that politicians are interested in *power*.[2]

1. David T. Bazelon, *Power in America—The Politics of The New Class* (New York: The New American Library, 1967), p. 1.
2. Hans Morgenthau, "Truth and Power," *The New Republic*, Nov. 26, 1966.

The assumption of both is that idealists cannot be practical and that practical men cannot be idealists, that intellectuals cannot be political and that politicians cannot be intellectual.

Despite the ease with which this line of division can be drawn on paper, the same line can rarely be drawn in reality. The truth is, indeed, quite the opposite. Most intellectuals whose names come to public attention are consummate politicians and shockingly practical in the conduct of their affairs. They have to be: to get college appointments, to rise to department heads, to land foundation grants, to get books published, to promote sales, to get nominations to government commissions. And vice versa, the politician who rises to top office is more often a man of ideas and ideals than not. He is generally somebody respected by his peers because he is something more than "one of the boys."

The examples of the men of action who are also men of ideas are numerous. In recent times, Britain had its Churchill and Gaitskell; the United States, its Stevenson and Kennedy; Rome, its Pope John and Giuseppe Saragat: Israel, its Ben-Gurion; India, its Ghandi and Nehru; Russia, its Lenin and Trotsky; China, its Mao-Tze-Tung; the U.N. its Hammarskjöld. In all these cases, the leaders were also men of ideals—albeit occasionally contradictory ideals.

Man, the political animal, does not stop being political just because he is an intellectual. In his community—whether it be the university, the government, or the trade union—he moves through political channels to realize his ideas, his ideals, and his identity. There are, of course, practical men who have no ideas just as there are so-called intellectuals who are equally devoid of thought. There are also intellectuals who are just plain power hungry just as there are politicians who want power for its own sake. But, in all cases, those who stand high in the decision-making process of an institution are men who have some ideas—good or bad—and possess political know-how.

Thus, in the trade union movement, there have always been

leaders who approximate the model: agitator, activist, and administrator, functioning best when all these personalities are clustered around a philosophic core. In many unions, these separate roles are played by separate men operating as a team. The top man may be predominantly any one of these, with his missing talents supplied by lieutenants. There are local unions run by muscle men who enlist the skills of the mental and managerial type. In other locals, the top man is a socially minded public figure who is backed up by a diligent administrator in his shop and a tough organizer on the streets. Hence, no one leader is likely to have all the qualities needed by a union; the leadership is very likely to be a compendium of needed union virtues.

It is, of course, no coincidence that unions should have such fortuitously fit leadership. Leaders rise and survive because the group they represent elevates them and perpetuates them according to the needs and moods of the institution. This is precisely what is meant by natural selection. Those who survive need not be the most virtuous, most learned, most articulate, or most courageous. Or they may be all of these. But they are the most *fit*. In the selection of leadership, the survival of the fittest is as applicable to unions as it is to the pleistocene.

Leadership is a class that arises in a culture. The culture (the "little republic") is the union. The class of leaders in a union, ilke any class in a society, does not suddenly disrupt the cultural continuum. The union elite reflects, refines, restates the values of the union culture.

What is this union culture? It is first a gathering of the folk in the *polis* into a group tied together by a "religion," the tribal knot that binds; hence, unions need men who are able to voice the faith, whether they be demagogues or scribes. Second, a union conducts a political struggle in the workplace; hence, unions need men who can fight, argue, bargain, whether they be diplomats or hagglers. Third, a union is a societal force, conducting its political struggles in the larger community; hence, unions need men who can "politic," whether they do so as wheelers and dealers or as statesmen paying tribute to noble ideals. Finally, a union is an institution, a polity, in need of men to make policy and to enforce it; hence, unions are run by "politicians," those who have been chosen by their people and by natural selection to lead.

The word *politician* carries a dirty connotation in America. Most politicians prefer to be known as statesmen or liberals or conservatives or representatives. In a college, they prefer to be known as president; in a church as bishop; in the court as judge. But they are all politicians who have the will and know the way to win the coveted post. A Prince of Wales could have been ruler of the British Empire but he willed to marry a lady from Baltimore instead. Each year, thousands of aspirants reach for public office in America only to find that their reach exceeds their grasp. The successful leader of an organization is the man who is oriented toward *power*. If he does not like the sobriquet of "politician," then he may be graced with the more lofty phrase of Harold Lasswell, *homo politicus*.

In his *Power and Personality*, Lasswell poses a key question on the nature of leadership. "Are there early experiences in childhood and youth which, impinging upon a basic biologic type, culminate in personalities oriented toward power? Is there, in a word, a political man, a *homo politicus*, a basic political type?"[3] Lasswell begins with the assumption that "men want power . . . in every society where power exists." The question is why the intensity of the power drive varies and whether the differences in intensity are innate or acquired.[4] In either event, the men who get power are those who want power. Contrary to the after-dinner speech about how the office sought the man, it is really the man who

3. Harold D. Lasswell, *Power and Personality* (New York: Viking Press, 1962), p. 19.
4. *Ibid.*, p. 16.

seeks the office. If he does not seek, he shall not find. For power is only one value after which men yearn. There are other values that rank higher with some men and with some communities than power. Lasswell suggests *respect* as a value held high in the distinctions of social classes: *affection* as a value held high in family; *rectitude* in church or home; *well-being* in the hospital or clinic; *wealth* in business; *enlightenment* in education; *skill* in education. *Power* is attached to the institution of *government*—including the government of unions.

What kind of man is it then who gives high priority to power in the scale of values? Lasswell offers a field theory about the type: "The political type is characterized by an intense and ungratified craving for deference. These cravings, both accentuated and unsatisfied in the primary circle, are displaced upon public objects (persons and practices connected with the power process). The displacement is rationalized in terms of public interest. We sum up the political type in terms of the development of motives as follows: Private motives displaced on public objects rationalized in terms of public interest."[5] The personality most likely to develop this sort of motivation, continues Lasswell, is that of a man who is compensating for deprivation. The deprivation may be real or imagined, but in either case the result is low self-esteem. Power is a way to overcome that sad state by changing self or the environment. Deprivation, by itself, will not necessarily stir a power drive. Indeed, quite the opposite is possible. If deprivation is overwhelming, the victim may turn to withdrawal —even suicide. Among the various ways to avoid being crushed by deprivation is to blame one's sorry state on others, to ascribe one's low estate to the oppressor. By doing so, the self is not destroyed. In due time, it will rise in revenge to compensate for its deprivation.

Lasswell puts forward this conception as "a means of unifying

5. *Ibid.*, p. 38.

the data of history, social science, psychology and medicine." Whether this sweeping hypothesis on the roots of the power personality is as all-inclusive as suggested, it is quite pertinent as applied to trade union leadership. The labor elite is composed of men whose ambitions were greater than their station when they came into the movement. They were not crushed by this "deprivation"—economic, social, or political. They pinned the fault on the boss, the system, the establishment. To revenge the injustice, they threw themselves into the struggle to compensate for the deprivation. The private motive (need to compensate) was displaced on public objects (the union) and rationalized in the public interest (the liberation of the laborer or even the elevation of the total society).

The power-minded personality does best in a community that is likewise power-minded. In fact, precisely the same factors that make the elite power-directed also make the union so oriented. The theme of unionism is its plaint of undeserved deprivation. Its drive is to compensate for this deprivation by exerting its own power. Its great break-through for recognition is a prime expression of power. Its daily political battle in the workplace is further assertion of power. Hence, power per se must rank high in the institutional values of unionism.

In one of the great classics on unionism in the United States, J. B. S. Hardman described the dominant element of power in the life of a labor organization at a time (1928) when unionism was relatively weak.

Trade union organization has become an exercise in power accumulation, and logically enough, all problems of labor organization must be subordinated to the aim of organization, the accumulation of power. Any method that points toward a possible increase in the power of the organization is the right method, even if the most sophisticated and difficult. Any procedure by which the central aim and the chief reason for the existence of the union is likely to be advanced will command approval. Power of, by, and for the union, is the issue and the acid-test of every trade-union organizing campaign.[6]

Hardman did not limit this power-drive to organizing:

Trade unions need power in order to materialize their most immediate daily objectives. In a social order in which groups and classes contend for power, trade unions cannot lead a vigorous, growing life unless they are powerful. Generally and objectively speaking, *trade unionism is a sustained and objective effort at power accumulation.*[7]

If you are a union member, you want the power to be used to protect and advance the interest of the members. You want a tribal chieftain. If you are a socially minded citizen outside that union, you want the power to be used to protect and advance the larger community—city, state, or nation. You want a societal statesman. But what if you are the leader: shall you serve the membership of the union, or the citizenry of the society, or—yourself?

Here the union elite is confronted with the eternal question of every governor since the beginning of time. Whom do you serve: your own class, the whole people, or—yourself? This is the agony of *homo politicus*—the essence of man, the political animal. The leader is trapped in the ancient dilemma of freedom versus organization, autonomy versus authority. He must believe in freedom and autonomy. If he does not, then his organization is not his sovereignty, his realm to rule without interference by the outside world. Hence, he must fight for the liberty to live his own institutional life. But, he must also believe in organization and authority. If he does not, then he is no power in his class or nation.

To cope with the contradictions inherent in his post, the leader must develop an *ethic*—even if he never heard of the

6. Bakke et al, *op. cit.*, in J. B. S. Hardman, *American Labor Dynamics* (New York: Harcourt, Brace and Company, 1928), p. 111.

7. *Ibid.*

word. He must decide what is good and what is bad. He must separate out what is good for the union, the country or himself. If his use of power turns out to be good for all three, his problem is simple. But if what is good for the union is bad for the country and of doubtful consequence to himself, he is torn. He has to take counsel with his conscience—a self-confrontation that is complicated by the fact that he is surrounded by his tribal conscience, his societal conscience, and his personal conscience.

A prime role of the union leader, his institutional *raison d'être,* is of tribal chieftain. It is this that gives added dimension to his person: a recognition, a distinction, a responsibility. It is also this that gives him added standing in the community: a voice, a treasury, an economic and political strength. Without his union post, he is less in the esteem of self and society, unless, of course, he gets some prestigious post of power elsewhere.

The necessary emphasis of a union leader on his jurisdiction is rooted in the logical and psychological. Logically, the leader can only survive as leader if he serves the real or imagined needs of his people. He cannot ask his members to commit economic suicide; as normal humans, they will not comply. If he even suggests it, then he—not they—will be the victim of the death wish. Nor is a leader likely to propose major sacrifices by his members for the alleged good of society. He may appeal for support of a humanitarian cause or for national purposes. But he would find it almost impossible to appeal for surrender of job, pay, or fringe benefits. When confronted with any question that would mean serious loss of membership (or membership standards) a union leader will instinctively paraphrase Sir Winston Churchill, "I was not elected to preside over the liquidation of this empire." Were he to act otherwise, he would be rendered inactive by his subjects.

Psychologically, a leader thinks instinctively in terms of his union. His views are shaped in the organization. He internalizes the anxieties and hopes, the attitudes and aspirations of his kind.

Indeed, as oracle for his community, he becomes attached to words, phrases, even full-blown philosophies that become the instinctive guidelines of his institutional behavior.

The more democratically run the union is, the more is the leader bound to reflect the opinions of his constituency. In a dictatorially conducted union, a leader may defy the attitudes and even the best interests of membership: he can sign "sweetheart" contracts, sell off a portion of the membership, transfer the jurisdiction for a consideration or—if idealistically motivated—can sacrifice his membership on the altar of some great god, like the "revolution" or the ideologic imperatives of a religious, ethnic, or political group. But, such playing free with the members is not likely where the members are free to oust the leader. Internal democracy limits leadership.

The tribal (or parochial) origins and limitations of union leadership are not peculiar to labor organizations. Consider the members of the United States House of Representatives. They are sworn to uphold the Constitution, one of whose cardinal premises is the promotion of "the *general* welfare." Despite this, a congressman from a dairy district can be counted on to promote butter against oleomargarine; or, if he comes from a silver-producing district, to favor mintage of silver coins at some fixed evaluation. If he is a liberal from the South, he may be expected to make concessions to Dixie mores on race; if he is a conservative from a northern city, to make concessions to union demands. He is a representative, subject to the will (more or less) of his constituents or at least those who are vocal and who vote.

Consider a corporate manager. His object is to produce profits or corporate growth. He is most unlikely to tell a shareholders' meeting that the corporation is pleased to report losses in the current year incurred gleefully in the public interest. However public-spirited the owners, they would prefer to show gains so that the individual recipients of corporate income might indulge their private charities or the public weal.

The leader is the embodiment of the body politic. He *is* the institution. As such, he is logically, psychologically, and ethically obliged to speak the will of his constituents, his tribe. The inherent institutional egocentrism of the tribal leader, whether of union, congressional district, corporation, appears very often as parochial and partisan, callous and even cruel. And indeed, it can be such. Yet to escape these built-in confines is an almost superhuman challenge. "The whole of history revealed," wrote Reinhold Niebuhr in his essay on "Tribalism and Inhumanity," that "even the most learned men would not be rational enough to penetrate and transform the unconscious and sub-rational sources of parochial loyalties, which determine the limits of community and which prompt inhuman brutalities to other human beings. All historians and political scientists have accepted the curious paradox lying at the heart of human universalist aspirations and at the same time making history the tangled story of endless forms of community and communal conflict.[8]

Disturbing as these tribalisms are, they have a positive role to play in the preservation of man's freedom. Each little community is an island of independence, standing firm against the waves of conformity. The limited visions and the fierce loyalties of those within the tribe make them a seperate people, able to resist the universe, to be different. Without such diverse communities, pluralism becomes an empty abstraction. It is tribal irrationality that ironically democratizes universalist rationality.

Because tribes tend to integrate into states and states into nations, leadership operates at ascending levels to discover ever greater horizons. In a union, the head of a local is generally compulsively parochial, he represents one sort of worker, as a rule; he meets them face to face; he is directly accountable to a fairly homogeneous group. But when the local leader becomes a national president of a union, he can begin to play the statesman. He

8. Reinhold Niebuhr, *Man's Nature and His Communities* (New York: Charles Scribner's Sons, 1965), p. 94.

has a diverse membership; he is dependent on no one group; he is not daily conditioned by a confrontation with the rank and file. When he rises to become president of a labor federation, he can speak as a national figure concerned with the national interest. He can afford to rise above limited sectors of the movement as long as he can put together an internal coalition to support his view.

Again, what is true of union leaders is true of other political leaders. When Kenneth Keating represented a district in upstate New York, he had the reputation of being a conservative Congressman; when he was elected as Senator from New York State, speaking for a new constituency, he was viewed as a liberal Republican. When Lyndon B. Johnson was the Senator from Texas, he acted in Congress as a Texan; when he became President of the United States, he acted for the American consensus, for the larger culture. Conscience conforms to constituency.

Although rooted in the "tribe," the union leader must branch out to the society. He can not afford to listen to his members alone; he must listen to the employers. What a union can get depends on what a company or an industry can give. Hence, the union leader is compelled to learn something about the economic situation in the firm and in the economy.

The union leader needs allies outside his union. Normally, his local will affiliate with a larger national union, where he will be exposed to a more generalized view of his problems. He will find himself working with other union leaders in city or national projects. He will engage in governmental elections and discover the importance of coalitions with other groups. He will find that what his union can or cannot do will be affected by public opinion, especially that body of opinion that may ultimately be transformed into law. All of these involvements with the outside world serve to widen his inside world. The higher up he is, the wider his society, in the same way that a man standing on a peak can see further than a man confined to a valley.

The personal ambition that makes a man a tribal leader also can make him socially conscious in a broader area. Having risen to the top of his district, he is likely to crave recognition from a larger circle. He may do this because his ego yearns for greater gratification, because he wants more power, or because he wishes to be the missionary for an ideal. But the drive to lead, whatever its conscious or unconscious motivation, does not end when a man wins his first post. As his ambition extends so will his contacts, his constituencies, his views.

As part of a class—the leadership elite—he will also look within this congregation for models, for men who have won wider acceptance. He will discover that they are men who can speak to a variety of audiences, who have knowledge about something more than their trade, who command respect among the "strangers," who have an image and a conviction about the role of the union (corporation, church, university) in the total society. He will begin to internalize the values of this leadership-within-the-leadership, as once he internalized the values of his clansmen.

The transition from tribal to societal view is not too difficult or abrupt for a union leader in a democratic society. The leader, like other citizens in a pluralist culture, is a plural individual. He is not just a unionist—central as that is to his being—conditioned solely by his union environment. He is a citizen of a nation: when that nation goes to a major war, the union leader is likely to urge a no-strike policy on his membership and they, in turn, are very likely to go along. The leader is affected by the sub-cultures of the nation: religions, regions, political parties, race. The union leader is necessarily the child of two parents: tribe and society. He cannot rid himself of that heritage.

Not all union leaders are equally tribal or societal. The so-called pure-and-simple unionist is basically tribal: the so-called social unionist is basically societal. Each, in time, must learn something about the relationship of the clan to the cosmos.

Those who do not are ultimately stunted by their own short-comings.

In the eternal interplay between freedom and organization, the union leader who lays out his jurisdiction as a distinct locus of power in a pluralist society (the *sine qua non* of freedom) must also lay out his place of power within the jurisdiction (the *sine qua non* of organization). At one and the same time, he fights for autonomy and authority—autonomy within the nation and authority within the union. Although the leader appears very often to be a hypocrite who denounces the vices of conformity in company or culture while demanding the virtues of conformity to the union, he is doing what is natural and necessary. He is doing what George Washington did when he put together an army, trained it in the ways of soldiery, established his discipline, and formed a body of authority with himself at the head, in order to win independence from the mother country of Great Britain. The union leader, likewise, shapes a political corporation with a polity and formal policy makers. He composes a private government.

As a leader exerting authority, he is very likely to be tinged by authoritarianism, whether he is primarily tribal or societal in his orientation. The authoritarian constellation is not limited to any one ideology. The inevitable ingredient of authoritarianism arises from the fact that the man who holds high office was, even before he took office, somewhat hungry for power. He was, therefore, corruptible by power even before power began to corrupt.

The forms in which authority expresses itself in corporate life vary greatly. Much depends on the nature of the institution, on its constitution, on the people in it, on the purpose of its work, on the environment within which it operates. The forms are as varied as the forms of government on the face of the earth, and for the same reasons. But, no matter the form, no man remains long in effective authority (although he may continue in nominal authority) unless he is willing and able to wield authority—a habit that can harden into authoritarian rule.

As examples of differences in form and style, consider the contrasts between authority in a business corporation and a labor union. In a business corporation, there is no pretense of one-man, one-vote, since voting strength is normally based on shares held. In a union, the officers are elected by members with each vote counting equally, except where there is indirect election by conventions in which each delegate is elected by popular vote. In the corporation, consequently, the top man with a majority of the voting stock in his possession is the undisputed boss; he need not campaign unless there is a proxy fight. In a union, on the other hand, the top man must politick—line up votes and organize a machine. In the business corporation, the owner can rule *in absentia*, removing managers, reallocating finances, redesigning products, restructuring production. In the union, the leader must rule in person and must make his presence known by building a personal image, grooming his charisma, making friends and influencing people. The business corporation is fundamentally authoritarian in structure: the company belongs to its owners. The union is fundamentally democratic in structure: the union belongs to the members. Despite these real differences, however, there is an underlying likeness since neither can function without the presence of a unifying instrument, an authority.

There are unions, of course, that are run as the personal property of a man or a little band of men. They are generally "racket unions," started by an entrepreneur in possession of a charter he may have issued to himself, who then approaches employers for "sweetheart" arrangements, whereby he automatically gets contracts and "membership." He may never hold a meeting; he may never run for office; his members may not even know they are members. His union is a "union" in name only.

Then there are unions that are a first cousin of such a paper local, starkly reminiscent of a paper corporation. This second type may be a legitimate union into which strong-arm men have muscled their way to take over the controls. Such unions are the labor counterpart of the political organization of some American cities where the machinery of nomination and election has fallen into the hands of the underworld, who bribe, beat, and bully voters and who, by their control of the counting places, count themselves into office.

Generally speaking, however, most unions are democratic in structure in the sense that they rest on majority rule and are governed with the consent of the governed. But this general democratic model varies considerably from union to union, from time to time. The model also varies greatly from the forms and practices customary in the government of the nation. Because of these differences within the labor movement and because of the even greater differences between the political structure of unions and nations, the nature of democracy in labor organizations is open to question. Union leadership often appears to be a bureaucracy imposing its personal will on a yea-saying membership.

Unions lack many of the forms, traditions and practices of the American government. They rarely have a clear separation of powers between legislature, executive, and judicial. A two-party (or multiparty) system is rare. A body of civil liberties, subject to independent judicial review, has not been elaborated. Measured by the Constitution of the United States and its formal and informal ramifications, union governments appear wanting in democratic fulfillment. Unions, however, are not national governments; they are private governments.

A business corporation is a private government. But its forms are starkly different from those written into the U.S. Constitution. By their very nature, they are undemocratic. As noted earlier, the majority stockholder (and it can be one man) runs the show.

A university is another kind of private government whose forms differ from those in public government. The university president is not elected by the student body, although he is the chief executive; neither is the board of trustees, although it may function as a kind of legislature. Attempts of faculty to become the decisive "democratic" citizenry in matters of curriculum, personnel, standards have been repeatedly repelled. Student demands for an adult voice in the running of universities have brought on crises bordering on riots. A two-party system, with formal campaigns and elections, is unknown.

A church is still another form of private government. Some denominations do not even pretend to be democratic in the choice of leaders: all appointments come from above. But even where it is the congregation that selects its minister or rabbi, the spiritual leader soon becomes political leader, generally re-appointed unanimously and often granted life tenure.

From these examples, it is clear that the structures of private governments do not copy the United States government, no matter how much the individual members, the leaders, or the ideals of the organization are dedicated to democracy. Private associations are different from a nation in two fundamental respects: they are narrower in *purpose* and more homogeneous in *composition*. These traits are inherent in their nature, since they are political corporations arising in a limited *polis*, where jurisdiction is marked off, objectives narrowly defined, and membership of common interest.

What is the *purpose* of the union? It is to act as a collective counterpoint to the company, which is also a collective. "We must bear in mind," points out David L. Cole, "that industrial democracy is primarily intended to establish equality in certain matters between groups of employees and their employer. Democracy is intrinsically tied to the principle of collective bargaining, and I emphasize the word collective."[9] From this premise, Cole concludes that the rights of the individual worker have to be balanced against the needs of the collective group.

When we explore the means of protecting the freedom of the individual worker, we must be aware that we are thinking of him within the framework of an organization that itself has a major function to fill on behalf of workers as a whole. The union is expected to do an effective job in promoting the economic interests of the workers and to be socially progressive and responsible while doing so. To expect it at the same time to operate as though it was an anarchy within itself would seem to present an impossible dichotomy.[10]

Although "anarchy" is not the only alternative to "autocracy," the fact remains that a union tends to subordinate the individual. The emphasis is on the labor organization as an active agent in the workplace rather than as an environment for personal expression. (To the extent that the union also becomes a place where workers develop their personalities as union or community leaders, the result is a by-product of, rather than the reason for, the union's operations.)

In the performance of its defined purpose, the union is involved in conflict—strikes, bargaining, grievances. Hence the union is always something of a garrison state, a quasi-military operation. This circumstance imposes tighter disciplines on the union as an organization, in the same way that any democratic state curbs individual freedom of action in the interest of national defense. "The union," said A. J. Muste, "is a fighting instrument and exhibits always more or less definitely a tendency to take on the characteristics of armed forces and warfare in its structure and activities. . . . Whatever be the manner of warfare, the union

9. Cited in Neil Chamberlain, *The Labor Sector* (New York: McGraw-Hill, 1965), p. 206.
10. *Ibid.*

must wage war to gain and to maintain tolerable conditions for its membership. It must develop something of the solidarity, discipline and capacity for swift striking that an army has."[11]

When a union is not warrior, it is policeman, enforcing contracts with employers. If it is not policing, it is administering: handling properties, investing funds, checking expense accounts, hiring personnel, managing offices, filing reports, keeping records, balancing budgets. These are all functions of a bureaucratic character—using *bureaucrat* in the formal sense of an agent performing a nonlegislative nonjudicial governmental function.

The relatively narrow, semimilitary, highly administrative functions of a union give rise to a leadership that, in the long run, tends to become bureaucratic in the pejorative as well as formal sense. And because the union is a fairly homogeneous organization, a heavy percentage of union officers do serve for a long run.

The homogeneity of a union is as much a part of its nature as is its limited function. A local union is made up of people doing approximately the same thing in the same place (plant or town). This is more true of a craft than an industrial local. Indeed, in some skilled craft unions, where there is little turnover in the local labor market or in union rolls, the membership is not only of the same skill but often of the same age, ethnic background, and political conviction. This homogeneity makes it unlikely and unnatural for a local union to divide into a formal multiparty system. The sociologic base is not present for a political pluralism. Hence, a union official, once elected, can be re-elected without major opposition for decades. This is a phenomenon not limited to unions. In congressional districts of a homogeneous character, the same man can be elected for decades. Emanuel Celler of Brooklyn, William Dawson of Chicago, the late Sam Rayburn of Texas, Graham Barden of North Carolina, Adam Clayton Powell of Harlem are just a few examples.

11. A. J. Muste, "Factional Fights in Trade Unions," in *American Labor Dynamics*, pp. 332–337.

In national unions and federations where there usually are genuine diversities among affiliates from a variety of trades, skills, and traditions, there is also a record of long tenure by union leaders. But, in most cases, such tenure is more a *reign* than a *rule*. The top man is a symbolic figure who may or may not use his post to influence his affiliates but who, as a rule, does not intervene actively in the life of his subordinate units. He continues to reign because he allows others to rule.

The man who holds union office for a long period becomes a professional. Union work is his business. He accumulates special skills, not the least of which is the political know-how to get re-elected. He is in a position to politic all the time. Indeed, that is one of his chief objectives when he bargains, services, speaks, scolds, or smiles. He develops a class point of view that is different from that of his members. He thinks institutionally and not just as an individual in the ranks. He must think that way because he represents many people and not just one. The leader is also likely to develop the stance of a mediator in that he is pressured by members to do the impossible and pressured by employers not to demand the impossible. The union officer is also more exposed to public opinion: press, politicians, people of community standing. The officer forms a self-image as an important industry and political figure. As a result, he envisions himself as a "papa who knows best" and therefore feels he has the right and duty to caution, restrain, admonish, and even punish the unruly or misguided member.

Society approves, even demands, a union leadership that controls the membership. The public wants unions that are responsible, that have stable relations with employers, that can curb strikes, that can win approval for proposed contracts. They want peace in the economy and expect leaders to preserve that peace. The public wants a near impossibility: a leadership that is both responsible and responsive. And some union leaders try to do the impossible: to be responsible in their industrial and societal relationships while being responsive to the mood of the membership. But to find such a balance between the bureaucratic function and the democratic ideals of the union requires a high degree of political skill.

While some union leaders perfect these skills, others find themselves slipping into the bureaucratic mold—in the unpleasant sense of the term. As institutional heads, they become institutionalized. In the vein of Louis XIV who said, "*L'etat c'est moi*," and of Mayor Hague who said, "I am the law," they come to think, "I am the union."

When a leadership believes this and acts accordingly, the *form* of the union begins to replace its *content*. The union, as content, is a political corporation: a body of people gathered in a *polis*. The union, as form, expresses its will through a polity headed by policy makers and enforcers. When form replaces content, unions begin to resemble the empty corporation, the paper charter without a going concern.

Although there is an inevitable temptation for some leaders to assert that they *are* the organization, for form to replace content, there are forces at work within and about a union that serve as countervailing influences. They arise from the membership, from within the leadership itself, and from government. A brief examination of these forces and their dynamics reveals why a political corporation such as a union is under constant compulsion to reassert its real content despite the tyranny of form, or perish.

A case of a political corporation that perished is that of the medieval guild. It started as a gathering of people with a common trade. They composed a formal institution—the guild—to regulate their mutual business. The guild elected leaders with broad powers. In time, the leadership became a separate class, a corporation within the corporation, that operated as if it were the guild. Eventually, the guild became nothing but a few influential men issuing licenses to practice certain trades. The guild was no longer a guild at all: it soon passed away, its form unable to survive meaningfully without content. "The craft gild," noted Davis, "developed, before the end of the sixteenth century, from a self-governing organization of men of a craft into a close corporation imposing from above a code of regulations to which the men of the craft should conform."[12] The head had replaced the body. Then came the logical next step:

After the middle of the sixteenth century, the gild or company was so plainly a body having merely a profitable control over certain fields of industry instead of an organization for the control by the tradesmen or craftsmen of their own conditions that Elizabeth and James I could see nothing objectionable in investing private individuals with similar powers in the "monopolies" created by them. The governing body of the craft had shrunk into a close corporation virtually outside of the craft itself and simply deriving revenues from it in the form of fees with little beyond a nominal control of it; most of the public functions of the body had vanished and in their place was a body of rights private in their nature.[13]

In sum, the corporation, as a live body of beings, had become a corpse.

The demise of the guild cannot be attributed solely to its internal development from a voluntary association with quasi-public functions into a piece of private property for personal gain. The times had already made the guild an anachronism. Trade and commerce had expanded to the point where it was both undesirable and impossible for a guild to exert the kind of controls over production and exchange that it had in previous centuries. If the guild had been necessary for the economic needs of the times, it may very well have been that the "private" possession of these vital bodies would have been challenged by both the practitioners of the trade and the government.

In summarizing the evolution of corporations in an introduc-

12. Davis, *op. cit.*, p. 187.
13. *Ibid.*

tion to Davis' classic Chayes notes the irony of how a congregation of persons can become an aggregation of things:

> The concept of the corporation began for us with groups of men related to each other by the place they lived in and the things they did. The monastery, the gild, the university were only peripherally concerned with what its members owned in common as members. The subsequent history of the corporate concept can be seen as a process by which it became progressively more formal and abstract. In particular the associative elements were refined out of it. In law it became a rubric for expressing a complicated network of relations of people to things rather than among persons.[14]

Could not the same things happen to unions? Could they not become "progressively more formal and abstract" with the associative elements "refined out," concerned with things rather than persons?

There are such unions, although the very few of them that exist today are caricatures. There are locals that have come into being because some national union issued a charter to some person in the manner of Queen Elizabeth bestowing a guild franchise on a favorite. Such locals make agreements with employers, collect dues through checkoff, hold no meetings, enforce no contracts. They are strictly formal and abstract, concerned with gathering things; namely, money for the owners of the union.

There are other unions that once were going concerns but whose members no longer exist because the company went out of existence. Left behind, however, was a treasury and union officials who live a kind of ghostlike existence: investing funds, drawing income, aiding the needy. They resemble the "incorporated charitable foundation" that Chayes sees as having "achieved the ultimate of a corporate body without any members at all."[15]

Cannot other unions ultimately slip into either of these molds?

14. *Ibid.*, p. xix.
15. *Ibid.*

The funds are there and so are the union officials. The officers take over more and more of the functions once performed by active members now turned apathetic. The elite becomes an administrator of things: treasury, property, personnel, pensions, contracts. In the abstract, the union as a corporate body presiding over corpse-like members is possible. In reality, it is most unlikely.

A union contract is put to the test daily by the membership. The individual member makes his judgment about his union by a manual measure: by the way life feels on the job. He counts his income; he watches the clock; he smells his surroundings; he voices his grievances; and he demands action. In the first instance, he turns to the shop steward—one of the workers in the plant entrusted with initial responsibility: the member may himself be that steward. He turns to shop committees, such as those entrusted with setting piece rates—he may himself be a member of the committee. He uses section and shop meetings to give his own "state of the union" address. It is at this level—the *polis* of the workplace—that union democracy is most vital, drawing its energy not from any abstractions about participatory democracy but from the compulsions of the occupational circumstance.

When the first step in the grievance procedure fails, the second step may involve a paid officer: local union president, business agent, delegate. When the steward fails, the "pie-card," the "pro," is expected to succeed. Unlike a member of the House of Representatives whose actions in Congress are generally unknown to his constituents, the paid union officer charged with servicing a shop is under repetitive review by his dues-payers, judged by the results of his doings.

For the worker in the shop, the great piece of legislation governing his work life is the contract. To enact this basic "law," the membership turns out to the meeting en masse. Here democracy often runs raucously and rampantly. Here leadership is on trial as the officers in charge of bargaining try to put together a consensus. The older members want better pensions; the younger members could not care less. The skilled workers want optimum scales; the unskilled want higher minimums. The male members want more pay regardless of hours; the women want shorter hours even at the expense of pay. They all want "more" and therefore, even if the contract as proposed looks good, the membership sees logic in rejecting it to get still more. Recommendations of bargaining committees are turned down regularly as hoi polloi takes "leadership" from the leadership.

The greatest challenge to the incumbent official comes from a heterogeneity among once-homogeneous members, as differences develop along trade, ethnic, age lines. In the mid-1960s a number of industrial unions were faced with internal strife through the revolt of the skilled trades. Formed in the 1930s, when skilled and unskilled were all in the same sinking boat, these industrial unions were able to unite all crafts in one union, through gains that brought benefits to all. But these gains were uneven: generally those at the bottom (who were also the most numerous) showed greater progress percentage-wise. The better paid jobs also went up, but not as fast. By the 1960s, the skilled trades felt that they were not being appreciated for their skills and their long apprenticeship, their level of responsibility and their key function. At local meetings, their problems were not given enough attention because they were in a minority. They were the forgotten aristocracy, and, as such, began to take measures to lift salary and restore status. Consequently, within such unions an articulate opposition came into being.

Ethnic heterogeneity in a union provides an inner dynamic that closely resembles the clash of diverse cultures in the total society. Union politicos run "balanced" tickets. Where those in power are insensitive to their membership changes, they run the risk of losing power. Ethnic diversity in unions, as in the nation, makes for political pluralism, its conflicts and coalitions.

The most serious challenge to American union leaders in the

next decades arises from a generational change in the composition of the labor force. The postwar "baby-boom" gave birth to a numerous youth that in the 1970s and 1980s will represent an unusually large percentage of the population. This age cohort will carry with it the normal hostilities of the young to the old, the fuel for any intergenerational struggle. Old heroes are just old men. The present is no longer measured by the fears of the past but by hopes for the future. The new generation wants its own heroes.

In these many circumstances—reminders that a union is a *body of people* and not just a *collection of things*—there are two courses open to labor leaders: to conform to the congregation, or to compel the congregation to conform to them; *to allow freedom in the organization, or to use the organization to bar freedom*. Where the governing elite can change with changing times, transitions in style, purpose, and personnel can take place smoothly, without fierce internal rivalry or sharp break. Where the leadership decides to make no change, decides to hold on by tightening the screw, transition can become trauma.

The story of the leader who is driven to arrogate all power to himself only to end up powerless reads like a Greek tragedy in which a majestic figure, as a result of his combat against a dire oracular fate, destroys himself. This leader is often a man of heroic proportions, arisen through many conflicts. He fought to establish the boundaries of his realm; he fought off invaders; he fought off challengers to the crown; he fought to enlarge his influence in the outer world. He is, by nature, a warrior—although he may also be statesman and administrator. His identification with the organization is absolute. He has long been the *spirit* of the collective; he feels as if he has also been the *body*. He has been called, "Mr. Union," and he has come to believe he *is* the union. He knows the insecurities of the mass because they were his own. He knows the new-won securities for they, too, have become his security. To challenge the organization is to challenge him, and vice versa.

Despite the security that the organization brings to such a leader, the very drive to build such security often creates its own sense of insecurity. Lasswell describes the leader as the man driven by deprivation to compensate by the push for power. Such a *homo politicus* assumes that his security lies in accumulating power: the more he accumulates, the more secure. Willy-nilly, he becomes a machine that cannot stop, racing toward an unattainable security, fueled by a sense of insecurity. Without the sense of nonarrival, the machine runs out of fuel, the juice of life is gone. If real insecurity is not there, it must be invented to give the relentless inner mechanism a reason to run.

The imagined fears are the prelude to political suicide. "The gods make mad those whom they would destroy." The old king refuses to look or listen: he will only open his eyes for those who smile and his ears to those who bring glad tidings. In this self-imposed isolation, he moves into a world of unreality. The old king turns suspicious. Those nearest him are the most dangerous because they know him best. He reads his own fears as their motives. The old king turns tyrant. He denigrates his court so that none may rise to his height. The fears that rule him make him use fear to rule others. In the end, the old king is surrounded by men who use flattery as a substitute for friendship, who relate for revenge not respect: the palace guard prepares for the regicide.

The story, of course, is as old as mankind: the potent man whose delusion of omnipotence ultimately makes him impotent. It is tragic yet hopeful, a promise that the *form*—the ruler—cannot eternally replace the *content*—the ruled.

Where the corporate structure is such that the membership can have no determining voice, the government ultimately steps in. The abuse of power by a private association invites the use of power by government. Legislation is enacted to restrain and remove leaders. The social order that recognized the institution for its public role as a private association moves to re-establish the original purpose of the political corporation.

Through these many-sided dramatic conflicts between form and content, man the political animal reasserts his primacy over the corporation he created. Substance subjugates shadow.

It is man's dilemma that in the search for freedom he comes together into organizations within which he must again begin the search for freedom. It is the leader's dilemma—and he, too, is a man—that the organization which has given him his freedom must also be allowed to be free.

In a theologic exegesis on man's relationships to his community—state or city, union or corporation, family or friends— Niebuhr brilliantly defined the dilemma.

Man's seeking and self giving are intricately related in the human self. Human freedom makes for a unique and dialectical relation of the individual to the community. On the one hand, it transmutes nature's instinct for survival into a variety of forms of self-realization, including vanity, the will-to-power and the desire for a full selfhood, which must include always relations to neighbors and communities. On the other hand, the freedom of self gives man an infinite variety of relationships with his community, from social dependence to social creativity. Thus man's selfhood is involved in an intricate relation of self-seeking and self-giving. The paradoxical observation of Jesus about this relation is accurate. He said, He who finds his life will lose it, and he who loses his life for my sake will find it. This aphorism might be interpreted as follows: consistent self-seeking is bound to be self-defeating; on the other hand, self-giving is bound to contribute ultimately to self-realization.[16]

Moving from this theologic concept back to our original theme of "man, the political animal," may we conclude:

16. Niebuhr, *Man's Nature and His Communities*, pp. 106–107.

The man who would stand alone, apart from his fellow men, is lost. The man who cannot stand alone, and remains indistinct from his fellow men, is lost. To find himself, man must find his role in his community and live that role in the here and now.

In the words of a Hebrew sage:

> If I do not speak for myself, who will?
> If I speak for myself alone, what am I?
> If I do not speak now, then when?

INDEX

Index

Gus Tyler has spent his life in a world of organizational conflict—as activist and author, as practitioner and thinker. He is assistant president of the International Ladies' Garment Workers' Union and directs its program of Politics, Education, and Training. He is the author of *The Labor Revolution* and of *Organized Crime in America*, a definitive study of the American underworld. His articles have appeared in *The Nation*, *The New Republic*, *The New Leader*, *New Politics*, *Dissent*, and other periodicals. Mr. Tyler has served as consultant to the President's Commission on Law Enforcement and Administration of Justice and is a member of the Advisory Committee of the National Commission on Reform of Federal Criminal Laws.

*T*his publication under the Arkville Press imprint was set on the Linotype in Janson, with display in Ultra Bodoni; presswork by Noble Offset Printers, Inc., New York, New York, and binding by The Book Press Incorporated, Brattleboro, Vermont. It was printed on paper supplied by The J&J Rogers Company of Ausable Forks, New York. The Colophon was created by Theodore Roszak.